CW01558982

The Study Abroad Murder

Trial of the Century

Will Savive

Del-Grande Publishing Inc.
New Jersey Hackensack

The Study Abroad Murder

Trial of the Century

Copyright © 2011 by Will Savive

All rights reserved. No part of this book may be used or reproduced by any means, graphic, electronic, or mechanical, including photocopying, recording, taping or by any information storage retrieval system without the written permission of the publisher except in the case of brief quotations embodied in critical articles and reviews.

Del-Grande books may be ordered through booksellers or by contacting:

www.delgrandepublishing.webs.com
1-877-249-1121

Because of the dynamic nature of the Internet, any Web address or links contained in this book may have changed since publication and may no longer be valid. The views expressed in this work are solely those of the author and do not necessarily reflect the views of the publisher, and the publisher hereby disclaims any responsibility for them.

ISBN-13: 978-0615456263
ISBN-10: 061545626X
BISAC: True Crime / Murder / General

Printed in the United States of America
Del-Grande - date: 3/25/11

TABLE OF CONTENTS

Chapter 1 - Who's That Girl?

Chapter 2 - Nightmare in Perugia

Chapter 3 - Initial Investigation

Chapter 4 – Prelude to a Trial

Chapter 5 - Trial of the Century (pt. 1)

Chapter 6 - Trial of the Century (pt. 2)

Chapter 7 - Trial of the Century (pt. 3)

Chapter 8 - Trial of the Century (pt. 4)

Chapter 9 - Trial of the Century (pt. 5)

Chapter 10 - Trial of the Century (pt. 6)

Chapter 11 - Trial of the Century (pt. 7)

Chapter 12 – Trial of the Century (pt. 8)

Chapter 13 – Forensic Analysis of the Evidence

For up-to-date, continued coverage of the Amanda Knox case, including the appeals, slander charges, and further analysis of the evidence go to:
www.willsavive.blogspot.com

You can also visit the author's website at:
www.willsavive.webs.com

Will Savive can be reached at:

willsavive@live.com

Also, to see the most comprehensive website on the case, visit:

True Justice for Meredith Kercher
http://truejustice.org/

Chapter 1 – Who's That Girl?

Edda Hagge and William 'Curt' Knox were married in April of 1987, in Seattle, Washington. Curt Knox, as he is referred to, had a promising career in the retail business, and the couple was expecting their first child within the next few months. On 9 July 1987, just three months later, Edda Knox gave birth to their daughter, Amanda Knox. One year later the growing family gave birth to another daughter, whom they named Deanna. Soon after, they packed-up their belongings and moved to a middle-class suburb in the south of Seattle—a city famous for its waterways, beautiful mountains, and low crime rate. However, less-than four years after the couple said "I do," Curt Knox petitioned the courts of Seattle for a permanent-legal split. According to court records, Curt Knox had been remarried by 1991. Still, Curt and Edda remained committed parents and on cordial terms for the sake of their daughters.

As a teenager Amanda attended the *Seattle Preparatory School*, located on Capitol Hill. This Jesuit institution is considered one of the elite schools known for sending many of its students to Ivy League and highly-selective universities every year. The school's tuition reflects this, currently exceeding $12,000 a year. Students were expected to study very hard, obey strict disciplinary policies, and recite daily prayers. Amanda was known as an exceptional student who enjoyed a pretty normal childhood—as normal as could be expected with parents who were divorced. Yet, many speculate that the first traumatic event in Amanda's young life came at the tender age of fourteen, when her 38 year-old mother sat her down and announced that she had fallen in love with a 26 year-old man. In March of 2002, Edda married the younger Christopher Mellas, naturally changing her name to Edda Mellas. A product of a dysfunctional family herself, Edda's own parents had an ugly divorce.

Edda and Curt chose to live close to each other for the sake of the kids. Amanda's grandparents, aunts, and uncles also lived nearby and she would see them all regularly. Killing two birds with one stone, Amanda would often perform *gymnastics* then run from house to house to say 'hello' to her various family members. She considered it an extension of her workout to go back and forth. The family steadily grew throughout the years, until Amanda eventually had three younger sisters and several male cousins, whom she considered her brothers.

Not long after her mother's marriage to a younger man, Amanda began to show signs of degeneration. Appearing to resent women, Amanda started hanging out with more boys than her female counterparts. According to the UK's *Daily Mail* (11/10/07), a long-time acquaintance of Amanda's family said, "We live in an age when a lot of people don't consider it goofy for a woman to marry a younger guy [speaking of Edda's marriage to Chris], but Amanda was at a pretty impressionable age when this happened." Although she did have a few girlfriends, some say that Amanda became one of the guys. The *Daily Mail* reported that fellow student, Philip Setran, said, "She [Amanda] did not seem to have many girlfriends. She would spend all of her time with the guys. She would come home looking like one of the guys, covered in mud after playing tag football."

Amanda soon graduated and went on to attend the *University of Washington*. Enrolling in German, Italian, and creative-writing courses, Amanda spent much of her free time on the soccer field and climbing the dangerous mountainous peaks that border the west coast city. It is hard to say if Amanda's drinking, partying, and men-chasing-ways were attributed to internal problems that she may have been experiencing, since it's fairly normal these days for young adults to exhibit this type of behavior. Yet, some speculate that these activities were spawned from the troubles she was experiencing internally.

On the surface, nothing out of the ordinary jumped out about Amanda's high school dating life. She dated a clean-cut, studious boy named Kyle Samek, only for a short time, but then Kyle was soon dating someone else. Amanda said that she then had a serious relationship with Ben Schock, but Ben said when they went out it was usually with a group of friends and that their romance was casual. Then there was Andrew Seliber, who was a drummer in a local Seattle band called *Missing Fingers*. Although they dated only for a bit, the two became close friends—a relationship that would last through thick and thin. Amanda, Andrew, and other friends made a YouTube video in which they were visibly drunk and possibly high. Amanda is seen slurring her words, giggling, swaying, and talking to the camera, as she explains only having consumed one-and-a-half shots. Another boy is seen in the background 'jokingly' making a racial slur, calling Amanda and the girl filming "dirty Jews" for tapping them, stating his belieif that they were going to put the recording on the internet.

Amanda had met David Johnsrud (who she and others call DJ) a month before their freshman year at the university. The two immediately became friends and shared their love of rock climbing, soccer, and other outdoor sports. They grew so close that after their sophomore year they decided to start dating. DJ describes Amanda as a good friend and someone who he has always relied on, even to this day.

Amanda also had a MySpace page that she had signed-up for back on 16 December 2004. Her page was cleverly titled "*Foxy Knoxy*," a nickname given to her while in high school; Amanda asserts that the name was given to her because of her prowess on the soccer field. On her page she portrayed herself somewhat differently than what she was in reality, some would say. According to her page, she didn't drink or smoke. She liked to fancy herself as a deep thinker, not bound by any religion, but bound only to the truth—which is probably why she listed her religion as Agnostic. Under her general interests and likings she listed tea, yoga, rock climbing, soccer, writing, reading, people-watching, day-dreaming, studying, playing, making coffee, dressing like a dork, eating, cooking for other people, music, inspiration, photography, and art. Amanda's favorite band was, by far, *The Beatles*, and she listed them first on MySpace. In fact, they were the only band listed in all capital letters. Other bands and artists included, *Led Zeppelin*, *Nina Simone*, *Cream*, *Eric Clapton*, *Outkast*, *Queen*, *Roxette*, *Cake*, and *The Red Hot Chili Peppers*. Her favorite movies were, *Help!*, *The Princess Bride*, *The Lion King*, *American Beauty*, *Fight Club*, *Hero*,

3

Shrek/Shrek 2, Garden State, Moulin Rouge, Finding Nemo, The Fifth Element, Spaceballs, Robin Hood: Men In Tights, James Bond, and *The Full Monty.*

Amanda didn't watch television much and she read too many books to mention, according to her profile. She listed her profession as a writer/novelist. One very odd and disturbing piece on her MySpace page was a short story that she wrote in her MySpace blog entitled *Baby Brother.* The story described a young woman who was drugged and raped, that concluded with two roommates in a bloody confrontation. Dominick Balsoma, who took Amanda to the senior prom and also attended WSU with her, told the UK's *Daily Mail,* "Normal people can write horror stories, but it does suggest a side to her that might not have been public."

In 2006, Amanda rented a house in *Greek Row,* situated just down the hill from *Bryan Hall* and *Hill Halls* on the WSU campus. Greek Row was well-known for its wild fraternity parties thrown by rich students letting-off steam. Amanda Achieved top grades, but she also started smoking potent 'skunk' cannabis (marijuana) regularly and declared to friends that her favorite poison was vodka. "She just went wild," said an acquaintance. "It was like the brakes were let off. She started smoking pot in the mornings before class and then partying at night. Even by student standards, she was wilder than hell." One student who stayed in the same halls of residence as Amanda recalled, "We all like to smoke a bit of pot and go out and get trashed on the weekends," Philip Setran, a medical student who shared a dormitory with Amanda, said, "but she *really* used drink and drugs. By that, I mean she didn't just take stuff to get high and have fun. It was like she wanted to get away from herself, as if she had some sort of chemical imbalance she could only cope with by getting wasted. She also developed a deep, abiding desire for casual sex. She was—how can I put it—very friendly, outgoing, and bubbly to all men she came into contact with. She had what in polite terms you'd call a lot of close male friends." Other students who spoke out were blunter, calling her a "man-eater."

As soon as she started at the university, Amanda started studying the German language as well as creative writing. Intrigued with both, she had decided that she would either become an interpreter or a writer of some sort. Either way, she soon heard about a program in which she could learn Italian as well as creative writing in Rome. Amanda took a course in Italian grammar and she liked it so much that she was hooked. Following the advice of a friend, Amanda decided that instead of studying in Rome—where there were so many tourists—she would study in a smaller town in Italy that wasn't flooded by so many Americans. Amanda wanted to meet Italians and learn their culture instead of hanging around people who spoke English. Amanda's German was better than her Italian, and she knew that she would need to spend time with real Italians in order to quickly acquire the language. Following up on this idea, Amanda had planned to attend the *University of Foreigners* ("the Università per Stranieri") in Perugia to study Italian language and culture for one year. Amanda and DJ had a big decision to make.

Amanda was going to be studying in Perugia and DJ was going to study in China. Although the two were great friends and very much in love, they both decided that a long-distance relationship wasn't a good idea. So, they broke up; but decided that they would keep in close contact, mostly through Skype conversations.

In August of 2007, Amanda decided to throw a going-away party for herself at her dorm on Greek Row. Things apparently got a bit wild and someone called the police and reported that some of the party-goers were throwing rocks at cars outside the party. According to Seattle police, there was a disturbance at a house near the prestigious University of Washington. When Patrolman Jason Bender arrived at Greek Row he witnessed "Gangs of students, drunk and high on drugs, hurling rocks into the road, and cars swerving to avoid them." Knox was the only one arrested that night. According to one party guest it was "bedlam, with drink, drugs, and bodies everywhere." The guest went on to say, "Some people were naked inside the bedrooms. There were people draped over each other. I've been to a lot of student parties in my time, but I've never been to a party like that. Everyone just wanted to get drunk, get high and get laid. There was also a lot of violence because everyone was so pumped up." Knox was fined $269 at the Municipal Court after the incident—Crime No: 071830624. According to court records, the first officer on the scene, Patrolman Jason Bender, said "the only excuse Knox gave for her behavior was that she was moving abroad."

"Sono Andato!" ("I'm Gone!")

On Tuesday, 14 August 2007, Amanda wrote a MySpace blog informing her friends that she and her sister Deanna were off to Hamburg, Germany to visit their aunt, Dolly. Hours later they boarded a flight that stopped briefly in Amsterdam. During another blog post, Knox joked that she wasn't able to smoke [marijuana] while in Amsterdam. Arriving in Hamburg after an extremely long flight, the girls were greeted by aunt Dolly and her husband, Manoj. Deanna and Amanda spent a lot of time shopping and bonding initially. Not long after that they met a coworker of Manoj's who informed Amanda that he would get her a job at the *Bundestag*; which is (along with the *Bundestrat*) the legislative branch of the German political system. Much like America's House and Senate, nothing can be passed in Germany without going through the *Bundestag*. The *Bundestag* is housed in Berlin, and Amanda was soon scheduled to work there as a clerk/secretary. Amanda's new plan was to work in Germany for a few weeks before starting school in Italy.

Deanna jokingly accused Amanda of being attracted to Manoj's coworker and friend, who she described as looking a bit like John Lennon. Amanda admitted that she had a slight crush on him, declaring that he had a "cute butt." Seemingly in her continuous flirtatious mode, Amanda also acknowledged that Manoj (Amanda's uncle), who was only twenty-five years old, "inadvertently made certain sexual advances towards her and Deanna. Amanda, however, downplayed the incident, alleging that, for some reason, it was more embarrassing for him than for them. That night Manoj took the girls out to Hamburg's *Red Light District* for some drinking and dancing. He warned the girls not to wander off onto the surrounding streets of St Pauli, as the seedy area carried several hookers, thieves, and drug dealers. Hookers in that area have been known to parade the streets naked and sometimes throw their urine on passing females.

Soon the entire family—Dolly, Manoj, their son Anil, Deanna, Amanda, and their grandmother (who Amanda called "Oma:" German for grandma)—piled into a car and were off to Austria to tour places where Oma had grown up. They stopped for a few days in Trofaiach (small town near Graz), where the girls were introduced to Oma's cousin, Hansi, and her husband, Peter. The family also spent some time in Graz, Wien, and then Munich, Germany. Amanda and Deanna parted ways with the family in Munich; from there they took a plane to Milan, Italy. The girls then headed to Perugia to find a place for Amanda to live in the coming weeks, as she had planned to attend the *University of Foreigners* there. From Milan, the sisters took a train to Florence. On the train Amanda met a man named Frederico, and the two became fast-friends. Once they arrived in Florence Frederico spent the day with the girls, even taking them to dinner; the three checked into a hotel in Florence later that night. Once Deanna had fallen asleep, Amanda and Frederico smoked [Marijuana]. Amanda boasted that this was her first time smoking in Italy; although, it would not be her last.

Off to Perugia

The adventurous girls hopped on a train to Perugia the next morning with high hopes of finding a place for Amanda to live. Perugia is a beautiful Italian city, located about 105 miles north of Rome, home to approximately 150,000 residents. The ancient Italian fortress city is lined with cobblestone streets and has a rich history and culture. Perugia is also home to two major universities: The University of Perugia (Enrollment of about 20,000) and the University for Foreigners (Enrollment of only a few thousand students).

Carrying everything on their backs in large, heavy back-packs; the girls entered Perugia on foot. They carried along with them a map of the area, setting-off to find the hotel room that they had previously booked. Upon viewing the map, however, they soon realized that the hotel was far from where they were currently located; they were unsure how far, but they knew it was farther than they had previously anticipated. With their heavy back-packs in toe, they struggled mightily up and down the hilltop streets of Perugia. After a grueling two-hours of hiking—with Amanda growing angrier by the minute and Deanna drowning in her own sweat—the girls realized that they were lost; so they flagged down a forty-something-year-old Italian man who was serendipitously driving by. The man took a look at their map and explained to them that their calculations had been way-off—the hotel was about another twenty-minutes, away by car. Deciding to take the chance and ride with the stranger, the girls hopped in his car and soon arrived safely at the hotel, without incident. Amanda did, however, need to explain to the man (in broken-English) that she was not interested in going out with him later that evening, as he had so graciously asked. After the long ordeal, the girls checked into the hotel and their brains checked out.

They spent the next three days getting acquainted with their surroundings and enjoying some leisure-time; they found a bus near the hotel that took them to Perugia's center (downtown) and made new friends at a local café. After familiarizing themselves with the area, Amanda had to get serious about finding a place to live; therefore, she searched tirelessly through the classifieds. One day Amanda and Deanna decided to buy a cell phone; on their way, they walked down a steep road leading to the university where Amanda would soon be attending. As they reached the university they noticed a very skinny girl putting up a page (reading: *for rent*) on the outer wall of the university. Immediately seizing upon the opportunity, Amanda introduced herself to the girl and began a conversation and a chain of events that would change their lives, and the lives of many others, forever! The young woman introduced herself as Laura Mezzetti, [27], and she informs Amanda that she has a room for rent that is just minutes away from the university. To Amanda's surprise, the Italian born Laura speaks fluent English. She has been living in Italy, working for a lawyer, and studying to be a lawyer herself. Within minutes of conversing, Amanda, Deanna, and their new friend Laura were off to take a look at the place.

The house is about a five-minute walk from the university. As the first glance of the house came into view, Amanda's dilated pupils reflected her viewing pleasure. *The cottage*, as it's called, is located at Via della Pergola 7, on an open hillside below the city's centre, near a motorway. Although it is actually on Viale Sant'Antonio, it is officially listed as being on Via della Pergola (which actually ends a few yards before the cottage). The cottage is situated at the top of a steep wooded valley, just below the level of a winding road near the city's historic centre. Part of a 17th-century palazzo, the house shares the neighborhood's heir of decadent opulence, with a terrace overlooking the red and gold foliage of the lush Umbrian valley and glimpses of the medieval wall from its green shuttered windows. Inside, the cottage included a foyer, a kitchen-living room area, two shared bathrooms with a sink, toilet, and bidet (one had a bathtub: the other an adjoining bedroom room and shower), and four bedrooms. There was also a laundry room containing a washing machine in the room adjacent to the bigger bathroom (the one with the tub), which was entered by a door opening from the living room.

The outdoor balcony extended along the main hallway. At that time, Laura lived in the cottage with two other girls, Italian born Filomena [27], who was also working for a lawyer in the same law office as Laura, and British born Meredith [21], who had arrived in August. Filomena's bedroom was near the larger bathroom and had a single window with outward shutters and two window-panels that opened inward. There was also a flat downstairs that covered a similar area, but had an enclosed room in place of the balcony above. Living down there were four boys who were in their early twenties.

Amanda and Laura hit it off immediately, becoming fast friends. There were several commonalities between the two that Amanda personally couldn't resist. Amanda loved that Laura had two acoustic guitars and, although she was just a novice player at best, Amanda loved playing guitar. Laura also informed Amanda that she would teach her yoga, something that Amanda had wanted to learn. Another big benefit to Amanda was that Laura smoked, which was probably the most compelling benefit, as she claimed that "they [Laura and Filomena] smoked like chimneys." After a very short time of talking and hanging out, Laura offered Amanda an open room right next to the smaller bathroom. If she moved-in that room she would be sharing the bathroom with whoever moved into the room next to her, which was unoccupied at the time. Laura was ecstatic to have a young American girl of a similar age and with similar interests as a roommate. Aside from the fact that the two girls really hit-it-off; Laura's quick acceptance of Amanda had much to do with her desperation to find roommates.

Just before Amanda's arrival, Laura had two others whom she was going to rent the room to, but both had disappeared since, with no hint of ever returning. Before that, Laura and Filomena had interviewed several people for the room, but found that most were rude, uptight, or simply not a good fit. Laura offered Amanda the room for €300 (approx. $409 in 2007) per month, and thus far Amanda had found nothing less than €500 (approx. $680 in 2007) per month. The two spent most of the day together chatting-it-up.

Amanda's carefree, infectious personality and English speaking must have seemed refreshing to Laura at the time. Before leaving, Amanda gave Laura a down payment to secure the room. After that Deanna and Amanda went to their favorite café to grab a bite to eat. There, Amanda claimed on her MySpace blog that she ran into "the most beautiful black man," but she did not mention his name. She spoke to the man for a bit and he informed her that they would see each other when she returned from Germany. Amanda also made friends with Nerti, an Albanian waiter at the café.

Back to Germany

When their trip had ended, the two spent a full day traveling, from a train to a bus, and then a plane back to Hamburg, Germany. Amanda had previously purchased the first *Harry Potter* book, written in German. The bright young American only spent the first chapter looking up words, but as she went on reading she easily picked up the vocabulary. By the end of the book she was reading it as if it were written in English. Amanda also bought the third *Harry Potter* book, written in Italian, but she wasn't good enough with the language at that time to read it. She had planned to go to a bookstore and purchase the second book in the series and read that one before reading the third anyhow. In any event, Amanda was determined to practice the Italian language and become fluent in both the written and spoken word.

Amanda spent a few more days in Hamburg with the family. Soon, however, it was time for Deanna and Oma to travel back to the United States, and for Amanda to travel alone to Berlin to begin working for the German government for a two-week gig. Amanda's uncle, Manoj, had set Amanda up to live with a couple that he knew in Berlin during her two-week job at the Bundestag. The couple did not actually own the place; they were watching it for a friend of theirs' who was away for three-months. Amanda took a three-hour bus ride from Hamburg to Berlin and she was picked up at the Berlin bus station by the couple on Sunday afternoon. The gracious couple stopped by their own house after picking up Amanda to loan her some household items—such as blankets, soap, *a lamp*, and so on— before dropping her off at her new, temporary residence, which was located in a nice neighborhood in the center of Germany's biggest city, Berlin. Amanda believed that she would fit right in—in a city that regularly observes sixteen-year-olds partying as twenty-one-year-olds do in America.

It was a small room, much like any average apartment in any major city, a bit shabbier than Amanda had expected. Amanda was so excited about her new adventure, however, that she didn't care about the condition of the apartment. Instead, she focused on some of the more attractive features of the place, such as the bedroom: which had a large window, a desk, and a set of shelves. As night approached Amanda realized that the lights in the kitchen and the bathroom were not working; the only light in the apartment was in the bedroom, her favorite room anyhow. Amanda set up her favorite music group, (*The Beatles*) on her laptop computer and rejoiced to their music while unloading her suitcase. She relaxed a bit after that, writing and thinking about her first day on the job, which she was to begin the following morning. She had directions to the office written down, but she had no idea where it was located otherwise; all she knew was that it had something to do with the Bundestag.

The next morning (Monday) it was pouring rain. Amanda got dressed presentably, triple-checked that the directions to the office were in her bag, and walked to the subway near her apartment. She left at 7:00a.m., although her start time wasn't until 10:00a.m. She wanted to leave herself enough time in case she got lost, not having much faith in her sense of direction. Once in the subway, Amanda purchased a €25 (approx. $30) ticket to ride the busses and trains within the center district of Berlin for seven-days. After a train and two buses later, Amanda arrived at the Bundestag with two-hours to spare. She decides to head into the Bundestag building to see if she could figure out where her office was located.

The Bundestag had not opened yet, so Amanda decided to wait in the lobby with a group of English tourists. After waiting a bit, Amanda and the group headed through security. She wanted to call the phone number that she was given and figure out the exact location of her office, but she was having trouble finding a phone within the building. As she walked upstairs to look for a phone she came upon the famous dome within the Bundestag building, which has an unbelievable view of the city. The dome has a circular walkway and, as Amanda walked on the platform, she got caught-up for a few minutes in the gorgeous view. Nevertheless, there was no phone up there. On her way back downstairs a gentleman in the elevator informed her that there is an information booth across the street from the building.

Once at the information booth, the woman inside tells Amanda that there is a phone booth at the corner. Amanda places a call to the phone number written on her directions, but it is only 8:30a.m., and no one is in the office yet. Amanda decides to have an espresso back at a café near the information booth to kill some time. After a delicious espresso macchiato, Amanda walked back to the phone to try the office again. This time a woman answered the phone and directed her, in German of course, to the office. After receiving a special entrance pass, Amanda sat near her new co-worker and waited for her boss to arrive. When her boss, Johannes Kahr, arrived, she was sweating as if she had woken up late and had rushed into the office. Barely paying Amanda any mind, Johannes shook Amanda's hand, asked her how long that she'd be hanging around with them, and then rushed off into her posh office. Amanda sat there for a long period of time writing emails to friends and family and wondering if she was already on the clock.

So Much for Berlin

On her second day of work (Tuesday) Amanda claimed that she wasn't feeling well; affects from what she claimed was a bad flu that had kept her in bed three days straight the week before; something that she forgot to mention in her long blog to friends detailing her trip. Amanda told her boss that she was sick and was going home. Amanda felt that there was nothing for her to do. With little work, Amanda would read *Harry Potty* in German to pass the time. Amanda rationalized her decision, claimed that she was "in the way" and that they didn't need her anyway. The next morning (Wednesday) she called the office and explained to them that she was not coming back. Amanda had scheduled her trip back to Hamburg on Friday, so she had two whole days to enjoy the sites of Berlin, which was why she wanted to be there in the first place. Amanda wanted to visit *Tiergarten Park*, a big park in the middle of the city, much like *Central Park* is to Manhattan. She spent the next two days wandering around Berlin and drinking wine in the park. From her decision to leave the job Amanda learned two things: how much fun Berlin could be when you don't have to work, and how angry her aunt and uncle would be that she did not simply work the full two weeks.

Amanda took the bus back to Hamburg on Friday. Upon her return she found that her aunt and uncle were very upset with her. Manoj had gone to a lot of trouble to get Amanda the job at the high-level security position, and Amanda's quitting in the way that she did made him look bad. As Manoj was explaining this to her acrimoniously, Amanda broke down and started crying. The site of tears certainly must have weakened Manoj, as he backed-off and told Amanda not to worry and that he'd take care of everything. Amanda spent the next few days in Hamburg with her aunt and uncle before heading off to Italy for good.

Back to Perugia

After her last MySpace blog on 15 September 2007, Amanda [20] disappeared from MySpace momentarily. Approximately a week later she arrived in the university community of the Umbrian hilltop town of Perugia, Italy, and moved into the cottage at Via della Pergola 7. Even before arriving in Perugia, Amanda ostensibly "lost control." Within hours of arriving in Italy, she had emailed a former Washington University student, writing excitedly about having sex with a stranger on the train. She also seemingly taunted her new roommates with this news as well. Early on in her stay she had also emailed friends in Seattle, saying that the party scene in Perugia was "great," and that she "could have any man she wanted."

Meredith Susanna Cara Kercher, known to friends as "Mez," had also moved into the cottage, a month before Amanda had. Meredith Kercher, like many Britons each year, had set off to the city of Perugia to study abroad for the 2007/2008 school year. The attractive twenty-one year old (born on 28 December 1985 in Southwark, London, England) living in Coulsdon in Surrey—a town on the southernmost boundary of the London Borough of Croydon—had come to Italy on an Erasmus scholarship. Named after Dutch philosopher, Catholic priest, and humanist, Desiderius Erasmus of Rotterdam, the *European Region Action Scheme for the Mobility of University Students* (Erasmus) Programme (Life-long Learning Programme) is a European Union (EU) student exchange program that is part of the operational framework for the European Commission's initiative in higher-education. The EU is a regional trade agreement—much like MERCOSUR or NAFTA—whose members include 27 European countries; the UK being one of them. Only students from countries within the EU trade bloc can partake in the program.

Meredith had checked into a local hotel upon her arrival while she looked for somewhere to live. A paper pinned to an Italian university notice board (put up by Laura Mezzetti) led the British student to the cottage at Via della Pergola 7. Back in the UK, the English girl with Indian ancestry majored in European Studies at Leeds University. Meredith Kercher had travelled to Italy to spend a year studying modern history, political theories and history of cinema at the University of Foreigners. Meredith was described by most who knew her as intelligent, witty, caring, and popular among her fellow students. As one of four children, Meredith had been educated at the £10,000-a-year *Old Palace of John Whitgift School*, an independent girl's school in Croydon.

Meredith was known as an ambitious, hard working girl who also liked to have a good time. She had hoped to become a journalist when she graduated and work in Brussels. One of the reasons she had chosen Perugia was its annual chocolate festival; during which many of the streets within the city walls are lined with stalls and packed with visitors. She had promised her mother that she would bring home some of the wonderful chocolate treats offered at the festival. Just weeks before her arrival in Italy, Meredith starred in the music video *Some Say*, a song by solo recording artist, Kristian Leontiou. Meredith was a friend of Kristian's and many of the people who worked on the video, all of whom were students at Leeds University. The song was quickly climbing up the charts and eventually reached gold with 150,000 sales.

The entrance to the cottage was through a gate that led some 75ft to the front door. The house was a two-floor converted cottage with one floor above ground and a basement complex that served as a first-floor. The meager accommodations of the flat were typical to college life. There were four girls on the upper level and four Italian boys on the lower level. The four boys occupying the downstairs flat—Giacomo Silenzi, Marco Marzan, Stefano Bonassi, and Riccardo Luciani—were all from Le Marche in central Italy. Each of the four girls had their own room. Romanelli and Mezzetti occupied the rooms nearest to the entry to the house: Romanelli still occupied the room to the left in respect of the person entering and Mezzetti the one opposite; these two rooms were separated from the living room by a kitchenette. From this room a corridor ran to a small bathroom located near Meredith's room. Amanda's room was in the middle, between Romanelli's room, which was the first in respect of the entrance door, and Meredith's room, which was the last. All of the rooms were located to the left of the corridor in respect of people entering. Only the room occupied by Mezzetti was located on the other side (i.e., to the right of the corridor). Soon after Meredith had moved in, she had begun dating one of the boys on the first-floor, Giacomo Silenzi. The relationship was not categorized as a serious one, just two youngsters who were in close proximity and were attracted to one another.

Kercher's room was located on the middle floor (2nd floor/ground level) and her room was right next to Seattle born, Amanda Knox, who she shared a bathroom with. All four of the girls spoke English (Filomena, not as good) and they all hit it off immediately. The odd configuration of the cottage comes because it is carved into a mountain-side. Because Laura's bedroom is the part of the cottage that is carved into the ascending part of the mountain, her window-drop (from the bottom of windowsill to the ground) was only about 7-10ft. However, Filomena's room, located on the opposite side of the cottage—on the same floor as Laura's room—was a window-drop of about 20-25ft (which is indicative of a typical second floor). This contrasting theme extended in several different areas of the oddly-shaped home.

Although all of the girls were a bit wild and liked to have fun, Amanda quickly distinguished herself as the "wild one" right from the start. She kept a pink vibrator inside a clear-bag in the bathroom, in clear view of the others. Some of the roommates described it as odd and uncomfortable. Amanda seemed to go out of her way to annoy other women. A fellow student at the Italian university said, "When she introduced herself to the class she just went up to one random guy and didn't go up to anyone else. She talked a lot and laughed at her own jokes." In Perugia, locals explained to UK's *The Times* that their town has two faces (rich culture and a rich nightlife), both of which appear to have seduced

Amanda Knox. It was apparent right from the start that Amanda was more concerned with other things than studying in Italy, as she spent most of her free time drinking, doing drugs, and having sex with different men.

Amanda quickly found a job in late September working at a local club by the name of *Le Chic*. The club had three floors and was located at the end of Piazza Matteotti in Perugia's center. The bar's owner was Patrick Lumumba, a native of the Congo who had moved to Italy 15 years prior when his family opened a chain of clothing stores there. Patrick had recently opened the hot-spot and had heard through a friend, Juve, (a friend of Patrick and Laura's) that the young American girl was looking for work. Amanda entered the bar dressed in flimsy trousers and full of bravado. Patrick thought that she was open and bubbly, and Amanda told him that she'd bring in more customers because she knew everyone. Patrick decided immediately that she'd fit the bill. Le Chic featured specialty rum cocktails and its dance floor was packed regularly. Amanda worked at Le Chic as a barmaid/waitress, collecting glasses every night from 10:00p.m., to 2:30a.m., except for Mondays. Juve also worked at the bar, and was Amanda's personal contact there. Juve would often translate for Amanda, as he spoke both Italian and English.

One day Meredith, Amanda, and a group of their girlfriends stopped by Le Chic as customers. Amanda introduced Meredith to her new boss and he immediately took a liking to her. Meredith's Italian was poor, but she smiled and commented on the special make of vodka that Patrick kept behind the bar, adding that she used to use it instead of rum when she was a barmaid making Mojitos back in Britain; Patrick was impressed. As Amanda and Meredith reconvened with the rest of their group, Patrick noticed that they all seemed like a close-knit bunch of girls. It was Latin and Reggae night, and the girls danced the night away, attracting the attention of all the guys around them.

Amanda's Italian was not very good when she first arrived in Perugia. With Meredith, Amanda spoke mostly English. They tried to speak Italian every once in a while, but when they really wanted to communicate, they would speak English. With Laura, Amanda spoke a mixture of English and Italian, as Laura was fluent in both. Filomena's English, however, was very poor. Amanda seemed to be besotted with Laura; she saw her as a lawyer during the day and a

16

guitar-playing free spirit in the evening, and this intrigued Amanda. In the short time since she had arrived, Amanda and Laura played guitar and practiced yoga together frequently. Amanda saw Laura as a person that she aspired to be like.

On October 15th, Amanda wrote her final MySpace blog, wherein she explained that they had just gotten a washing machine. Although it was broken, she explained, a handyman came over and fixed it. The next morning Amanda was startled by the handyman, as he came walking out of the bathroom in his underwear. Apparently he had spent the night with Laura. Amanda let out a chuckle when she saw him, as she recalled that Laura had told her that she had not had sex in a long time.

Amanda had started school on October 1st. Her classes had been divided into grammar class, culture class, oral/talking class, and pronunciation class. All of her classes were scheduled for Tuesdays and Thursdays, so she had plenty of time during the week to study, work, and party.

Meet Raffaele

On 25 October 2007, Amanda and Meredith decided to attend a classical music concert together at the University of Foreigners. During the concert, Amanda noticed a boy who she thought looked a lot like Harry Potter. For an unknown reason, Meredith had left the concert during intermission, and Amanda continued playing eye-footsies with this intriguing young man. Finally, the boy came and sat near her and introduced himself as Raffaele Sollecito [23]. Introverted and calm—as his friends would later call him—Raffaele was born and raised in Giovinazzo (Southern Italy), a town just up the coast from Bari. Raffaele found Amanda fascinating—no doubt for her wild, charismatic, and care-free American bravado—and he was smitten with her right from the start. The romance was in full-swing as the two connected immediately. They spoke a mixture of English and Italian, with Raffaele often having to translate things to Amanda in English. Amanda was scheduled to work at Le Chic later that night, and she told her new friend to stop by.

Later that night Raffaele, along with a few of his friends, arrived at Le Chic. The flirty and enticing Knox had piqued

Raffaele's interest, and had him stick around the rest of the night. When Amanda's shift had ended (around closing time), Raffaele took her back to his studio apartment at 110 Corso Garibaldi and the two spent the night together. Raffaele's flat was only a ten-minute walk or so from the cottage. Amanda must have been impressed with the fact that Raffaele could afford the rent in the affluent area, as well as with his black Audi that he had parked outside. From the first night on they were all but inseparable; Amanda stayed at Raffaele's that night and every night thereafter, according to Raffaele in his diary. Each morning Amanda would return home to shower and change her clothes, and do whatever else that her daily schedule required.

In the ensuing weeks, leading up to November 1st, there were a few confrontations between Meredith and Amanda over Amanda's lack of work around the cottage. The tension became so that just days before November 1st, Laura and Filomena had organized a program or system for cleaning the cottage that involved a rotation of household chores. At work, Patrick was becoming frustrated with Amanda. For weeks Patrick had quietly tolerated Amanda's unprofessional behavior, but he felt that firing her could generate as much negative word-of-mouth publicity as bringing her in had intended to create. "Every time I looked around she was flirting with a different guy," Patrick told the UK's *Daily Mail*. "She was always causing trouble," said Patrick. "Even my girlfriend thought she was strange. Whenever she met her she'd [Amanda] death-stare her and turn her nose up. I don't think she was jealous? She never came on to me. She just felt so threatened by other women."

Chapter 2 - Nightmare in Perugia

October 31, 2007 - Halloween

The Halloween celebration was in full-swing all over Italy. Street salesmen were out selling roasted chestnuts, and kids ran from door-to-door yelling, "*Dolce!*" ("Sweets!"). And just like in the United States, smiling pumpkins sat outside many houses. Meredith had decided at the last minute to dress up as a vampire for Halloween, with a long black cloak, fake blood on her lips, and vampire teeth. Before heading out, Meredith logged into her *Facebook* page for the last time. She attended her favorite bar, *Merlin's Pub*, with her British girlfriends, Sophie Purton, Robyn Butterworth, and Amy Frost. The Calabrian bar owner, Pasquale Alessi (Pisco), had also decided to dress as a vampire that night. For that reason, Pisco specifically remembers talking to Meredith earlier that day about purchasing vampire teeth to complete their costumes. Apparently there was only one local shop and only one set of teeth left for these last-minute night creatures. Picso had always been friendly with the four British young ladies as they were frequently seen at his pub and were particularly pleasant to be around. Somehow they both managed to complete their outfits and both had a wonderful evening. For one of them, it would be the last night of fun they would ever experience.

That evening Amanda Knox sent Meredith numerous text messages. At 7:00p.m., Meredith responded to Amanda writing, "I have to go to a friend's house for dinner." Amanda persisted, sending Meredith another message. "What are you doing tonight? Do you want to meet up? Have you got a costume?" Receiving no response, Amanda then sent another message saying the she was going to the club *Le Chic*. "Maybe we'll see each other," Amanda concluded with her last message. Amanda arrived at Le Chic (which was also hosting a Halloween party) sometime after that message and took advantage of the free red wine that was being served, but sported no costume.

Just one day earlier the 37-year-old Congolese bar owner of *Le Chic Night Club*, Patrick *Diya* Lumumba, had reduced Amanda's role significantly. Lumumba was fed-up with her, because he had seen her flirting and dancing with several different male patrons (on numerous occasions) that had come into the bar. "Things didn't go very well," Lumumba said when referring to Amanda's employment at the club. He would frequently have to remind her to take care of the customers. Amanda would apologize, but would then go right back to the same destructive behavior. After nearly four weeks of quietly tolerating her wild mood swings, obtuse sexual innuendos, and unenthusiastic work ethic; Lumumba had finally had enough. On Tuesday, 30 October 2007, he told Amanda that she could carry on handing out flyers for the club, but could no longer work inside the bar. Amanda just looked at him blankly and walked away without a response. The club was busy at that time and he didn't see her again that evening.

They ran into each other briefly on Halloween night and momentarily exchanged pleasantries. Lumumba recalls seeing Amanda "all over two American boys…and Sollecito was nowhere in sight." The three-level club was jumping that evening, and Lumumba had much to look after; he could not recall what time Amanda had left that night. Lumumba locked up his club at 3:00a.m., and headed over to *Merlin's Pub*, which was close-by. There, he ran into Meredith Kercher and the two spoke briefly. Since he now had a job opening—after limiting Knox's role—Lumumba mentioned the idea of having Meredith work for him. Meredith smiled sweetly and said she couldn't wait and that she'd bring all her friends back to the club for him. At some point, either before the bar closed or after, Amanda headed over to Raffaele's flat (late night) and slept over. "I told her [Amanda] I'd asked Meredith to come and work for me and her face dropped and there was a big silence," Patrick told the UK's *Daily Mail* (in an article published on 11/25/07). "Then she said, 'Fine,' and stomped off. I knew then she was extremely jealous of Meredith. She [Amanda] obviously thought she [Meredith] was invading her territory."

November 1, 2007 – All Saints Day

The next day is officially known as "All Saints Day," in Italy. Many Catholics attend church services in honor of the saints, the martyrs, and those who have died for the Catholic faith. It is a two-day celebration; although only November 1st is a National holiday. Amanda and Raffaele woke up at his flat at 10:00a.m., the next morning and had breakfast there together. There were scores of students in the city of Perugia—a city that was thronged with young people who partied the night before—who were undoubtedly nursing hangovers.

After breakfast Amanda left and arrived home at around 11:00a.m. Meredith was still sleeping after the wild Halloween celebration the previous night. Amanda took a shower then went into the kitchen and began making herself something to eat. As she was fumbling around in the kitchen, Meredith emerged from her room with the blood of her costume still on her chin and jumped into the shower. Another roommate, Filomena Romanelli, and her boyfriend, Marco Zaroli, arrived at the cottage at 12:30p.m. Filomena had returned home, with Marco, to change clothes; because they were going to lunch at the home of a friend of Marco's, Luca Altieri. When they arrived they witnessed Amanda sitting at the kitchen table wearing a white and dark grey-striped top. Filomena changed quickly and the couple was off to meet their friend for lunch.

At 1:00p.m., Amanda had begun eating when Raffaele entered the cottage. Hungry as well, Raffaele made himself some pasta and joined Amanda at the kitchen table. While they were in the kitchen eating, Meredith came out of the shower, grabbed some laundry, and returned to her room. At about 4:00p.m., Meredith again emerged from her room; this time she left in a hurry and did not say where she was going. Nonetheless, Meredith was walking to her friend Robyn Butterworth's flat (Via Bontempi 22) to meet Robyn and her other Halloween cohorts, Sophie Purton and Amy Frost. There is no direct route to Robyn's house, but there are several ways to get there; keeping in mind that everywhere in Perugia is uphill from the cottage at Via Della Pergola 7. All of these routes to Robyn's, nevertheless, would first start by walking up past the car-park (which is across the street from the cottage), passing the basketball court with only one hoop (at Piazza Grimana); on an uphill trek to meet her girlfriends. Since she was walking alone she probably would have taken a different route to Robyn's apartment on the way there than she did on the way back.

Meredith would have either made at left at the basketball court onto Via Pinturicchio then a quick right up the stairs of a small alley that leads directly to Via Bartolo. She would take Via Bartolo all the way to the end. From there she would have made a left (Pizza Danti-Piazza Piccinino) and followed this street, which soon turns into Via Bontempi. Or, for argument sake, back at the basketball court she could have walked through the Etruscan Arch and continued up Via Ulisse Rocchi. As she ascended she would pass Pizzeria Etrusca and several strangely intersecting streets and alleyways. Via Ulisse Rocchi ends behind the *Cattedrale S. Lorenzo*. From there she could have cut across the plaza, by the cafés, and onto Via Bontempi; where Butterworth's apartment was only a few feet ahead. During the walk to Robyn's apartment, Meredith decided to call her ill mother, Arline, as she did everyday during her stay in Italy. The two discussed her plans to return home to England the following week to celebrate Arline's birthday. Meredith told her mother that she was tired from the night before and was headed to a friend's house to watch a movie. Meredith also explained that she planned to return to the cottage early that evening as she had an essay to finish and a lecture at 10:00a.m., the following morning.

Raffaele and Amanda stayed at the cottage until 5:00p.m., at which time they left and went on a walk through the center of town before returning to Raffaele's flat. Once at Raffaele's the couple ate a fish dinner that Raffaele had prepared. After dinner Amanda told Raffaele that she wanted to watch a movie; so they went up to his room and watched the movie *Amelie* while downloading the film *Stardust* to watch at another time. Amanda sat on the bed as Raffaele sat at his desk preparing a marijuana cigarette so that they could smoke and watch the movie. There are conflicting stories regarding what the couple did next and for the remainder of the night. So conflicting in fact, that even they have both changed their stories about what they did for the rest of the evening. They both have claimed that they smoked hashish and that they don't remember many details of the night (*See chapter13 for speculation regarding Knox and Sollecito's whereabouts from this point on during the evening*).

Either way that Meredith took to get there, she arrived at Robyn's apartment at sometime before 4:30p.m., where Sophie and Amy had already been since about 3:30p.m. They were all tired from partying the night before, so they decided to spend a quiet and uneventful evening inside. The four young girls all piled onto Robyn's bed and spent the night watching the movie *The Notebook* on a laptop DVD, eating pizza, ice cream, and drinking soda. At sometime just before 8:30p.m., Meredith told the others that she was tired and was going to go home. Feeling a bit fatigued from the prior nights' events, Sophie also decided to call it a night and agreed to walk home with Meredith. Before they left Meredith borrowed a book from Robyn on medieval history for her next exam. It was a cold night, so the girls made sure to throw their scarves around their necks to keep warm. Robyn's flat was located at the top of the hill, in Perugia's center, where all the buildings are connected.

After exiting through Robyn's large wooden door they stepped onto the narrow street of Via Bontempi and moved east. Darkness had begun to fall upon the historic hilltop city by then. Instead of taking the same route that she had taken to get there, Meredith decided to walk the flatter route that led to Sophie's house; from there it would only be a short walk home. Although the route would take a little longer for Meredith, she would at least walk most of the way with her friend. They conversed casually as they walked down the windy road that soon turned into Via de Roscetto. It was a short walk for Sophie from there, who lived just about half-way down Via De Roscetto. They soon came upon Via Del Lupo, the street where Sophie lived (on the corner of Via De Roscetto and Via Del Lupo). It was there that Sophie bid Meredith farewell for the very last time.

Meredith continued on alone down Via de Roscetto and soon reached Via Pinturicchio, which runs alongside the medieval wall. At number 31 is the former Oratory of St. John the Baptist; Meredith made a left on Via Pinturicchio, going in the opposite direction of the Oratory. Just beyond the Pesa Gate she passed under the historic Dei Tei Arch, which marks the end of Corso Bersaglieri. Just past the arch is the entrance to the Santa Maria Nuova Church. Just a few steps ahead of that on the oddly small sidewalk and she came up upon a small sign on her right that reads, "*POST centro della scienza.*" This is a small and narrow alleyway that leads to Via Del

Melo. Meredith could have taken this shortcut to get home, as Via Del Melo is just above the cottage. The shortcut is a dimly-lit alley that leads to metal stars into the car park. It is unlikely; however, that Meredith would have taken this shortcut, as it would be a risky proposition at night.

Meredith most likely continued walking down Via Pinturicchio for a very short distance, until she came upon a sign that reads: "Hotel San Sebastiano." There she made a right and walked down the hill of stairs that starts at the basketball court (The same court with one hoop that she passed on the way to Robyn's house). She continued down the stairs, ultimately walking straight into the intersecting Viale Sant'Antonio. Only mere steps before she reached the intersecting road, she passed the car park, which was on her right side. A CCTV-camera from that car park *allegedly* captured a fleeting image of Meredith passing at 8:45p.m., that very evening. From there it is only about 50 yards to the front door of her cottage. Meredith made one last call to her mother at 8:56p.m., but the call was interrupted (for some unknown reason) and ended before they had a chance to speak.

November 2, 2007 – 'Il Giorno dei Morti', (The Day of the Dead)

November 2nd, "*Il Giorno dei Morti,*" or "Day of the Dead," is a holiday celebrated in Mexico and by Latin Americans living in the United States and Canada. The term has since been adopted by Italy and is the third-straight day of celebration in honor of the dead. It is the day when churches and families remember and celebrate all who've passed. Special celebrations are held, which includes taking flowers and candles to the graves of loved ones wherein children find presents given to them by the dead (assorted candies). A real treat on this day in Italy are "Bones of the Dead" cookies, which are made of powdered almond macaroons, sweet wine, dried fruit, chocolate, pignoli, and spices. They also make cakes in the shape of beans, which are amply titled "Beans of the Dead." This ironically titled day, however, would soon be overshadowed by a tragedy that would almost immediately garner attention across the globe.

Amanda Knox had allegedly spent the night at Raffaele Sollecito's flat, and then returned home to a troubling scene. At 12:08p.m., Knox decided to call her roommate Filomena Romanelli, who had spent the night at her boyfriend, Marco Zaroli's house. Filomena left Marco's house earlier that morning to attend 'La Feria de Morti' ('Fair of the Dead') with Paola Grande. *Fair of Dead* is a historic Italian Market Fair held that night at the Umbria Jazz Square, in the valley of Pian di Massiano. Filomena and Paola had just arrived at the fair and were parking their car when her phone rang; on the other end it was Amanda Knox.

During the phone call, Knox told Filomena that she had slept at Raffaele's house the previous night, and when she had gone back to the cottage that morning she found the door open and blood in her bathroom. She told Filomena that she'd had a shower, yet she was scared and that she was going to call Raffaele. Filomena urged Amanda to take a better look around the house, call the police, and get back to her. Filomena was puzzled how Knox could have taken a shower under such circumstances. After parking the car, Filomena and Paola proceed to the fare. Worried and confused, however, Filomena calls Knox back at 12:12p.m., and 12:20p.m., but Knox does not answer.

Earlier that morning the Polizia Postale (Postal Police)— Branch that deals with communication crimes—received a call from a nearby elderly neighbor, Lana Elisabetta, who had found two cell phones in the garden of her home at the Via Sperandio 5b (which was about two-hundred yards from Meredith's cottage). One of the phones was listed as belonging to Meredith and the other to her flat-mate Filomena Romanelli (SIM-card of Vodafone 348-467-3711). Meredith's phone was registered in the United Kingdom, while Romanelli's was an Italian registered device. Postal police dispatcher, Filippo Bartolozzi (Head of the Umbrian postal police), radioed officer's Michele Battistelli and Fabio Marzi, who retrieved the cell phones and headed over to Via Della Pergola 7.

The two officers responded by retrieving the phones from Via Sperandio 5b then going to Meredith's house to find out if the phones had been stolen and to return her property. They arrived at the cottage at approximately 12:30p.m., and found Amanda Knox and Raffaele Sollecito waiting outside. Officer Bartolozzi radioed back to headquarters and advised that they had arrived at the house. When Inspector Battistelli approached the couple he noticed that they seemed embarrassed and surprised; he also noticed that Knox and Sollecito were whispering to each other. At the time he didn't think much of it, but the couple was also holding a mop and bucket; which when later examined contained the contents of bleach. They told Battistelli that they had just arrived back at the house together. Knox claimed that she was at Sollecito's, came back, and noticed the front door open and their flat mate's window (Filomena Romanelli) smashed. Knox then claimed that she rushed back to Sollecito's and they returned together. Knox and Sollecito then told the Inspector that they were waiting for the Carabinieri, a.k.a. "The Flying Squad," (formally part of the army, they now operate as an all-purpose national police force) to arrive, but they didn't say when they called them, just that they were waiting for them to arrive.

Battistelli followed the couple inside to Filomena's room where they showed him the broken window, and ransacked room with clothes all over the floor. The inspector was immediately struck by the fact that the glass lay on top of the clothes as though the window had been broken after the clothes were scattered. Being a seasoned officer, Battistelli immediately thought that this had been an attempt to make it look like a break-in. Battistelli told Knox and Sollecito of his suspicions, but they did not respond. Battistelli also noticed that there was a lap top in that room and an expensive digital camera in the kitchen. He believed that these items would most likely have been taken if this was a legitimate break-in. Battistelli also noted that the washing machine was running at the time of his arrival.

At 12:34p.m., Filomena calls Knox again and this time she answered. "Come home immediately!" Knox commands Filomena. Knox tells her that she had found the window in her [Filomena's] room broken and her room was a mess and looked like it had been buglarized. Filomena tells Knox to call the police and Knox claims that she already had, but makes no mention that the police had already arrived. In a panic, Filomena called her boyfriend, Marco Zaroli, who lived closer to the cottage than where Filomena was physically located at the time, he could get there quicker than she could. She asked Marco to rush over to the cottage, because there had been a break-in. Marco then calls his buddy Luca Altieri, and tells him that his girlfriend's place had been robbed, and asks him for a ride over to the cottage.

Not realizing at the time that this chance phone call was leading him directly into a hellish scene, Altieri accepts and rushes over to get Zaroli. Sollecito is pulled away by a call from his father at 12:40p.m. In the meantime, Altieri and Zaroli rush over to the cottage and arrive at roughly 12:46p.m. When the boys arrived the postal police briefed them on the situation. The two boys noticed a post-it-note in the kitchen with Meredith's phone number on it, which Knox had written earlier for police. Meanwhile, Knox and Sollecito had slipped into Amanda's room to make some phone calls (*more on this later*). Knox came out of her room briefly and told police that it was common for Meredith to lock her door, even when she took a shower. Altieri overheard Knox telling this to police. She then disappeared back into her room.

Just before 1:00p.m., Filomena Romanelli finally arrived, accompanied by Paola Grande. Filomena confirmed that she had lent Meredith her phone so that Meredith could use it to make calls within Italy. Filomena said that she was concerned because she had called Meredith several times that day and the night before, but there was no answer: which she confirmed was uncanny. Knox and Sollecito were in Knox's room when the girls had arrived. They remained there for some twelve-minutes before emerging. Battistelli had been speaking to the group when Knox and Sollecito came strolling out of her room—as witnessed by Paola Grande—and greeted the new arrivals just after 1:00p.m. Filomena went into her room to assess the damage and noticed that her computer was on the floor, on top of a pile of clothes, and covered with pieces of glass. The first thing that Filomena thought when she saw her room was, "What a stupid burglar." As the group was discussing the situation, Altieri told them that Knox had claimed that it was common for Meredith to lock her door, even when she took a shower. Filomena adamantly objects and says that Meredith never locks her door.

It was then that it was decided to break down Meredith's locked door (approx. 1:15p.m.). Knox and Sollecito withdrew into the kitchen; the other six individuals walked through the corridor towards Meredith's room. The officers did not want to break down the door because they feared a lawsuit from the landlord; so Luca volunteered to do so. Luca wanted reassurance, however, that he would not be responsible for the damages. While in the corridor Paola told him, "Everybody is witness that I'm allowing you [Luca] permission to kick-in the door." Marco and Marzi (the other policeman) were in the corridor behind Battistelli and Luca. Behind them were Paola and Filomena.

Luca Altieri positioned himself and gave the door three good kicks. Suddenly the door swung open, but almost as soon as his momentum pushed him forward, he immediately drew-back in horror. Battistelli was standing behind Altieri at the time when he heard him scream, "There's blood! There's a foot!" Battistelli looked in the room and saw blood everywhere, a lot of blood, but he did not go in. Paola was also in position to get a quick peek inside the room. Marco screamed "Sangue, sangue!" ("Blood, blood!"). Marco then grabbed Filomena and said, "Via, via!" (Away, away), and the two exited the house. Battistelli was the first to witness Meredith Kercher's lifeless body lying on the floor; she was almost entirely covered by a duvet, leaving visible only a part of her head stained with blood and her left foot, which was sticking out from the lower edge of the duvet. Her head lay between a small nightstand next to the bed that was against the back wall and a tall wooden wardrobe that was also positioned against that same wall. Meredith's throat had been cut on one side, and had a very deep knife wound on the other side. She had no clothes on other than a t-shirt that had been pulled up to her neck, exposing her breasts.

Battistelli orders everyone out and they all hastily leave the house, escorted by officer Marzi, except Battistelli and Luca. Luca sees Battistelli stepping into the room, but Paola immediately goes outside with the others. Luca peeks in and sees Battistelli lift the duvet to see Meredith's face. In that moment Luca turns and goes to the others, who have reassembled in the garden outside. Officer Marzi goes and guards the entrance so that no one can come back into the house. No one but Battistelli had gotten a look at the body and no one was aware or told any of the details of the finding, other than the confirmation that the girl in the room—who was most likely Meredith—was dead. It all seemed to happen so fast; confusion and shock overwhelmed the group. Battistelli quickly meets the others in the garden, where he calls the operations room to notify them of what he had witnessed and he requested medical aid and a *volante* patrol (flying squad).

Strange Behavior

The press soon swarmed the area, as murders of this nature are very uncommon in Perugia. Almost immediately, police and reporters began to notice strange behavior exhibited by Knox and Sollecito. Cameras caught the two kissing outside of the house in what some would describe as inappropriate for the circumstance. Police rounded-up several of Meredith's friends and requested their presence down at headquarters for questioning. It was decided that Sollecito and Knox would ride with Paola Grande and her boyfriend, Luca Altieri, to the Perugia police station. During the trip Paola and Luca felt very uncomfortable with the couple. Sollecito was constantly asking them questions regarding the murder and investigation, in a very odd manner. So much so, it caused them to become concerned and suspicious enough to thoroughly check the interior of the car after Knox and Sollecito had gotten out. Paola and Luca were afraid that the couple might have "planted incriminating evidence" in the car.

As the interviews continued at the police station, so too did the couple's strange behavior. The owner of the Merlin's pub, Pisco Alessi, was at the station during questing. He claimed that Knox and Sollecito were laughing, joking, and kissing. "It just seemed completely wrong in that situation," he said. Robyn Butterworth also witnessed Knox's strange behavior at the station, and thought that she seemed unmoved by the events. "I remember Amanda also kept going on about how she found the body," Robyn said. "It was as if she was proud to have been the one who found it. I just remember thinking at the time at the police station that Amanda's behavior was very strange. It was as if she wasn't bothered at all." At some point while sitting in police headquarters the discussion then turned to speculation over Meredith's death.

One of Meredith's friends, Natalie Hayworth, said, "I hope she wasn't in too much pain." Knox replied smugly, "What do you think? She fucking bled to death." Knox appeared to be boasting about finding the body and giving explicit details that only the murderer(s) could have known at that time. "How do you think I feel? I found her in the closet covered by a blanket," Knox stated. Hayward also quoted Knox as saying Meredith would have "died slowly and in a lot of pain." Robyn revealed, "At that point no one had told us how Meredith had died." Opinions seemed to be unanimous as Amy Frost stated, "Their behavior [Knox and Sollecito] at the police station seemed to me really inappropriate...Amanda put her feet up on Raffaele's legs and made faces at him, such as crossing her eyes and sticking her tongue out. Everyone cried except Amanda and Raffaele." The picture painted of Knox and Sollecito during this time, by all accounts, was clearly that of cold and unemotional.

When it was her turn to speak, Knox told police that she had seen Meredith at 1:00p.m., at their apartment with Sollecito the previous day and that she saw her leave between 3:00p.m., and 4:00p.m., but did not know where she was going. Knox claimed that she stayed with Sollecito at the cottage until 5:00p.m., at which time they went to his apartment, where they spent the whole night. She told police that the next morning she had returned home at 11:00a.m., and found the front door open. She then tried to call her housemates, but heard no response.

According to Knox, she found traces of blood in both bathrooms and the toilet of the bathroom furthest from Meredith's room was full of feces. Knox said that she didn't think much of the blood, because she thought that one of her roommates might have had a menstrual situation and had forgotten to clean up. She claimed that she left the apartment at 11.30a.m., (after taking a shower). Upon leaving she closed the front door, locked it, and then returned to Sollecito's flat. Knox said that she "tried to contact Meredith several times, but no answer." It was later confirmed that Knox had called Meredith's phone twice that day, but at 12:07p.m., and 12:14p.m. Both calls only lasted a few seconds.

Knox then claimed that she went back to the apartment at Via della Pergola 7 accompanied by Sollecito. It was at that time she says she first noticed Filomena's window had been broken, and that she also discovered the door, of the room occupied by Meredith, locked. She then said that she decided to call the Carabinieri after Sollecito called his sister to ask what they should do. She said that after calling the Carabinieri, she and Sollecito were waiting outside for them to get there when the postal police had arrived.

Sollecito told police a similar story with a few inconsistencies:

"When she arrived the front door was wide open. She thought it was weird, but thought maybe someone was in the house and had left it ajar. But when she went into the bathroom she saw spots of blood all over the bath and sink. That's when she started getting really afraid and ran back to my place because she didn't want to go into the house alone. So I agreed to go back with her. When we walked in together, I knew straight away it was wrong. It was really eerily silent and the bathroom was speckled with blood like someone had flicked it around, just little spots"

The only two exceptions to Sollectio's version was that he left out the part about Knox's shower, and appeared to paint the picture as if Knox immediately fled back to his place in fear once she saw the blood. His account also differs in the fact that he told police that he found the water in the toilet by Filomena's room clean, instead of with feces in it. When the military police had arrived, on the other hand, they noticed that the toilet was still filled with feces. Both Knox and Sollecito maintained that after they had returned to the house, he then called his sister who advised him to call 112 (Italy's version of 911). Despite the fact that Sollecito informed the postal police (when they arrived at 12:35pm) that he had already contacted the Carabinieri, records would later indicate that Sollecito's two calls to 112 came at 12:51p.m., and 12:54p.m. The first time he called they put him on an indefinite hold, so he hung up the phone and called back at 12:54p.m.

Raffaele's Phone Call to 112, (2 November 2007) - English Translation:

Raffaele: Hello, good morning, listen, ah, someone broke into the house through a window and made a big mess. There is a closed door. The address is Via Della Pergola number 7 in Perugia.

Police: They managed to enter that way, they broke a window? And how do you know that's how they entered?

Raffaele: You can see the signs. There are also stains of blood in the bathroom. *They didn't take anything.* The problem is the door is locked. There is a lot of blood.

Police: There is a locked door? Which door is locked?

Raffaele: The one belonging to the roommate who isn't here and we don't know where she is. Yes, yes, we tried to call her, but she does not respond to anyone.

Police: Okay, good, now we will send a patrol so we verify the situation.

Forensic Investigation

Meanwhile, back at the house, the forensic investigation had gotten underway. The graphic scene of gathering crime scene evidence always seems like a scene out of a Hitchcock movie. The Italian Crime Scene Investigation (CSI) was operational at approximately 15:10:45 on 11/2/07. The Crime Scene Investigators were covered from head to toe with white protective clothing to prevent contamination while examining and bagging evidence. Also notable, close attention was paid to the small cabinet next to the toilet in the bathroom closest to Meredith's room, which had a roll of toilet paper on it and several blood stains. The time of the final clip on the video was 2:02:18 on 11/3/07, which showed nearly eleven-hours of crime scene processing. There was certainly more video that was taken, but here is a glimpse of some of the things that were recorded during the eleven-hours of footage.

11/2/2007:

15:10:45 - Quick pan of the living room
15:20:56 - Looking under duvet
15:30:15 - Small bathroom with zooms noted above
15:31:52 - The Victim under the duvet
15:31:53 - Zoom of corner made by left side of wardrobe and wall
15:31:57 - Zoom of visible blood spots on wardrobe doors
(There is a pair of jeans folded on shelf of wardrobe)

19:46:42 - Footprint in bedroom by evidence marker "A"
(Zoom of bra and dark colored underwear on the floor at victim's feet)

11/3/2007:

00:20:05 - Special light on floor by evidence marker "3", and wiping some substance on floor (Hopefully not luminol, as it destroys blood evidence and is supposed to be applied after it is thoroughly examined and collected)
1:22:28 - Putting bra into evidence bag
1:46:18 - The victim with duvet pulled back
1:52:42 - Zoom of Victim under the duvet
2:02:18 - Viewing and bagging a pair of bloody jeans found on the floor

During the Polizia's forensic search of the crime scene they collected several key clues, including:

In Meredith's room:

- Bloody shoeprint on a pillow that had been found half under the pelvis of the body
- Bloody jeans
- Two bloody Footprints (Sneaker)
- White Bra
- Black under wear (female)
- Duvet with blood stains that covered the body
- White towel on the bed with blood on it
- Drop of blood on the bed
- Another drop of blood on the bed (about 2 or 3 ft. from the other)
- Blood on the nightstand
- 19 unidentifiable fingerprints in Meredith's room (Partially smeared as if wiped clean)
- Broken window
- Red purse on the bed
- Pillow with blood stains on it

- Bloody handprint on the wall in Meredith's room (between the bed and the small nightstand – approximately 6ft high on the wall)

Found Elsewhere in the cottage:

- Bloody footprint (barefoot) in the bathroom on a blue mat on the floor (Along with several other spots of blood on the mat)
- A few small drops of blood on the small cabinet next to the toilet in the bathroom next to Meredith's room
- A swath of blood around the drainage of the bidet in the bathroom next to Meredith's room
- A smear of blood on the bottom, outside of the bathroom door of the bathroom next to Meredith's room
- Small amount of blood on the sink facet and on the side of the Q-tip box in the bathroom next to Meredith's room
- Smears of blood on Meredith's door handle—on the corridor side of the door
- Five footprints (barefoot) in the rest of the house (Found later using the chemical: Luminol)
- Afore mentioned broken window in Filomena's room
- Rock found in Filomena's room under a chair (believed to be what broke the window)
- Feces in the toilet in the bathroom next to Filomena's room
- A smaller stone on the ground outside of Filomena's window

Meredith's door was found locked from the inside, and one initial theory from police was that her attacker may have exited the cottage by climbing out through her ground floor window, which led to a small rear garden. Police had also theorized, however, that Meredith might have known the killer and might have met him at the bar she attended on Halloween night and that the killer may have exited through the front door. During their examination police began to formulate that Meredith had been involved in a sexual act before death, although they could not confirm at that time whether it was consensual or rape. Conversely, there was no murder weapon present.

Back in England, the Kercher family was notified and obviously devastated by the news. They all gathered in their home to morn together behind closed doors on 7 November 2007. John Kercher, Sr., [64], arrived at the family's home on Friday night. He and Meredith's mother, Arlene, were separated at the time; however, their unfortunate loss brought the family together once again. Meredith's other brother, Lyle [28], and her sister, Stephanie [24], lived with their mother at the time. Meredith's brother, John Kercher, Jr., [31], drove in from North London with his wife to be with his family as well. John Kercher, Sr., said that when he heard on T.V. that a British student was killed in Perugia he called Meredith's phone 20 to 30 times, but no one answered. His worst fears were later confirmed.

Chapter 3 - Initial Investigation

Killer(s) on the Loose – November 4, 2007

The next few days were traumatic and tense for the residents of Perugia, particularly for those living in the surrounding areas of the cottage. Word of the murder spread quickly in the shell-shocked city, and many residents feared the killer(s), who was/were still on the loose. Police had completely sealed-off the cottage and had a patrol protecting it day and night. Back at headquarters police continued their investigation—going through Meredith's diary and computer for any clues. They also took to the streets, sending out separate patrols into the city to investigate. This included a thorough sweep of the area residents, local shops, and bars associated with the murdered victim. Police were also tracking down the friends and family of the victim for further analysis. Right from the start police were working on the theory that Kercher had known her killer, which they identified as possibly being male. The theory was that Kercher had met a man at the Halloween party that she had intended on meeting up with the following night. This led them to a bar named Merlin's Pub, where Meredith and friends had been partying on Halloween night.

Plain clothes policemen canvassed student bars around the city the Saturday following the murder, interviewing anyone who might have encountered Meredith on Halloween night. Police already had knowledge of Meredith's whereabouts during the early evening hours of her death. They knew that she was at Robyn Butterworth's flat, and they believed that she may have left there to

36

meet-up with her killer. Police theorized that the killer exited the crime scene through the front door, staging the 'alleged' break-in. Police were also looking into the possibility that the killer may have been a heroin addict who frequented the area; although, this was a secondary theory. The underground car park, which is located across the street from Kercher's cottage, was known to be used by drug-dealers to make their transactions. The BBC reported on Sunday, 4 November 2007, that a teacher from the nearby University informed them that a former housemate (at the cottage) had complained the previous term that addicts were often seen in a nearby street and syringes had been found in the garden.

Raffaele Sollecito gave a detailed and cavalier account of their (Knox and Sollecito's) discovery of the body in his first public statement to UK Newspaper, *Sunday Mirror,* which was published the Sunday after the murder.

"It is something I never hope to see again…There was blood everywhere and I couldn't take it all in…My girlfriend was her flat-mate and she was crying and screaming, 'How could anyone do this?'"

Already, Sollecito had begun to spin his story with bizarre inconsistencies in comparison with the version that Knox told police and any of his versions. In this version he spun himself as the hero and Knox as outwardly distraught and frightened.

"It was a normal night," Sollecito said. "Meredith had gone out with one of her English friends and Amanda and I went to a party with one of my friends." Sollecito never identified this "friend," nor did he ever mention this "friend" or "party" in any other version. He claims that the next day around lunchtime Knox went back to the flat alone to take a shower, but:

> "When she [Knox] arrived the front door was wide open. She thought it was weird, but thought maybe someone was in the house and had left it ajar. But when she went into the bathroom she saw spots of blood all over the bath and sink. That's when she started getting really afraid and ran back to my place because she didn't want to go into the house alone. So I agreed to go back with her. When we walked in together, I knew straight away it was wrong. It was

really eerily silent and the bathroom was speckled with blood like someone had flicked it around, just little spots. We went into the bedroom of Filomena and it had been ransacked, like someone had been looking for something. But when we tried Meredith's room, the door was locked. She never normally locked her bedroom door and that really made us frightened."

Sollecito claims that he thought maybe Meredith was ill, but their panic grew as he banged on the door and no one answered. It was at that point that he claimed he attempted to knock the door down. He made a dent in the door he said, but he was not strong enough to break it down so he called the police. Once police got the door open, Sollecito claims to have witnessed the terrible scene along with Knox.

"I couldn't believe what I was seeing," he said. "It was hard to tell it was Meredith at first but Amanda started crying and screaming. I dragged her away because I didn't want her to see it, it was so horrible."

This version must certainly have caught police's attention as neither he nor Amanda were allowed to look into the room, according to police and everyone else at the cottage at the time of the discovery. Moreover, by all witness accounts, Knox and Sollecito were nowhere near the door when it was opened and the police had kicked everyone out of the house the minute they realized it was a murder and not just a '*case of the missing phones.*'

Post-Mortem Examination

Meanwhile, Pathologist, Dr. Luca Lalli, was in charge of the post-mortem examination. Dr. Lalli's examination was conducted three days after the body was discovered. The examination took six-and-a-half hours, and revealed evidence of sexual activity at some point before Kercher died. However, Dr. Lalli would not confirm at that time whether she had been raped or not. "We've completed our work and there are interesting elements which I must now discuss with the magistrate," Lalli said, but wouldn't elaborate. Dr. Lalli did not make clear when the results of the examination would be made public. Dr. Lalli claimed that Meredith was killed with a penknife (a small pocketknife).

November 5, 2007

The next day the Kercher family issued there first public statement. Nothing could have prepared them for the news that they were given the previous Friday evening. The shock and horror of the family was clearly evident in their heart-felt statement. "Words cannot even begin to describe how we feel right now, other than utterly devastated…" The family described Meredith as a "genuinely caring person" who "touched the lives of everyone she met." To make matters worse, if possible, Meredith had been scheduled to fly home the following weekend for her mother's birthday. Her suitcase was already packed and she had chocolates in it as a gift to her mother. In closing the family asked that if anyone had any information on the killer, to come forward and help them "bring to justice the person who has destroyed so many lives." Meredith's father John, a freelance journalist, made immediate plans to fly to Italy to identify the body. He would be accompanied by the British embassy staff.

Knox returned to the University for Foreigners, where she had a writing exam. Some students who saw Knox that day claimed that she was acting strange. Elena Scacchi (classmate of Knox) felt a strange feeling when observing Knox. "She [Amanda] didn't seem shocked," Scacchi said. "She seemed sad, but not like I'd imagine a person or I'd imagine myself after a person that is close to me gets killed in that way." Scacchi seemed to share the same sentiments of many others. While in class Amanda wrote a letter to her mother claiming that she was stressed over Meredith's death and wanted to go shopping to ease her mind.

Students and friends of Meredith in Perugia showed their humanity by organizing a torch-lit procession for her that led them through the city streets in her memory. The procession was paid for graciously by local bar owners. The atmosphere in Perugia was tense, subdued, and suspicious that evening. Of the many students from the University for Foreigners who attended, some knew Meredith and some did not; regardless, most of them seemed devastated. Several students told reporters that they were going to go home for break and probably not return as a result of the tragedy. The large procession toured the town with a giant portrait of Meredith hoisted high in her memory. Everyone who knew Meredith spoke extremely highly of her. Polish student, Tom Bednerek [22], sang Meredith's praises and shared the opinions of many. "She had a lot of friends of all nationalities," he said. "We all just feel so sad for her family."

Police reported that there was an unusually small amount of blood found at the scene for the type of crime that was committed. They believed, from that and other evidence, that the perpetrator had cleaned the house thoroughly after the murder. Police also suspected that the murderer must have had a key to the first level of the cottage—where the boys lived—because the bathroom down there was also used to clean-up. They also realized that there was no sign of a break-in at that level of the cottage. Moreover, police reported that the killer(s) appeared to have tried to incriminate the four Italian boys who lived on that floor, because they found smears of blood in their rooms after the killing had taken place. Coincidentally, Meredith had been given the keys to the first-floor level by her boyfriend, Giacomo Silenzi (who lived down there), to check on their cat who had a torn ear, and also to water his Marijuana plant. Police theorized that the killer(s) knew this and took the keys from Meredith during the murder. The keys were never recovered.

Media scrutiny soon brought police under intense pressure to come up with a suspect. Since the truth was not coming out naturally, police felt the need to use more invasive methods to find out what had happened. So police decided to tap-into Knox's mobile phone. On the evening of Sunday, November 4th, police overheard Knox telling Sollecito, "I cannot do it any more, I cannot bear it." Police had also placed a bug on Raffaele Sollecito's phone that night. They captured a conversation that Raffaele had with his father Franco, a urologist from Bari. Raffaele explained to his father what was going on and they had a conversation about a flick-knife that Raffaele was known to carry around. At one point during the conversation Mr. Sollecito said, "Raffaele don't walk about with a knife, if police find it on you who knows what they may think." Raffaele responded by saying, "Well they have already questioned me and they didn't find it on me, those stupid policemen." Feeling that this was sufficient enough for further interrogation, police asked

Sollecito to come to headquarters the next day. Although her presence was not requested by police, Knox had arranged to meet Sollecito at the station that night. As Knox waited at the police station for Sollecito to arrive—just before 10:30p.m.—she placed a phone call to Filomena to discuss future living arrangements. Sollecito arrived at police headquarters sometime after 10:30p.m. When police asked Knox to remain in the waiting room while they took Sollecito in for questioning, the couple asked if they could remain together. It was clear that the two did not want to be separated. Unfortunately for them, they had no choice.

The Arrest

While police were questioning Sollecito, Knox waited in a side room. Policewoman Lorena Zugarini walked into the room to check on Knox and caught her doing cartwheels and the splits. Zugarini told Knox that it was "not the right place for such activities." At around 11:00p.m., Inspector Chief of Perugia police's narcotics unit, Rita Ficarra, came out of the lift into the waiting room of the city's Flying Squad on the third floor of the police station and witnessed Knox "showing off her gymnastic ability," turning cartwheels and doing back bends. This angered the inspector, and she scolded Knox, telling her "This is the police station, not a dance theater!" Knox and Ficarra began talking about the night of the murder, and Ficarra told Knox that the answers she and Raffaele had given don't add up and are filled with several contradictions. Ficarra tried to explain to Knox, "If you tell me a lie one time, that is comprehensible, but if you lie again—even if it is a small lie—it makes you less credible." One reason for the officer's warning was that Knox had originally told police that she had not smoked cannabis, but then said that she had, according to Rita.

Ficarra then decided that since Knox was already present, she would like her to detail a list of people that had visited the house in th two months since she's been there. Knox agrees, takes out her ce l phone, and begins to go through the list of names. 'He's been there; he hasn't been there, etc.' Rita begins taking notes, but soon realizes that she needs an interpreter. When the interpreter arrived shortly after, Knox again began giving Ficarra names of people who had visited the flat, including "A South African man" she had met at a party in the flat underneath hers. Knox said that she didn't know his name or phone number, and had never seen him again after that night (Rudy Guede). At this point, Knox willingly hands over her phone to Ficarra, who begins scrolling through Knox's text messages and asking her who these people were and when she had met them— she wanted to know everything: "Peter, Juve, Spiros, Shaggy…" Ficarra continued, rattling-off names and quizzing Knox. Inspector Lorena Zugarini enters the room and begins observing silently.

Suddenly, the head of the Perugia homicide unit, Monica Napoleoni, enters the room and says, "*He [Sollecito] doesn't cover her anymore, so you'd better ask Amanda again her whereabouts on the evening of the murder.*" It turns out that Raffaele Sollecito had changed his story, claiming that he was with Knox only until 9:00p.m., on the night of the murder. Sollecito claims that he and Knox left the cottage at 6:00p.m., at which time they went into the centre. "At 9:00p.m., I went home alone and Amanda said that she was going to *Le Chic* because she wanted to meet some friends," Sollecito told police. "We said goodbye and I went home, I rolled myself a spliff [Marijuana cigarette] and made some dinner." Sollecito goes on to say that Knox returned to his flat at around 1:00a.m., at which time the couple went to bed.

Amanda Knox's alibi had abruptly evaporated! As Ficarra continued through Knox's messages, she came to a text that Knox had sent to her boss, Patrick Lumumba. Ficarra shows her the message and asks, "Who is this person?" Ficarra believed that the message read like a date—to meet up later that night. "Did you go out with him that night?" Ficarra asked. Unexpectedly and without warning, Knox put her head in her hands, started shaking her head, as tears streamed down from her eyes. "*He's bad, he's bad…*"— Amanda says as if she is in a trance—"*He's the murderer…I can hear him in Meredith's room…I can hear him killing Meredith!*"

Knox was a waitress at the bar *Le Chic,* which was owned by a Congolese man by the name of Diya Patrick Lumumba [37]. Lumumba was also a musician who was married to a Polish woman named Ola, with whom he had a baby boy named David. On the night of the murder Knox said that she had originally sent him a text message asking him if he wanted her to come into work that night. Patrick sent a reply back at 8:19p.m., saying that she was not needed. Knox then replied back to Lumumba at 8.35p.m., "*Certo. Ci* *vediamo piu` tardi. Buona serata!*" There has been many discrepancies as to what this statement actually means in Italian, or what Knox meant by the statement; particularly the *"più tardi"* in the sentence. A rough translation of this phrase in English is *"Certainly. See you later. Good evening!"* However, "più tardi" in Italian actually indicates a schedule or an appointment. This expression in Italian assumes that after a lapse of time, with many actions in between, we will meet up later. If you use the words "più tardi" it is assumed that you are going to meet-up with someone on the same day or evening, not tomorrow or at another time. It is possible to suppose that Knox did not understand the language well enough and this is just a simple misunderstanding, but police did not give her the benefit of the doubt; axiomatically because she had already stated that Lumumba was the murderer.

Once Knox had made this accusation, police immediately notified the Pubblico Ministero (Public Prosecutor) of Perugia, Giuliano Mignini, who gives the order to "Stop." Questioning for the evening was then suspended at 1:45a.m., as is prescribed by Italian law—in articles 386 & 566 of the Italian *Codice di Procedura Penale* [Code of Criminal Procedure] (*CPP*). Knox signs a one-page statement that recounts her new story, and she is then informed that her status has officially changed from witness to suspect. Italian law differs from the law here in the United States in several respects (civil law system vs. common law system), but many aspects are strikingly similar. Italian criminal law, which is codified in the *CPP*, states that Defense counsel's presence is mandatory during the interrogation of the accused. One way around this, however, is not to officially change the status from witness to a suspect until after getting a sufficient amount of information out of her/him during questioning or to get a confession before changing the status. This is a common police 'trick,' per say, in Italy as well as in America.

Italian law does, however, have several differences. According to a provision introduced in 1978, it is not compulsory for the defense counsel to be present when the continuation of an investigation requires the immediate and urgent interrogation of a suspect. The statements made by the suspect, however, may not be minuted for use in judicial proceedings. Basically, this can be seen as a loop-hole that gives Italian police more leeway to do as they see fit in order to extract what information they need from a suspect. In

Knox's case, she obviously did not have a lawyer as she was not even called into the police station, let alone was she under the impression that she would be arrested at some point during that evening. In any event, it was Knox that allegedly waived her right to an attorney at that time, according to police. Nevertheless, the absence of a defense attorney during interrogation does not guarantee that the information provided by the suspect will be admissible in court. This decision will be up to the two judges and six jury members upon trial in Italy, or the Italian Supreme Court.

The officers were completely astonished and dumbfounded by Knox's admittance. Here was a girl who hadn't even been asked to come in for questioning, and has—not only declared to have been at the house during the time of the murder, but—identified the killer! Mignini headed over to *questura* (police headquarters) to witness and question Knox further. Once he arrived—at 3:30a.m.,— questioning resumes at Knox's compliance. Knox repeats her story for Mignini, but this time she goes into great detail. This is considered the official interrogation. Questioning is halted at 5:45a.m., at which time Knox signs a five-page statement detailing the events of the interrogation.

In the report, regarding the text message that Knox sent to Lumumba, police changed the text to read: *"Ci vediamo."("See you later")*. Mignini later used this statement to persuade the judge that Knox and Lumumba met up just before the murder. This information was then fed to the press, who reported the half-text "See you later" (by no fault of their own). An example of this is the story in the London Times on 13 November 2007, entitled, *"Meredith Kercher murder: why the timings are critical."* It wasn't until Lumumba's subsequent release that the full message was correctly reported to the public. In any case, police theorized from the text message, and Knox's statement, that the two met-up shortly there afterwards at the basketball court at Piazza Grimana before heading to the cottage. Shortly after signing the report, Knox is formally arrested then taken for breakfast. Sollecito had also been formally arrested and retained.

Meanwhile, a police task force had already been assembled and sent to arrest the dangerous murderer, Patrick Lumumba. At 6:30a.m., Patrick Lumumba sat in his fourth-floor apartment when he heard his doorbell ringing. Before he could even respond he heard a woman's voice outside demanding that he open the door. Patrick went to open the door, and as he did, the impatient police officers forced their way in. About 15–20 officers wearing plain clothes and carrying guns aggressively attacked. Shocked and terrified, Patrick thought that an armed gang had just barged into his home and were going to kill him for some unknown reason. [1]The scene got ugly quick, as the officers hit him over the head and called him a "dirty black." Patrick's fiancé, Aleksandra, and their son, David, were also terror stricken, and were screaming at the officers. Patrick was handcuffed and shoved out the door, where he was met by a fleet of seven police cars.

With Lumumba in custody, the procession headed to Perugia's police station with sirens blaring. The worst was yet to come for Patrick, who then had to sit through a ten-hour interrogation. During his questioning Patrick claimed that five men and woman, some of whom were punching and kicking him, forced him to his knees and up against the wall and shouted at him, "You should be in America where you would be given the electric chair for your crime." Humiliated and petrified, police kept yelling at him, "You did it, you did it!" Patrick was confused and scared, and police would not even tell him what he had just been arrested for. It was only after several hours that police showed Patrick a picture of Meredith's lifeless body. It was only after seeing the picture that Patrick had made the connection between his arrest and Meredith's death. "You think I killed Meredith?" Patrick uttered. Lumumba had been handing out flyers publicizing Meredith Kercher's candlelit vigil just one day earlier. Police told him that if he confessed right then and there that they would only give him half of the 30-year sentence that he would get otherwise. Nevertheless, Patrick continued to declare his innocence.

After Lumumba's arrest, Knox calls over Ficarra and asks her for a pen and paper. Knox says to her, "I want to give you a gift." Knox then proceeds to write a two page statement, confirming what she said earlier; but this time she posed her accusations against Lumumba and her presence during the murder as a "vision." Her statement is legally known as a voluntary, spontaneous statement,

---

[1] It was originally reported in UK's Daily Mail (DM) that Patrick was hit by police. He did several interviews thereafter denying that he was ever mistreated physically or verbally by police and that he was misquoted in his DM interview.

referred to as 'The Memoir' (Memorial or Two Page Note). When she is done she hands the memoir to Ficarra and says that it will help them in case they have some doubts. Little did Knox know at the time, but it would be the most damaging ink she would ever inscribe!

Key points in Knox's statement ('The Memoir'):

"This is very strange, I know, but really what happened is as confusing to me as it is to everyone else."

Knox starts off claiming that she was at Sollecito's flat *"smoking marijuana, having sex,"* and *"might even have fallen asleep."*

"The next thing I remember was waking up the morning of Friday November 2nd around 10am and I took a plastic bag to take back my dirty cloths to go back to my house."

As she goes on, she begins to tell a different story of what might have happened, in which she claims her boss, Patrick Lumumba, was probably the murder. According to this version of events Knox met Patrick Lumumba at around 9:00p.m., on the night of the murder at the basketball court in Piazza Grimana then went to her house. This is significant, because a homeless man later testified that he saw Knox on that very basketball court at around that time.

"In my mind I saw Patrik in flashes of blurred images. I saw him near the basketball court. I saw him at my front door. I saw myself cowering in the kitchen with my hands over my ears because in my head I could hear Meredith screaming...these things seem unreal to me, like a dream, and I am unsure if they are real things that happened or are just dreams my head has made to try to answer the questions in my head and the questions I am being asked."

The following statement is telling because Knox does not rule out the possibility that there may be evidence against her at the crime scene. Here she contradicts and back-tracks as she tries to talk her way out of trouble.

"The police have told me that they have hard evidence that places me at the house, my house, at the time of Meredith's murder. I don't know what proof they are talking about, but if this is true, it means I am very confused and my dreams must be real."

In his account to police that night, Sollecito tried to distance himself from the murder, telling police that Knox asked him to lie for her and say that she was with him the whole night.

"In my previous statement I told a load of rubbish because Amanda had convinced me of her version of the facts and I didn't think about the inconsistencies," Sollecito told police

Knox responds to this by writing, "I also NEVER asked him to lie for me. This is absolutely a lie...What does he [Sollecito] have to hide? I don't think he killed Meredith."

Knox then acknowledges that her story seems far fetched, yet she stands by both of her stories, each contradicting the other.

"I also know that the fact that I can't fully recall the events that I claim took place at Raffaele's home during the time that Meredith was murdered is incriminating. And I stand by my statements that I made last night about events that could have taken place in my home with Patrik, but I want to make very clear that these events seem more unreal to me that what I said before, that I stayed at Raffaele's house."

Knox reaffirms that she is not sure what she was doing the night before the murder.

"I'm very confused at this time. My head is full of contrasting ideas and I know I can be frustrating to work with for this reason. But I also want to tell the truth as best I can. Everything I have said in regards to my involvement in Meredith's death, even though it is contrasting, are the best truth that I have been able to think."

Knox reaffirms that she is not sure what she was doing the night before the murder, and that Patrick may have been the killer.

"In these flashbacks that I'm having, I see Patrik as the murderer, but the way the truth feels in my mind, there is no way for me to have known because I don't remember FOR SURE if I was at my house that night."

Knox then asks herself a very puzzling question, which is basically like saying that she was not there unless they have proof that she was, and if so then she doesn't remember.

"Is the evidence proving my pressance [sic] at the time and place of the crime reliable? If so, what does this say about my memory? Is it reliable?"

It wasn't until 5:30p.m., that day—still handcuffed and bruised—that Patrick was informed of the evidence against him. Police showed Patrick the hand written statement of Amanda Knox accusing him of being Meredith's killer. It was only then that Patrick had realized just how mad Knox was with him for firing her. Patrick filled-up with rage and contempt toward Knox, but continued to keep himself calm and composed in front of police. After Patrick was fingerprinted and his blood was taken, he sat in a holding cell awaiting his first hearing.

Police then turned their investigation to Raffaele Sollecito's flat on Corso Garibaldi. Police entered the premises looking for a pair of shoes that matched any of the bloody prints left at the crime scene, and a possible murder weapon. Armondo Finzi, an assistant in Perugia PD's organized crime unit, entered the home and immediately noticed a "strong smell of bleach." As police began the inspection of the flat, Mr. Finzi opened a drawer in the kitchen and noticed a shiny knife lying on top of the silverware tray. The Marietti knife with a 6 ½ inch stainless steel blade, was the first knife that he saw and his investigative intuition led him to believe that it might be the murder weapon. Officer Finzi grabed the knife, with gloves on, and placed it into an envelope and taped it shut, and then placed it into a folder. No other knife was taken into evidence. Back at police headquarters, homicide unit captain, Stefano Gubbiotto, removed the knife from the envelope—with gloved hands—and placed it into a cardboard box, and it was scheduled to be sent to Rome for further analysis.

[2]During the search, reports surfaced saying that police had also found a pair of Sollecito's sneakers (*Nike size 42½*) that they announced was a perfect match with the footprint left at the crime scene. Police also discovered a receipt in Sollecito's flat for cleaning products from a local supermarket, which they claimed included bleach. [3]This bleach, police believed, was used to clean the knife found in his apartment, according to many news reports. Police also examined Sollecito's car (Audi) for any traces of blood on the pedals, but found nothing. They confiscated Sollecito's collection of violent Japanese comic books as well. Knox, Sollecito, and Lumumba all spent the next two days and nights in isolation— behind bars in *Capanne prison,* about a ten-minute drive from Perugia.

---

[2] In fact, police retrieved these sneakers from Sollecito at the station, as he was wearing them.

[3] These receipts were later found not to be for bleach and irrelevant.

November 8th Hearing

According to Articles 390 & 566 of the *Codice di Procedura Penale* (Code of Criminal Procedure), a hearing for the "validation of the arrest or detention" must be scheduled within forty-eight hours of the arrest. This hearing, however, took place on Friday, November 9th, and was presided over by *Judge Claudia Matteini.* It was a tense seen as Amanda Marie Knox, 20, Raffaele Sollecito, 24, and Diya "Patrick" Lumumba, 37, entered the courtroom for the first time. Judge Matteini ordered the three to be held in *Capanne prison* (near Perugia) for up to one year without any formal charges being filed while the investigation continued. Under Italian law the Public Prosecutor can ask for preventive detention (*fermo di indiziato di delitto*) while an investigation is pending, if there is very serious incriminating evidence against the accused or if there is a danger that s/he might flee the jurisdiction. The three suspects each were confined to 6ft by 12ft cells in Capanne prison while police continued their investigation. In her 19 page written ruling, Judge Matteini stated that she feared the three might flee if released. "They could easily leave the territory of the state to escape the investigation," the judge wrote.

Knox had retained a lawyer, Luciano Ghirga, and it appeared that even he was 'in the dark' in regards to Knox's version of events. After the hearing Ghirga confirmed that his client [Knox] had given "three versions." He also made the comments, "…it is difficult to evaluate which one is true." Even Knox's own lawyer appeared in disbelief of her stories when he issued her a warning: "We told her [Amanda] that it would be worse than assassination to accuse an innocent person. We explained to her [Amanda] what slander means in Italy and we'll see." Slander is a much more serious offense in an inquisitorial justice system as opposed to an adversarial justice system, because the accused does not enjoy a presumption of innocence.

Lumumba had retained his own lawyer, Carlo Pacelli, who called Knox's statements against his client "Slanderous." While one of Sollecito's attorneys, Tiziano Tedeschi, told the court that his client "wasn't at the crime scene." Another of Sollecito's attorneys, Luca Maori, said that they didn't expect such a harsh ruling from the judge and that they planned to appeal the decision. In her report, the judge gave her version of the crime, stating that Knox had let Lumumba and Sollecito into the cottage. "Then something went wrong," Matteini wrote. "The two [Lumumba & Sollecito] demanded some kind of sexual act, which Kercher refused to do. She was then threatened with a knife, which Sollecito always carried with him, and with which Meredith was stabbed in the neck." Not by coincidence, the judge's theory seemed to be in line with prosecutor Giuliano Mignini's theory.

In Judge Matteini's report she stated in detail the evidence against each of the three suspects that brought about her decision. Obviously Knox had incriminated herself, claiming that she was at the cottage during the murder. Lumumba was incriminated only by Knox's admissions, but his alibi was also in question. The fact that Sollecito had lied (covering up for Knox) and being the owner of the possible murder weapon and sneakers that left a print at the scene—which were also found in his home—were plenty to hold him while the investigation continued. Judge Matteini's report expounded on her judgement:

Amanda Knox:

"As far as the presence of Knox Amanda is concerned in the place of the murder, there are the statements from Sollecito who has lately confirmed that he was always together with her and in the objective circumstances that only the aforementioned had access to the keys of the apartment in via della Pergola and had therefore the ability to open the front door without leaving any signs of breakage."

Raffaele Sollecito:

"In fact, the checks by the forensic police, under the duvet that covered the body of Meredith show three footprints of which one, the only one which it was possible to analyze because of the others where indefinite, shows itself to be compatible in shape and dimensions with the sole of the shoe taken from Sollecito Raffaele. This objective fact cannot but represent a grave indication of guilt on the part of Sollecito Raffaele which is deepened further if combined with the removal from his person of a flick knife with an

8.5cm blade, defined by the pathologist as compatible with the possible murder weapon."

Patrick Lumumba:

"Referring to the position of Diya Lumumba, the statements on 6 November of Knox Amanda are of extreme relevance, considering that his presence in the inside of Meredith's bedroom at the moment of the murder while Meredith screamed. In fact, while Lumumba was in the court hearing he confirmed that he had opened the pub in the afternoon of November 1 at around 1700 to 1800. The first receipts are shown to start from 22.29 and the suspect was not able to give any logical explanation for these circumstances, and was not able to furnish precise indications of the eventual clients who could attest to his presence in the pub before 22.29, and was not able to provide precise and therefore useful indications for the meeting with a person known only as Usi who would have come into the bar at 2000, or was able to give a telephone number or other identifying elements, despite calling him a friend."

Judge Matteini's report also revealed more specifics from Dr. Lalli's post-mortem examination, which detailed the brutality of the murder:

"From reading the first summary of Dr Lalli's report, deposited at the court on November 8, 2007, after the autopsy on the corpse of Meredith Kercher, it emerges that the wound had not hit the carotid artery so the death was preceded by a relatively slow agony, circumstances which allow us to date back the time of the criminal act to between 21.30pm and 11.30pm on the day of November 1, 2007, a timetable which tallies with the consumption of dinner in an hour before 9pm."

According to Judge *Matteini's* 19-page report, Knox and Sollecito "had been seeking to experience extreme sensations, intense sexual relations which break up the monotony of everyday life," and had attempted to persuade Kercher to participate in a sexual encounter. "They went together to the apartment on Via della

Pergola 7, to which only Amanda had the key," *Matteini* continued. "It was roughly at this time that both Sollecito and Knox switched off their mobile phones until the following morning." Judge Matteini also rejected a demand that Knox be moved from jail to a shelter run by the Catholic charity Caritas. Judge Matteini wrote that Meredith was "subjected to several violent acts characterized by extreme cruelty in a hideous crescendo, surely a sign of personalities who were perverse and without any inhibitions". The judge added; "There was first an act of suffocation, probably to stop her shouting; then strangulation, given the marks of ruptured blood vessels found on her neck; then repeated cuts with a sharp weapon also in the neck area—one of which brought about her death." The judge wrote there was "serious evidence" against Knox and expressed her "dismay and apprehension" at her cold, detached manner following the murder; the judge was struck by a woman so young "finding it so easy to govern her state of mind."

Media Hype

The victim was British and the murder occurred in Italy; so the English and Italian presses were all over this story from the beginning. The headlines kept coming in on this case, as journalists scrambled to get the next detail. When police reported the news of Knox and Sollecito's arrests, this story eclipsed any other, and in a town with more 40,000 college students, Knox and Sollecito had become household names! Journalists' began a massive manhunt to get any dirt they could find on the suspects. Reporters had soon dug-up a tabloid treasure on the web when they found Amanda Knox's MySpace page with the username *"Foxy Knoxy."* On it she had posted a short story/blog entitled *Baby Brother*, which described a young woman who was drugged and raped. The story ended with a bloody confrontation between two roommates. This story and other strange writings by Knox became front page news in Italy and in the United Kingdom and fueled speculation that Knox and her friends were "lust-crazed pals." The British press also jumped all over an internet blog that featured a photograph of Sollecito dressed as a mummy and waving a meat cleaver while proclaiming his desire to try "extreme experiences." The American media followed suit, but were a bit more apprehensible about calling out her guilt; they played footsy with the subject, reporting the story in a dyer manner, reporting only the known facts of the case without much spin.

Soon after, security footage from a fashionable clothing store on Via Calderini named *Bubble* surfaced. Knox and Sollecito were seen kissing and purchasing two-pairs of sexy thong under wear just one day after the murder. The owner, Carlo Scotto di Rinaldi, told journalists that he overheard the two talking and giggling about the *Sesso selvaggio* (wild sex) that they were going to have. The incident was cited as another example of Knox's unemotional response to Kercher's death.

The UK's *Daily Mail* took a fancy to Knox; portraying her as a self-obsessed party girl. The UK newspaper recounted how Knox had been fined $269 at Municipal Court in Seattle some four months prior to the murder. Arturo De Felice, Chief of police in Perugia, was quoted as saying Kercher's murder was "concluded." Having now apprehended Amanda Knox, Raffaele Sollecito, and Patrick Lumumba; he was of the opinion that "all three took part in the act," and that Meredith had been "morally upright," and no traces of drugs or alcohol had been found in her blood. "She was a victim, nothing more," he said. De Felice proclaimed that Kercher had died during the course of a sexual act that "must be considered of a violent nature" and carried out in "a particularly intimidating context." One UK newspaper, *The Sun*, called it the "Orgy of Death," and said that Kercher had been killed by "three lust-crazed pals as she fought off a savage sex attack." Italy's Interior Minister, Giuliano Amato, said, "It's an ugly story in which people—friends in her home—tried to force her into relations she didn't want."

More details began leaking out about the viciousness of Meredith's attackers. Italian Professor and Forensic Pathologist, Carlo Torre, claimed "The death can be attributed to more than one factor." He says that "There was a major neck wound and an inhalation of blood in the lungs which can be attributed to a constriction of the neck or a strangling," which Torre believes happened before the knifing. Other experts estimated that Meredith suffered a slow, painful death; drowning in her own blood. She bled to death after what some officials estimate was an agonizing two hours.

Knox had incriminated herself almost beyond repair in her written statement to police, putting herself at the house during the time of the murder. Police believed that they had the murderers apprehended in record time and it was as they say in Italian: *Caso chiuso* (Case Closed). One of Italy's leading crime journalists, Meo Ponte, soon joined in on the investigation. The police had already begun theorizing, and their main theory was that Amanda and her friends killed Meredith in a drug fueled sex game gone wrong. Ponte, however, was not convinced. "We still know nothing for certain," Ponte claimed in the documentary *Sex, Lies & The Murder of Meredith Kercher*. "It's still a mystery why Meredith was killed, especially how and by whom…with no motive" Ponte was one of the first skeptics of police in this case, and when he first visited the crime scene, his concerns grew.

Ponte believed that the police had not been as thorough as they should have been. "Why were there no traces of blood stains found during the escape of the killer(s) along the escape route?" Ponte was in close contact with police and the lawyers, receiving constant updates. Ponte contacted Professor Torre and asked him to get involved in the investigation. Ponte wanted Torre's theory on whether there was a single killer or multiple assailants. Torre is a seasoned pathologist who has performed over 6,000 postmortems. After his investigation, Torre believed, based on how Meredith had died, that the murder had been committed by one person and not multiple.

Yet it was Investigating Magistrate, Giuliano Mignini, who wholeheartedly believed that it was Amanda Knox who was the cunning ring leader of the three. Mignini was one of two prosecutors in the case, and he was determined, early on, to get a conviction based on this philosophy. Mignini's scenario was that Patrick was sexually assaulting Meredith while she was being held down and threatened by Knox and Sollecito; and Mignini believed that it was Knox who slit Meredith's throat, the fatal blow. Ponte asserts that Mignini's theory is "fiction, not reality." The polarizing nature of this case was only just beginning.

Evidence Mounts

More evidence began coming in against young Amanda in the form of eye-witnesses. Allegedly Knox had been seen by two men washing some clothes and a pair of shoes at a laundry mat in

Via Fabretti with an African man the day after the murder. It was reported that CCTV cameras in a car-park across the way from her house had captured images of Knox entering the cottage just before Meredith arrived that fatal night. There were also reports from neighbors living in the flats overlooking the cottage that they had seen two people running away from the house at the time of the murder.

Authorities reported that only hours after telling police definitively that Patrick was the murderer, she recanted her story and then provided the above hand-written statement in which she describes seeing Patrick "in flashes of blurred images." However, she goes on to say, "these things seem unreal to me, like a dream, and I am unsure if they are real things that happened or are just dreams my head has made to try to answer the questions in my head and the questions I am being asked." Patrick's nightclub was searched thoroughly and nothing was found. Moreover, there was absolutely no physical evidence linking him to the crime scene.

Nearly three-weeks after Lumumba's arrest, witnesses (including Swiss professor, Romano Mero, and his Senegalese friend, Usi) were tracked down by police that had an alibi for Lumumba, claiming that he was at the club (at 9:00p.m.) during the time of the murder.

The nightmare for Lumumba was over, and he was finally released and exonerated of all charges. Lumumba was obviously upset, and he later explained that police would not tell him why he was there. He claimed that they just kept saying, "You know what you did!" Lumumba thought he was there because they suspected him of being a terrorist. After his release Lumumba claimed that he thinks that the reason why Amanda claimed that he was the murderer was because he is a black man and an easy target for suspicion coming from the lips of a "scared" young white girl. Lumumba claimed that Knox had probably killed Kercher because he had recently hired Kercher in her place.

The Forth Suspect

The fact that Knox originally implicated Lumumba sidetracked police's investigation and caused them to use resources and focus away from the other factors. After Lumumba's release police continued their investigation, still believing that three people were involved. Three weeks after the murder, they made a startling discovery. Police soon discovered that someone else was in Meredith's room during the time of the murder. Fingerprints of local drug dealer, Rudy Hermann Guede, were located in Meredith's room, including a bloody handprint on the pillow that rested half under the pelvis of the body when she was found. More than sixty prints were found in Meredith's room; none of which could be attributed to Knox or Sollecito. Guede had fled Perugia days after the murder. Police contacted friends from his Face-Book (FB) page. When Guede made a voice-call to one of his friends from a computer using *Skype*, police tapped in. Rudy told his friend that he was with Meredith the night of the murder and that they had been fooling around. He claimed that he "tried something on her," but nothing happened, because neither one of them had a condom. Puzzled, his friend says, "But they said in the newspapers that you had done something to her." Rudy interjects, "I'm telling you the truth, we didn't do anything."

Meanwhile, Kercher's funeral service was held on 14 December 2007, in a service held at Croydon Parish Church in south London. Meredith's parents, Arline and John Kercher, along with her sister, Stephanie, and brothers, John and Lyle, were the last to arrive at a funeral service (at about 10:50a.m.), attended by around 400 mourners. The service was led by Vicar of Croydon, Rev. Colin Boswell; who handled the proceedings more like a celebration of her life rather than the awfulness of her death. The family also wanted this to be the theme, as they believed that there was much happiness in Meredith's life, and her family wanted that to be in big part what they celebrated and remembered on this dreadful day. Many of Miss Kercher's friends, and her sister Stephanie, carried a single white rose in tribute. Among the many bouquets of flowers brought in by mourners, was a basket of flowers signed "From the City of Perugia" and an arrangement of yellow flowers spelling out "Mez." After the funeral, the family followed the coffin—which was surrounded by colorful floral tributes and a photograph of Meredith—to Croydon Cemetery for a private burial.

Chapter 4 – Prelude to a Trial

The Baron

Rudy Hermann Guede, the 21-year-old immigrant from the Ivory Coast, had spent most of his life in Italy. A somewhat tragic story to say the lease, Guede arrived in Perugia with his father as a child. After being abandoned by his father at some point, Guede was adopted by an Italian family and he lived with them in Perugia. Guede played basketball and tried to work normal jobs. However, his adopted family also abandoned him, citing his poor behavior as the reason. Guede moved back to Milan for a short time, and then back to Perugia, living on Corso Garibladi; a stones throw away from Raffaele Sollecito's flat. Guede admitted being at the scene when Meredith was murdered, but he denied involvement in the crime. In his prison diary, Guede explained his involvement with Meredith, Amanda, and the rest of the residents of the cottage.

The first time Guede met Knox was at *Le Chic*. Guede had known Patrick Lumumba; so to speak, from a meeting they had at the *Domus Volumnia* (hotel & nightclub) where they took a picture together. Guede described Patrick as a "nice, normal guy." Guede entered *Le Chic* alone one night prior to the murder and Knox approached him with a big smile on her face. The two spoke for a while, getting acquainted. After that night they ran into each other many times, but they never stopped to converse; it was always just "hi" and "bye."

Soon after that Guede and a bunch of his friends went out to celebrate their friend, Owen's, birthday. The birthday boy got pretty drunk that night, so Guede and friends took him back to Alexis's house (another friend in attendance) to sleep it off; leaving Owen behind, the guys went back out to party. As they arrived at the *Shamrock Pub*, Guede was approached by two Italian gentlemen. Guede recognized them, as he had played basketball with them months earlier on the small court at Piazza Grimana. Little did he know at the time; the two Italians were first-floor residents of the cottage. After a while Guede had lost track of his friends, so he decided to continue to hang out with the Italian boys. Suddenly, a young woman approached him and started chatting with him. He did not recognize her; but when she said that her name was Amanda and that she was from Seattle he made the connection that they had spoken a couple of times before. They all walked home together from the bar that evening, and when they reached Piazza Grimana they were about to part ways; but the group convinced Guede to accompany them back to their house.

It was that evening that they gave him the nickname "The Baron," because he looked a lot like Baron Davis: the professional basketball player who at that time played for the Golden State Warriors. Guede and the rest of the guys went to the first floor and Knox had gone up to her place on the second floor. Immediately, the conversation turned to Amanda and how they all fantasized about having sex with her. One of the guys rolled a joint and they continued critiquing Knox and fantasizing about sleeping with her. As they began smoking Amanda walked into the room and they all let out a chuckle. Knox came in and began smoking as well. According to Guede, Knox smoked an inordinate amount of marijuana. He claimed that she walked around for the rest of the evening with a joint in her mouth, and compared to her, Guede claimed he was a novice smoker.

Guede claimed that his glance and Amanda's glance kept meeting a lot, alluding that she may have been coming on to him through constant flirtatious glances. As they continued to converse a young English woman walked in; it was Meredith Kercher. Guede immediately turned his attention to her and he said to himself, "Damn, she is Beautiful!" Like most people, Guede was struck by Meredith's dark skin and he said to her, "You don't seem to have anything English about you." Meredith informed him that the reason for her dark complection was that her mother had American Indian blood. This was the first time that Guede had met the beautiful

English woman. They spoke at length; according to Guede, they spoke all night. At approximately 5:00a.m., they had all decided to call it a night. Guede was too tired to walk home, and the guys told him that he could sleep on their sofa. The girls returned to the second floor to retire and it was lights out soon after that.

Guede awoke at about 9:30a.m., awoken by the resident black cat, which propted him to be on his way. He met up with the guys at the basketball court soon after that, and he also ran into Amanda and Meredith another time as well. One day (Saturday night) the guys invited him out to eat, but he wound up being late and he missed them. From there he went to the cottage looking for them, but they weren't there. Then he went to *Le Chic* to see if Amanda knew where they were, but she was not working that night. The next day Guede showed up at the cottage and found out that they had all went to *The Red Zone* the night before. *The Red Zone* is a popular nightclub in Perugia on Via Fratelli Cervi, about 16 kilometers southwest of the cottage. The club is wildly popular for the local university crowd it draws. It was that night that Meredith first kissed her downstairs flat mate, Giacomo. It was also the night that Amanda had sex with Giacomo's friend, Daniel de Luna.

On October 20th (Saturday night), Guede went to a bar to watch the rugby championship, which featured England and, his own, South Africa. There, Guede ran into Meredith and her English friends. Guede seemed infatuated with Meredith, and he turned frequently throughout the game to glance at her. South Africa won the game in a route by the score of 16–5. After the game, Guede jokingly teased the English girls about the outcome of the game. A little over a week later—on Halloween night—Guede claims that he ran into Meredith again. Guede declares that Kercher approached him, as he was not in costume and she was, and he did not recognize her at first. According to Guede, they spoke for a long period of time. Guede also claims that the two "flirted" and that he even "stole a kiss" from her that night. They made plans to see each other the following day, according to Guede, and Meredith informed him to meet her at the cottage at around 8:30p.m., the next night.

Guede was excited about his impending meeting with Meredith. At around 7:30p.m., the following evening, Guede stopped by his friend Alexis's place. The two friends conversed for a bit and then made plans to see each other later that night, but no time

59

was identified. From there Guede went into the town's center where he met up with his Australian friend, Phillip. There he decided to eat a kebab right next to *La Tana dell'Orso* (restaurant) on Via Ulisse Rocchi. Geude ate the kebab and conversed with Phillip for a while. Guede told Phillip that he was going to meet a girl, and they decided that they'd meet up later at Alexis's house. Guede did not have a watch, but he believes that he had arrived at the cottage at about 8:30p.m. When Guede arrived he noticed that a white car was in front of the house and its headlights were on and he also noticed a drug-dealer that he frequently saw on Garibaldi Avenue, but he paid neither any mind. Guede knocked on the door, but there was no answer. Then he went to the first floor apartment and knocked there as well, but again, there was no answer. After that he decided to wait in the yard. Meredith showed up sometime soon after and greeted him with a smile. They entered the dark cottage together and Meredith called-out, "Anybody here?" but the place was empty. Guede was thirsty—because of the spicy kebab he had just eaten earlier—and asked Meredith if he could have something to drink, to which she replied, "Help yourself." Guede proceeded to opened the fridge and drink some apricot juice and water; and since Meredith wasn't looking, he drank them straight from the containers.

Guede took a seat in the living room, but minutes later he heard Meredith complaining from her room. He got up and entered her room to see what the problem was. When he entered her room he saw that she was furious. "What's wrong?" he asked. "That whore of a doper," Meredith replied, referring to Knox. "What happened?" Guede asked. Meredith couldn't find the money she had recently withdrawn from the bank to pay her share of the rent and she believed that Amanda was the most likely candidate to have lifted it. "Maybe it was a thief," Guede said. But Meredith was convinced that it was Knox who had stolen her money. According to Guede, Meredith knew where Knox had kept her own stash of money. Meredith went into Knox's room to see if her money was there, but no luck. Meredith became even more furious after that. Guede finally calmed her down and convinced her to wait until the others got back home to see if they knew anything about the stolen money.

They put off the stolen money and began getting to know each other better. Meredith told Guede that her parents were separated and that this had a big affect on her teenage years. Guede understood; he too came from a broken home, and he had been abandoned as well. After a while of conversing, Guede informed Meredith that he had to go to the bathroom. The spicy kebab that he had eaten earlier was starting to bother his stomach. Meredith advised him to go to the bathroom near the fridge, near Filomena's room. While Guede was on the toilet, he heard the doorbell ring more than once. Ignoring it, he put his headphones on and began to listen to music. Guede had his three favorite songs queued up on his ipod, and he proceeded to listen to each of them. While he was listening to the third song he heard screaming; even though the volume on his ipod was loud, he heard the louder screams. Guede rushed to finish up and go check on Meredith. As he entered her room he saw the back of a man standing in her room. "Hey, what happened?" Guede asked.

Then he noticed that Meredith was on the ground and that there was also blood on the floor. "What the fuck have you done?" he yelled. The man turned around and insulted him in Italian. Guede recognized that the man was Italian, because he had no foreign accent. The Italian man then attacked Guede with the knife that he had in his hand. As the man swung the knife at Guede, he blocked it with his hands, causing small deep cuts, even though the sharp knife had only grazed him. Guede grabbed a chair in an effort to fight off the attacker. However, not having zipped his pants up fully after rushing in from the bathroom, his pants fell, causing him to fall as well. Guede held up the chair to defend himself; it was then that the attacker turned and fled the house screaming, "Black man found, guilty man found!" Guede quickly rushed over to help Meredith and noticed that she was covered in blood. Guede knelt beside Meredith and held her hand. Her neck was flowing like a river, so Guede ran to the bathroom and grabbed a towel to try and soak up the blood. There was so much blood that the towel became immersed with blood very quickly; so Guede ran and retrieved another towel. So much blood was flowing that the wound was no longer visible. Guede asked the struggling girl what had happened, but she couldn't get a word out, she could only mouth the sound, "AF, AF, AF."

Not knowing what to do; Guede panicked. He had no phone; and worse yet, he didn't think that the police would believe that he wasn't the killer. Meredith gestured to Guede to stay with her, as she struggled to stretch her arms out at him. "Why did all this happen to her, why?" he said to himself, in complete shock. Then Guede made a decision that even he claims was shameful and cowardly at best. Covered in blood, Guede fled the cottage and set-off for Germany. Although he said that he was distraught and suicidal over what had happened, he was seen later that night at a nightclub in Germany, dancing. A witness in the club said that he smelled really bad. While in Germany, Guede went into hiding, allegedly sleeping on a barge on the Rhine, and in empty train carriages.

Five days before the murder of Miss Kercher, Guede was discovered to have broken into a nursery school in Milan, where he had spent the night. Guede was also brandishing an 11-inch kitchen knife and was arrested and booked for this incident. From this arrest, police were able to match fingerprints taken from the crime scene to his fingerprints in their database. Once this was done, Guede was the object of an international manhunt. Police investigated his *Facebook* account and contacted his close friends. One of his friends, identified as Alberto, worked with police to persuade Guede that the longer he remained abroad the guiltier he would seem. German police tracked Guede through his computer's IP address after a three-hour conversation with Alberto on *Skype* (the internet telephone service)—a conversation that Guede was unaware that police were listening. During the conversation, Guede told Alberto, "I was not there that night. If they found my fingerprints, it means I had left them there before. I had been in the house before, but not on the day of the killing." Rudy Guede also had a Skype conversation with his friend, Giacomo Benedetti, which was intercepted by police. Guede told Benedetti a similar story to the one he wrote in his diary, in which he claimed he was there during the murder and fled after being attacked by an Italian man. When Benedetti asked Rudy whether it had been Amanda who had killed Meredith, Rudy replied, "No," claiming further that his mind at the time was concentrating only on the male figure with the knife. Guede concluded the conversation by saying that he felt responsible for not saving the life of a dying girl, but that he had nothing at all to do with the murder.

Guede had decided to return to Perugia to talk to police and declare his evidence, although he had not told police his plans yet. On November 20th, Guede boarded a train headed for Milan, Italy. The train was expected to arrive in Milan at 2.35p.m., that day. However, Guede was stopped just after 7:00a.m, on the train for not having a ticket. Guede told police that he was wanted in connection with Kercher's death and that he was returning to Italy to speak with police. Guede was arrested on the train near Mainz, Germany, the capital of the Rhineland-Pflaz region (between Mainz and Wiesbaden). Guede was taken into custody in Germany. The day following his arrest Guede attended his first hearing in Koblenz, Germany. The proceeding was the first hearing in legal procedures for Guede's extradition back to Italy. At the hearing Guede denied any involvement in the killing, claiming that he was not present at the cottage where Kercher died on the evening of the murder, and that his fingerprints found at the scene date from earlier visits. Arturo De Felice, the Chief of Police in Perugia, said that there was a "reasonable expectation" that Guede would be extradited "in about ten days." He said that the arrest was a joint Italian-German police operation, and had followed "days of investigation."

Diary of a Mad Man

Over the course of the next month, Raffaele Sollecito wrote a series of letters to his father from jail. With the version that he gave in the UK's *Sunday Mirror* and the two different versions that he gave to police—one initially after the murder and the other during his interrogation/arrest—this was his fourth version. In one letter, Raffaele seemingly slams Knox for being a care-free pleasure seeker. "She lived her life like a dream," he says. "She was detached from reality, she couldn't distinguish dream from reality…Her life seemed to be pure pleasure, she had a contact with reality that was almost non-existent" In regard to Amanda's role in the murder, Raffaele leads his father to believe that he is unsure. He also points-out that the version Knox gave police in regard to the events of the night of the murder is skewed or simply untrue. "I try to understand what Amanda's role was in this event. The Amanda that I know is an Amanda who lives a carefree life; her only thought is the pursuit of pleasure at all times. But even the thought that she could be a killer is impossible for me…I have read her version of events. Some of the things she said are not true, but I don't know why she said them."

Sollecito writes clearly about his whereabouts and all of his activities the day before and the day of the murder. However, when speaking about the events of the night of the murder, Sollecito makes a caveat, stating that "his memory is confused" about some of the events.

> "First, Amanda and I went downtown to Piazza Grimana to Corso Vannucci; around the university for foreigners and ending in Piazza Morlacchi (the way we always do). Then I do not remember but we probably went shopping. We returned to my house around 8:00 to 8:30p.m., and there I rolled another joint...and I had no intention of leaving because it was cold outside. I remember that I surfed the internet for a while and maybe watched a movie, and then I saw that you [his father] called me at home...I remember it was Thursday, so Amanda had to go to the pub where she works, but I do not remember how long she was absent, and I remember after she had said that the pub was closed...I'm trying to remember other details but they are all confused. Another thing that I can be certain is that Amanda stayed with me that night."

Raffaele then claims that Amanda woke before him the next morning. He continued sleeping while she went home to take a shower; he could not recall if he had breakfast before or after Amanda had returned. When she returned, Amanda had brought a Vileda mop to clean the mess on the floor left by the leaky sink pipe. He claims that they may have had breakfast at around 11:30a.m., or 12p.m., and then they left the apartment together. As they descended down Corso Garibaldi, Amanda informed him that when she had returned to the cottage earlier, she found strange that the front door was open and that there were feces in the toilet and blood in the bathroom; she asked him to go back to her place to take a look and see what he could make of it.

When they arrived, Amanda opened the door with her keys and they entered. Raffaele placed the mop in the hall and headed to each room to take a look around. He remembers these events well, he says, because he was upset and alarmed. As he was going to take a look around, he saw Amanda take the mop and bucket and carry it into another room. He first noticed that Filomena's door was open. When he entered he saw that the room was "an absurd mess," with broken glass on the floor, the side window broken and left open, and clothes everywhere. He then went and checked Meredith's door and noticed that it was locked. Then he witnessed the bloodstains in the bathroom. At that point he decided to go outside and climb through Meredith's window but, because of the height of it, he though it impractical. Meanwhile, Amanda had opened a window and was climbing over the railing (of the balcony) to get a look, but Raffaele stopped her, saying that he thought that she might fall or hurt herself.

Amanda then began knocking on Meredith's door repeatedly and shouting her name; she believed that Meredith might have been sleeping. At that point, Sollecito advised Amanda to call her friends. She did, informing him that "Laura was in Viterbo (which is located in the Lazio region of central Italy about 80 kilometers (60 mi) north of Rome); Filomena was with her boyfriend and would come later." Sollecito had decided that it was time to break down Meredith's door. He tried several times, but the door would not budge. At that point he claims that he called his sister and she advised him to call 112. Sollecito claims that he called 112 and briefly explained the situation and they said they were sending help. Next, they went outside and were approached by two postal officers who informed them that Filomena's phones had been found. Amanda tells them that the phones belong to Meredith. Sollecito then claims that he asked the officers to break down Meredith's door, but they refused. He says that it was only after Filomena and the boys arrived that they were all able to persuade them to break down the door. As they broke down the door, Sollecito says that he heard someone scream, "Oh God! A foot! Blood..."

In each of his four versions, Sollecito left out at least one key element from previous versions; as well as adding random elements that he later retracts.

- In *version one*—given to police the day that Meredith's body was discovered—he told police that Knox was with him the night before, and that they had not parted-ways that entire day.

- In his *second version*—given to the UK Newspaper, *Sunday Mirror*—Sollecito claimed that he and Knox went to a party with one of his friends. He omits this in his other three versions. He also claimed that Knox was afraid when she noticed spots of blood in the bathroom upon returning to the cottage the morning after the murder. He says that she "ran back" to his flat in fear after seeing the blood, not mentioning that she calmly took a shower first. He also claims to have seen the body once the door was broken-down.

- In his *third version*—during his interrogation/arrest—Sollecito tells police that he and Knox had parted-ways before returning to his flat; at around 9:00p.m., on the night of the murder, and that she did not return to his apartment until 1:00a.m. In version four he claims that they returned to his flat together at 8:30p.m.

- In his *fourth version*—written letters to his father—the public gets the first glimpse of Sollecito's entire alibi in his own words. In it, Sollecito writes that he and Knox arrived at his flat at 8 – 8:30p.m., rolled a joint, surfed the internet, watched a movie, his father called, and Amanda had left for work (he writes this in that order). He claims that he does not remember how long Knox was gone. In this version Sollecito seemingly contradicts himself, writing that Knox had left and that he wasn't sure how long that she was gone, but he is certain that Knox had stayed with him the entire night. It is likely that he meant that Knox had left him for a time, returned, and stayed with him the rest of the night. Also in *version four*—Sollecito claims that he asked officers to break down Meredith's door while it was only him, Amanda, and the officers present.

Judges Report # 1

On December 5th, Judge Massimo Riccarelli outlined his reasons for denying Knox and Sollecito bail. In the damning report, Judge Riccarelli said, "From the reconstruction there is the concrete possibility of reoffending and the [alleged] role of Amanda Knox was by no means secondary…Amanda Knox is crafty and cunning with a multi-faced personality, unattached to reality with an elevated, one would say fatal capacity to repeat her offence…the severity of the proof at hand legitimized the custodial measure applied to the pair who are accused of murder and sexual violence."

Judge Riccarelli also theorized from the evidence presented to him that the crime was committed by more than one person and that Kercher likely knew the killer(s) due to nature of the evidence.

"There is also the very real probability that this murder was committed by more than one person – the injuries suffered by Meredith suggest more than one culprit. The fact that there was no sign of forced entry also strengthens the theory that Meredith was killed by someone she knew. This element suggests that the murderer did not need to use any violence to enter maybe because they had keys or maybe because the door was opened by the victim…To conclude I have to impose a custodial measure."

Judges Report # 2

On December 6th, Rudy Guede was extradited from Germany to Italy. Several judges were in attendance during a subsequent hearing to determine Guede's detention status. On December 19th, Judge Maurizio Bufali released a report explaining their decision to reject an appeal by Guede against his continued detention. In the report by Judge Bufali, written to confirm Guede's arrest, he wrote that Guede's testimony—in which he claimed to have fought-off an unidentified Italian man moments after Kercher was stabbed, was "full of decisive falsehoods." Judge Bufali also wrote that a group of people actively participated in the murder, writing: "There was group participation in the heinous crime in which a passive role does not appear plausible for any of those present."

In another section of the report, Judge Bufali reiterated, "the presence of more people in that house at the moment in which

Meredith was killed," adding, "And the quick departure of all of them after the tragic conclusion of the evening." One day earlier (December 18th), Knox told Perugia prosecutor, Giuliano Mignini, that she had "read a few pages" of a Harry Potter book at Sollecito's flat on the evening of the murder. That Harry Potter book that Knox claimed to have read at Sollecito's flat had been found at the cottage where Kercher was killed.

Supreme Court Hearing April 1, 2008

On April 1st, the Supreme Court rejected the requests of Guede, Sollecito, and Knox to be released from jail at that time and until commencement of the trial. On the grounds expressed by the Judging College of the First Penal Section of the Supreme Court of Cassazione (with President Torquato Gemelli and Counselors Emilio Gironi, Maria Cristina Siotto, Umberto Zampetti, Margherita Cassano), the court upheld the Italian Court of Freedom's decision to keep the three suspects detained through trial.

The grounds expressed by the Supreme Court for continued detention of Knox are as follows:

"The restrictive measure cannot be denied due to the gravity of the crimes; your negative personality, which we have deducted from the investigation and from your behavior during investigation and court hearings. Your freedom could threaten the collection of evidence and the completion of the next steps, such as further testimony, face-to-face sessions, etc. Not to mention the flight risk due to your status as a foreign citizen and the fact that the sentence if you are found guilty could possibly be more than 2 years of incarceration."

The grounds expressed by the Supreme Court for continued detention of Sollecito are as follows:

"In light of the forgoing, as for gravity of the charges the Court of Freedom was correct. The possibility of altering the evidence has not ceased just because Guede has been brought back. The investigation is evolving continuously and the positions of the suspects have yet to be defined. Their behavior has shown reluctance to cooperate and lying. You yourself admitted that you told "un sacco di cazzate" [a load of bullshit]. You are a flight risk because

of the gravity of the charges. Your danger to society matches your weak character and your personality, which we can't define in terms of harmless juvenile stereotypes, since the context includes the habitual use of drugs."

The grounds expressed by the Supreme Court for continued detention of Guede are as follows:

"The Court has also ruled that all the precautionary requirements of art. 274 c.p.p. (requiring that there be a concrete danger - by reasons of the particular circumstances of the case and of the personality of the accused - that the latter would commit further offences) were satisfied and could be guaranteed only through continued detention."

More Problems for the Sollecito Camp

In late June, with prosecutor Giuliano Mignini reporting that he had officially completed the investigation; more problems arose for the Sollecito camp. While tapping the phone of Raffaele's father, police allegedly overheard him discussing plans to persuade senior politicians to use their influence to get two detectives— whom the Sollecito's considered to be hostile—taken off the case. First obtained by Italian newspaper *Corriere della Sera*, Dr. Franco Sollecito was reported as saying, "'We've got to flay the Perugia flying squad…If we can get rid of the head of homicide and that other one, we'll be OK." Relatives of Sollecito—including his sister, a Carabinieri-Lieutenant at the time—were also overheard discussing politicians who could help their case.

Sollecito had recently hired Giulia Bongiorno, a lawyer and MP for Italian Prime Minister, Silvio Berlusconi, to represent him. The phone taps had been sent to Mignini and Bongiorno, and charges were expected to be filed against Dr. Sollecito. This event followed a previous incident in which Dr. Sollecito was accused of providing local Bari TV station, *Telenorba*, crime-scene video of Meredith Kercher. The video, which *Telenorba* broadcasted on January 4, 2008, showed Kercher lying half-naked on her back on the floor, with the wounds to her throat clearly visible. The Kercher family expressed their horror over the contents of the tape, and the indiscretion shown by Dr. Sollecito. The Sollecito family was expected to be charged for both acts at some point in the near future.

Formal Charge

On 11 July 2008, Perugia's public Prosecutor, Giuliano Mignini, made a formal request to have Amanda Knox, 21, Raffaele Sollecito, 24, and Rudy Herman Guede, 20, charged with the crime of conspiring to kill Meredith Kercher. After closing the investigation some three weeks earlier, Mignini sent the murder indictment request file to Judge Paolo Micheli—[44] a former Carabinieri officer who has been a magistrate since 1990—who will decide at a preliminary hearing if there is enough evidence to commit the trio to a full trial or whether to release them without charge. Just two days before Amanda Knox had celebrated her milestone 21st birthday behind bars in Perugia's Capanne Prison, with her mother and a bunch of flowers sent by Raffaele. Upon ending his investigation, Prosecutor Mignini deposited evidence on June 19th that included 10,000 pages; in those pages were autopsy reports, interrogations, evidence and phone taps. Among the many charges, Mignini accused the three suspects of voluntary homicide and sexual assault, with Knox and Sollecito also being accused of simulation of a crime for allegedly faking a break-in. The three were also accused of steeling 300 euros ($475 in cash) and two credit cards from Kercher.

Pretrial Hearing # 1 (September 16, 2008)

Media from the UK, the US, and Italy besieged the Renaissance-era court building in Perugia's Piazza Matteotti for the first preliminary hearing for the three defendants. Dressed in blue jeans, a white embroidered top, and her hair pulled back neatly in a half-ponytail, Amanda Knox was escorted into the courtroom by two female prison guards for the first preliminary hearing on Tuesday, 16 September 2008. Rudy Hermann Guede was led into the courtroom in handcuffs, and sat just a few feet from co-defendant, Amanda Knox. To add to the drama, Meredith's family—including her parents, John and Arline and her sister, Stephanie—had arrived in Perugia one day earlier; and were present in court as part of a civil suit against the defendants. Also in the courtroom for the same purpose were Patrick Lumumba and the owner of the cottage, Aldalia Tattanelli-Morrone, which the girls had shared.

With Raffaele Sollecito absent (allegedly because he was ill), Knox and Guede came face-to-face with the Kercher family for the first time since being accused of the murder. Knox sat in front of Kercher's family, but she never turned to meet their glances. The day's hearing is expected to be the first of six before the end of October, by which time judge Paolo Micheli is expected to rule whether or not there is enough evidence to send Knox and Sollecito to trial. Judge Micheli's first ruling of the day was that the Kercher family was entitled to attach a civil suit to any criminal proceedings; meaning that if there is a conviction then the family will be awarded monetary civil compensation. This ruling—prescribed by Italian Law—also allows the Kercher family to monitor the proceedings more closely, and get information usually reserved for defense lawyers and prosecutors.

The judge also ruled that the trial will be split, at the request of Guede's lawyers, with Rudy Guede receiving a *fast-track trial* starting on September 26th. The request came out of fear that the defense teams for the other two defendants would try to pin the crime on their client. Guede's lawyers had heard and had suspected that there was an alleged "secret pact" between both Knox and Sollecito's defense teams to frame Guede for the crime—this was really no secret. A *giudizio abbreviato ("Fast-track trial")* consists of several preliminary hearings whereby at the end of the hearings the preliminary judge—in this case, Judge Micheli—gives a final ruling on the guilt or innocence of the suspect. In short, there is no real trial, no jury, and the defendant gives up the right to present new evidence. The reward for the defendant in a fast-track trial is a reduced sentence. So if the defendant is given a life sentence, the sentence is reduced to one-third or 30-years. Unlike a full trial, a fast-track trial is closed to the public. In this case, Judge Micheli is expected to issue a verdict at the same time that he determines whether to indict Knox and Sollecito. Judge Micheli also granted defense lawyers the right to participate and have full access to Guede's trial.

During the intense hearing, Meredith's older sister Stephanie stood and gave a heart-wrenching statement to the court:

"Each time we arrive in Perugia we wish we were here for a different reason. It is so easy to understand why Meredith loved this city. She loved everything about Italy, but the fact that she chose Perugia above all others showed that it was a special place for her. We only wish she had had more time before she was brutally taken from us. We are all struggling to understand why she was so cruelly taken from us. We are pleased that we have reached a new phase in the process, hoping that justice will soon be done for Meredith."

Pretrial Hearing # 2 (September 26, 2008)

Dressed in a sky-blue V-necked sweater and jeans, Amanda Knox was again escorted into the courtroom by blue-bereted prison guards. As opposed to her calm demeanor at the first pre-trial hearing a week earlier, Knox appeared nervous, tense, and pale as she entered the courtroom. Wearing a black T-shirt and with his head almost completely shaven, Rudy Guede was also escorted by three blue-bereted prison guards and carrying a somber poker-face into the courtroom. Twenty minutes after Knox had arrived; Raffaele Sollecito entered the courtroom wearing a white cotton jacket and jeans, with wavy long hair. It was the first time that he and Knox had come face-to-face since being arrested ten-months earlier. The two exchanged smiles as Sollecito entered, but no words were exchanged. To ensure that the three suspects do not communicate, they were all seated in different rows; Sollecito in the front row, Knox behind him, and Guede in the third row behind Knox.

Defense lawyers spent the morning challenging the testimony of Albanian witness, Hekuran Kokomani, who claims to have seen the three together on the night of the murder. During his four-hours on the stand, Kokomani was questioned by Judge Micheli, prosecutor Mignini, and the defendants' lawyers. Kokomani told police back in January that he had parked his VW near a dumpster in view of the cottage when he had seen Knox emerge from the cottage waving a knife and screaming at him. Kokomani also claimed to have seen Sollecito wearing a cap and a dark-skinned man (Guede); all three were agitated and threatened him.

He claimed that he later recognized the three—Knox, Sollecito and Guede—from photographs in the newspapers. Kokomani reiterated his account for Judge Micheli. Lawyers for the defendants claimed that Mr. Kokomani's testimony was confusing and unreliable. For example, one discrepancy that they had with Kokomani's testimony is that he had told police that it was raining on the night of the murder; however, video footage taken from a CCTV camera at the car park above the cottage shows that it hadn't rained that evening. It did rain October 30th in Perugia; however, it did not rain on October 31st or on November 1st. Mr. Kokomani's cell phone records show him in the vicinity of the cottage on October 31st at 11:00p.m., and on November 1st (night of the murder) at 8:00p.m. Kokomani also remembers seeing a tow truck in front of the cottage, which was at around 11:00p.m.

Rudy's elementary teacher, Ivana Tiberi, and her son, Gabriele Mancini, both gave testimony as character witnesses for him. Ivana explained that Rudy is sensitive and good-natured. Ivana testified that she had let Rudy live with her for a short time and that he had become good friends with her son. Rudy Guede, Amanda Knox, and Raffaele Sollecito were proven to be in the same room on this day. The question that remains going forward is, were they in the same room at the time of Meredith Kercher's murder?

Pretrial Hearing # 3 (September 27, 2008)

Several witnesses came to the stand on this day. The only witness that was a possible threat to Guede's character was proven to be a liar, and his testimony was discredited and dismissed. First up was Stefano Bonassi, one of the boys who lived on the first floor of the cottage. His testimony mirrored Guede's diary for the most part, claiming that Guede occasionally hung out on the first-floor of the cottage, that Guede had a crush on Amanda, and that Guede thought Meredith was beautiful.

The next witness was Abuker 'Momi' Barrow, A tall, stylishly-dressed Somali man called in by the prosecution. Momi was a former basketball partner of Guede's. Momi described Rudy as a thief, drug addicted and violent with girls. Barrow testified that Rudy, above all when he was drunk or under the effects of drugs, "bothered people, especially young women. He blocked them off physically and tried to kiss them." However, he was shutdown famously by Guede's main lawyer, Walter Biscotti. Coming to Guede's defense, Biscotti asked Momi if he had ever received money from media, to which Momi answered, "No." Biscotti then wielded a videotape recorded September 17th by Studio Aperto of the Mediaset Group showing Momi negotiating in a van with a female reporter, Anna Boiardi, for cash to tell his story. Biscotti also presented evidence that Momi had also received 2,000 euro from *La Nazione* for his testimony as well. This information prompted Judge Micheli to dismiss the witness. Momi was taken away by guards and faces possible prosecution for perjury. Biscotti wrapped up the hearing by producing several character witnesses who described Guede's very sad childhood. Collectively, they said he was "like any other child."

Pretrial Hearing # 4 (October 18, 2008)

During the fourth preliminary hearing, Amanda Knox gave a statement proclaiming her innocence. Sounding at times as if she was acting, Knox's teary proclamation tells of the abuse and mistreatment she experienced during her interrogation; which she claims led to her false statement. The statement to the court—in English—was made on 18 October 2008, before Judge Paulo Micheli during the trial of Rudy Guede and the fourth preliminary hearing for Knox and Sollecito:

Amanda Knox: "I want to clarify what it is that happened to me in the um, the quest, the um, the day that I made the declarations that didn't make sense, that changed. After the discovery of Meredith, I had spent days collaborating with police trying to give as much information as I could. (Sigh) The day of the fifth, I wasn't called to the questore, Raffaele was called, but I decided to go with him to keep him company, but also because I was scared to be alone. When I was there I just planned to wait, but the police came into the waiting room and wanted to talk to me more about what I knew, people that I had knew that had come to my house; I gave them phone numbers, and, after that they moved me into another room and started asking me the same questions, what I had done that night; asking me for times, exact time periods, exactly what I did. It was, it was difficult for me because it was the middle of the night that I, we had been called. I was very tired and I was also quite stressed out, and I, so I. They kept asking me the same questions, time periods, um, exactly sequences of actions. And I did my best to give the same information over and over and over again."

"Um, at a certain point, um, at a certain point (sigh), the police began to be more aggressive with me, they called me a liar, and they told me that I was, of all the things that I kept saying over and over again they said that I was lying, they said that (hmm) they said that I was going to go to prison for 30 years because I was hiding something, but I (hmm), but I felt, I felt completed stressed out—blocked—because I wasn't lying, I didn't know, I didn't know what to do. Then they started pushing on me the idea that I must have seen something and forgotten about it. They said I was traumatized. I didn't understand; I became really confused. I tried to re-express, re-explain what I had done, the fact that I didn't have to go to work. At that point they, I gave them my phone so they could see that I didn't have to, [short pause] because I received an SMS and for that reason they kept repeating to me that I was lying about, ah, I was confused."

"So, what ended up happening was the factor that I had been pressured so much [begins getting teary] I was hit in the back of the head by one of the police officers who said she was trying to help me remember the truth. I was terrified; because I didn't know [starts crying] I didn't know what to do anymore. And so what ended up happening was [pause, more crying] they said they were going to take me to jail. And because of all this SMS, because of all this confusion, they kept saying, 'You sent this thing to Patrick, we know that you left the house, we know!' I just said his name; it wasn't because I was trying to say anything it was just because they were [pause - Composes herself]."

"After that (sigh) I asked if I should have had a lawyer, and they said that it would have been worse for me. So they asked me to make declarations about what I remembered, but I told them that I didn't remember anything like this, because I was confused. What I remembered was different from what they asked me to say. They asked me for details and I didn't have details to give them. So they just asked me questions and I just responded [short pause], I was stressed so what I, in that moment I was trying to think of something else. My memories of just random events: seeing Patrick, for instance, one night or ah (sigh)."

"I wrote these memorials that everyone is putting so much pressure on only because I wanted to express the fact that I was confused. I felt like no one was listening to me anymore, and so I wrote these to express the fact that didn't, I didn't, I wasn't for sure about anything anymore. I want to stress the fact that I'm innocent. Meredith was my friend and I would never have hurt her! I'm not the person that the prosecutor says I am. [Sheds teary voice and says in a completely low, soft, and composed voice] And that's all I want to say, thank you."

As the session rapped up, prosecutor Mignini proclaimed his certainty that the three suspects raped and killed Meredith. Prosecutor Manuela Comodi requested that the judge sentence Rudy Guede to life in prison and for Amanda Knox and Raffaele Sollecito to stand trial for the charges of murder and sexual violence.

Pretrial Hearing # 5 (October 27, 2008)

The fifth hearing was filled with high-stakes drama, and certainly packing the most excitement and surprise thus far. The prosecution and all defense teams were set to present their closing arguments on this day; but before they had a chance to do so, there would be one jaw-dropping moment. At one point, prosecutor Mignini presented the court with a 14 page report submitted by forensic specialist, Professor Francesco Vinci. Having been initially retained by Sollecito's legal team to research the bra clasp that allegedly had Sollecito's DNA on it; Vinci's report suggested a shocking revelation. In his report, Vinci stated that—not only was Sollecito's DNA found, but— Knox's DNA and Guede's DNA were also found on Meredith's bloodied bra clasp. The shocking revelation appeared to be the second time that Sollecito has turned on Knox, and the media later squawked about the tacit pact between them being broken.

Professor Vinci said that the DNA traces were "too contaminated" to be useable as evidence, but showed the presence of "all three suspects." Sollecito's main lawyer, Giulia Bongiorno, told the court that the torn bra clasp was not found until mid-December,

47 days after the murder, at which time two police searches had already taken place at the scene. Bongiorno did not dispute the DNA findings of professor Vinci, but insisted that it is there due to contamination owing to mishandling by police and forensic specialists. So, what sounded at first as though it would be a gift from the defense to the prosecution, Bongiorno spun to be a statement on behalf of the defense confirming contamination occurred. This was a good-play for Sollecito's defense, but the prosecution would surely try to use this evidence to their advantage to place all three suspects in Meredith's room during the murder.

During their closing arguments, Knox's defense team requested that if a trial date is set, she be released from prison into house arrest. Knox's lawyers asked to have her housed at *San Fatucchio*, a supervised community and farm in the Umbrian countryside for recovering drug addicts and young offenders, which is run by the Catholic charity Caritas. She has been offered a place at the Caritas hostel at Castiglione dell Lago on the shores of picturesque Lake Trasimeno, 25 miles (40 kilometers) north of Perugia.

Pretrial Hearing # 6 (October 28, 2008)

The Day of Judgment has arrived; not just for Guede, but for Sollecito and Knox as well. Meredith's parents, John and Arlene, her sister Stephanie, and her brothers, Lyle and John, were in court in Perugia to hear the ruling by Judge Paolo Micheli. With their fates hanging in the balance, the three suspects entered the courtroom for what was surely going to be an emotional day either way. As she awaited the verdict, Knox scribbled a note and passed it to her lawyers that read: "This is a horrible moment for me. I feel terrible. I am not a killer." Judge Micheli heard the closing arguments from Guede's lawyers before retiring to his council chamber (alone) to deliberate a verdict. Retiring around 9:00a.m., the suspects and their families would have eleven tense hours of waiting; as Judge Micheli gave an 8:00p.m., appointment to deliver his verdict.

Knox and Sollecito waited the eleven hours behind bars in the basement of the courthouse for Micheli to return. When Judge Micheli returned to give his verdict, the courtroom held their collective breaths. Judge Micheli stepped up to the podium and delivered the worst possible news for all three suspects. Rudy Guede was sentenced to 30 years of jail, and was ordered to pay 2 million euro to each of Meredith's parents and 1.5 million euro to each of her siblings. Amanda Knox and Raffaele Sollecito will be tried for murder, sexual violence, theft, simulation of crime, transportation of knife, and Knox will be tried solo for slander against police and Patrick Lumumba. All of this, according to Judge Micheli will take place starting on 4 December 2008. Judge Micheli informed the court that he would give a ruling on whether or not to have Knox and Sollecito confined to house arrest within the next five days. However, just a day later they would get more bad news. In a 17-page report, Judge Micheli turned down both requests for house arrest, explaining that they were flight risks and that there was a possibility of "reiteration of crime."

As the verdict was read, Knox began crying and got emotional. She was comforted by her lawyers, one of whom replied, "Don't worry, we will fight on." Sollecito, however, gave a much different response, seemingly in shock from the surreal situation. Apparently not understanding the verdict, Sollecito turned to his lawyers and asked if he could go home. Sollecito's lawyer, Luca Maori, later said that "He seemed like a lost bird" after the verdict was read. Sollecito had been fighting sickness prior to the verdict, a decision that would likely make his condition worsen. Meredith's family described the sentencing of Guede as "really important in our steps towards justice for Meredith." Lyle Kercher said, "We are as satisfied as we can be with the decision we have received. It is important to remember at the end of the day we are here because our sister Meredith was murdered."

Because Guede is appealing his own guilty verdict, the testimony from his trial cannot be used in the case against Knox and Sollecito. This means that the witnesses that have testified at this trial would need to be recalled for Knox and Sollecito's trial. Also, Guede is not required to testify in the upcoming proceedings, even though he would be given the opportunity to do so. Judge Micheli has 90 days from this ruling to provide a full report on his ruling, as prescribed by Italian law. For now Knox would return to Capanne (the 40 acre prison) to await trial.

Approaching Trial

The year leading up to the murder trial of Knox and Sollecito was no-less action-packed than at any other time. The story had already taken on a life of its own and that life was alive-and-well leading up to the trial. In fact, public anticipation was at an all-time high as the trial approached. New websites were opened, including one for Knox that allowed people to donate money to her family. New witnesses came forward, including another super-witness that far exceeded the expectations of Mr. Kokomani. Knox and Sollecito had gone from possibly going home and ending their nightmare to an indictment and an impending trial that was expected to be at least 6 to 10 months long. Their infamy and popularity grew with the indictment. Amanda Knox's popularity, particularly, grew to an all-time high after the pretrial hearings. Knox had become a tabloid celebrity in Italy the likes of Paris Hilton in America at her height, and beyond. Knox was voted "most interesting person of the year" in a 2008 online *poll* by a major Italian T.V. station. Knox nudged out her second place opponent—Italian-born French first lady, Carla Bruni—to get the honors.

The prosecution's case was made much stronger in the months leading up to the trial. In fact, they acquired a few mysterious witnesses that were expected to fill the holes in their theory. These new witnesses were pieces of the puzzle that the prosecution believed would complete the picture of events surrounding the murder. With just a few days left until the first day of the trial (December 4th), delay became inevitable. For one, the prosecution had not met the deadline that was set for them to deliver their witness list. That, coupled with the fact that defense teams wanted more time to analyze their cases made it apparent that a rescheduling was to take place. Moreover, the court was still addressing concerns of public safety, as the popularity of this case was unprecedented. And with the Christmas-break fast approaching, Raffaele and Amanda would need to sit-tight in their cells a bit longer. With all these considerations in mind, the court announced that the new trial date was set for January 16th. On December 4th the judges were sworn in, and the court began jury member selection in the month leading up to the start date.

Chapter 5 - The Trial of the Century

Meredith Kercher Trial Day 1 – (Jan 16, 2009)

Fourteen months after the brutal murder of Meredith Kercher, Amanda Knox and Raffaele Sollecito would face their first day in court. Millions throughout Italy and the UK had been following this story religiously, and they were finally going to get a trial. Sollecito's lawyer expressed similar sentiments on the part of his client. "He [Raffaele] is happy that the trial is finally starting, but extremely unhappy that he has spent over a year in jail waiting for it," said Marco Brusco. Kercher family lawyer, Francesco Maresca, responded by saying that Sollecito would need continued patience as, "Every shred of evidence must now be heard in court and the trial will run until July or even September." Although the media circus and banter from opposing sides was just beginning, at least the remainder of this saga would now be played out in a court of law. Rumors will be replaced by testimony; speculation over the evidence replaced by expert testimony. Yet, just as fast as fantasy can become reality it can revert back with the same swiftness.

Italian Professor and Sociologist, Franco Ferrarotti, asserted that Italians have been mesmerized and hypnotized by this case. What Knox eats in prison, says to guards, or wears into court has captivated Italians. The sheer scope of this trial was astonishing. One-hundred-thirty newspapers and T.V. stations from around the world had applied for press passes to be seated inside a court room that could only accommodate about that many people in total. More than 250 witnesses were expected to be called, including dozens of investigators, forensic specialists, and computer experts. Bars and restaurants around Perugia were swarmed with outsiders from all over the globe looking for local Italian comforts and hospitality during court recessions. More than 140 reporters squeezed into *The Court of Assizes (criminal court)*, at Palazzo di Giustizia; for what would surely become known as Italy's trial of the century.

The controversy surrounding the murder and the events leading up to the trial would also play out when it was time to determine who was allowed into the courtroom. The maximum capacity of the courtroom is only 150 people, so only a handful of media and a handful of the general public would be seated in the actual courtroom itself. The media allowed into the courtroom would have to sit inside a cage reserved for terrorists, which almost gave the appearance as though they were the ones on trial. A separate large room next to the courtroom with one large T.V. monitor was set up for the remaining credentialed media representatives. The decision whether to switch the T.V. on or not would be the first order of business of the court.

Two judges, six jury members, and six jury alternates had been selected to hear the testimonies and the evidence in the case. Selecting the jury was the job of the chief judge in the trial, Judge Giancarlo Massei. Judge Massei had previously narrowed the jury pool down to fifty people and then down to twelve only days before the first day of trial. The verdict will be determined by six flanking lay-jurors and two judges, each with an equal vote. As prescribed by Italian law, the six jury members will have the "same weight and the same responsibility" as the two professional judges. By the ordered of Judge Massei the six jury members—all between the ages of 35 and 57—would be paid between €25 and €70 (Euros) per hearing, according to their professions. The deputy judge in the trial would be Judge Beatrice Cristiani, who would be seated to the right Judge Massei during the trial.

All eyes, however, would be on the "star of the show;" the attractive, young American girl Amanda Knox. As she entered the courtroom—wearing a grey hooded sweatshirt over a black, gray, and white striped top and jeans—Knox seemed relaxed and even appeared gleeful in certain photos. She looked diligently around the room for her aunt and uncle, who were seated in the back of the courtroom. Her mother was scheduled to be a witness and therefore she was not allowed to be present in the courtroom before she testified. After Knox's grand entrance she took her place beside a court-appointed interpreter and her two Italian lawyers.

Then it was Sollecito's turn to take his place in the courtroom. Wearing a bright green sweater and beige trousers, Sollecito entered looking more subdued and tense, despite his lawyer Bongiorno telling the press beforehand that he is "absolutely unafraid of what might happen here at this trial, because he knows he is innocent." Sollecito and Knox shared a glance, but nothing more as a previous court order forbids the two from communicating. Sollecito took his seat just a few meters to Knox's left.

Italian law allows victims of a crime, or their family members, to attach a civil lawsuit to a criminal trial, asking for compensation to be considered if a suspect(s) is convicted. Patrick Lumumba was seated in the courtroom, there as part of a civil suit against Knox for *slander*. Lumumba was seeking £462,000 in damages from the Italian state and up to a million pounds from Knox for slander. Another civil suit included the Kercher family, who were asking for a total of $33 million in damages from the suspects. Even the cottage's owner, Aldalia Tattanelli-Morrone, was there with her lawyer seeking monetary redemption for unpaid rent. Francesco Maresca had attached the civil lawsuit for the Kercher family back in September (2008). Representing Rudy Guede was his lawyer, Walter Biscotti. Everyone was geared-up to see the Kercher family and the two suspects come face to face; but they would have to wait for another day, as the Kercher family was not in attendance on this occasion.

Trial Principles:

Judges	Giancarlo Massei	Beatrice Cristiani	
Prosecutors	Giuliano Mignini	Manuela Comodi	
Amanda's lawyers	Carlo Dalla Vedova	Luciano Ghirga	
Raffaele's lawyers	Giulia Bongiorno	Luca Maori	Marco Brusco
Meredith's lawyers	Francesco Maresca	Serena Perna	
Guede's lawyers	Walter Biscotti	Nicodemo Gentile	
Patrick's lawyer	Carlo Pacelli		
Aldalia's lawyer	Letizia Magnini		

*Note: number next to name, going forward, indicates order of testimony

The prosecution will attempt to make the case that there were multiple killers and that Knox and Sollecito were two of the three involved. Moreover, the prosecution would say that Amanda Knox struck the fatal knife blow that killed Meredith Kercher while being held down by Guede and Sollecito. The defense will contend that there was only one killer and that he (Guede) has already been convicted. In a report sent to the pre-trial hearing, Medical examiner and renowned forensic consultant, Carlo Torre, hired by Knox's legal team, said the wounds pointed to "one robust man attacking from the front—who wounds, who pushes the girl to the ground, who immobilizes her by straddling her, who grabs her neck with bare hands and then stabs her in the neck." This contradicted Pre-trial judge Paolo Micheli's report, which said that he found the single killer theory "rather difficult to prove." However, even Micheli described Mignini's theory of an orgy inspired by "satanic rites and manga comics" as "fantasy."

The crowd inside the courtroom waited anxiously as if at a rock concert awaiting the main attraction after hours of tailgating. Many voices spoke just above a whisper in anticipation for the proceedings to begin. Abruptly, and without warning, the speaker (a curly haired blonde woman) announces *Signor presidente della corte* ("Mr. President of the court"), and everybody stands. The presiding judge, Giancarlo Massei, the side judge, Beatrice Cristiani, and the lay persons enter the room. Facing the intimidating panel, it was easy to notice the large crucifix directly behind and slightly above judge Massei. Security officers with black attire and blue berets would be on hand to deliver the suspects and secure the scene for the entire trial. Judge Massei wore a black robe over his suit; and around his neck—a white dickey, a small white bow-tie, and a frilled collar. On each shoulder of the robe hung gold tassels. The *procuratori* (prosecutors) and the *avvocati* (lawyers) both wore robes with a sliver tassel on each arm of their robes.

Only minutes after the trial was underway, the first decision had to be made. More than a month earlier the Kercher family (Francesco Maresca) had filed a formal request asking that the trial be held behind closed doors away from the watching eyes of the media. The defense attorneys were all adamant about having a public trial. Knox's attorneys argued that an open trial would lead to greater transparency "without preconditions." The first decision for the jury is presented to them within a matter of minutes of the start of the trial. The jury leaves the court room to deliberate for the first time. Not long after, the jury returns with their first decision: a public trial with no video cameras. It seems that the first of many decisions to be made goes to the defense teams. The judge orders that when something disturbing is to be shown in the courtroom he will order the T.V. monitor (being watched by reporters in another room) to be disconnected. Massei banned cameras from filming, but ruled the trial would remain open to print journalists. Then he allowed for a three-minute photo shoot before proceeding. The frenzy of flashing cameras and running of video recorders turned bizarre when prosecutors literally had to push journalists out of the courtroom to get them to finally stop filming.

With that out of the way the real trial could finally begin. The speaker stands and announces the charges against Knox and Sollecito, which included murder, sexual violence, theft, transportation of weapon, and slander, among other things. After both the prosecution and the defense made their announcements of new material and new witnesses, it was time for the preliminaries. The concerns of the defense were made very clear, and those were the questions of admissibility. Giulia Bongiorno took the stage first. In dramatic fashion Bongiorno claimed that Sollecito's first interrogation was held without the opportunity for him to consult his lawyer; therefore, it shouldn't be admitted. Then she went one further, saying that since the interrogation led to his arrest that the arrest should also be revoked.

Bongiorno then went on a tirade, protesting her client's innocence. It was an obvious attempt to immediately impress the jury. Bongiorno criticized the prosecutions' theories indirectly, claiming that the couple had only met on 25 October 2007, and were not longtime lovers looking for new sexual experiences. Bongiorno called the couple "Little lovebirds" who were only "in the first week of their love story." It was one of the many memorable and headline-worthy sayings that Bongiorno would exhibit throughout the trial. Bongiorno's early aggression angered *procuratore* (prosecutor) Giuliano Mignini, who objected to her discussing evidence that had not yet been introduced. "Then where were the wine glasses?" Mignini asked sarcastically. However, the judge overruled and had to quiet the visibly flustered Mignini. Luca Maori added his own comments, claiming that Rudy Guede and only Rudy killed Meredith; a statement that Guede's lawyer, Walter Biscotti, called "Cowardly." It would be the only temper flair-up of the day, but the first of many throughout the trial. The battle lines had been drawn and everyone braced themselves for the inevitable skirmishes to come.

Then it was Knox's lawyers turn, and the question raised would turn out to be a very pivotal decision in the trial for both sides. Knox's lawyers asked that the voluntary statement given by Knox on 6 November 2007 (The Memoir) be ruled inadmissible, because it was not a confession and it was given to police after the interrogation had officially ended (5:45 a.m.), as indicated in the police report. The prosecution objected and an interesting legal battle ensues. The jury again goes back to the chamber to deliberate, but this time for nearly two hours. When they return they rule that Raffaele's interrogation was permissible. This is not really a big shock to his defense. However, the question of the admissibility of Knox's 'memoir' needed further examination as to where it lies under Italian law. Court is then adjourned until 6 February 2009, at which time this ruling will be made. For Knox and Sollecito it's back to Capanne prison, their home for now.

Meredith Kercher Trial Day 2 – (February 6, 2009)

The ice had been broken and it was time to get down to brass taxes. Someone was horrifically murdered and it was time to find out if the two accused had a hand. As with any trial the ebbs and flows play out much like a basketball game, wherein a ten-point lead could be erased in less than a minute. In a trial a huge deficit can be erased with one word from a witness. It is a moment that could make the whole courtroom gasp aloud all at once and the hairs on the back of their necks rise, such as in *A Few Good Men* when Nicholson admits to ordering the *code red*. Then there is the steady pounding of testimony that paints a consistent picture of the events; the battle won by attrition. This day would be the latter and would not be a good day for either defense team. The prosecution would establish the tempo right from the start, showing Knox in particular as callus and remorseless just hours after the murder. To do so they would call to the stand several of Meredith's close friends who witnessed Knox's bizarre behavior at the police station on 2 November 2007.

The first order of business, however, was the 'to be continued...' decision from day one: the admissibility of Knox's voluntary statement. So the second day of trial starts out with a council chamber at which point the decision is discussed among the lawyers first, followed by the official announcement of admissibility.

First decision: It was determined that Knox's statement made to police at 1:45a.m., when she first accused Lumumba of the murder was inadmissible, because it was made while she was still a witness.

Second decision: It was ruled that Knox's statement made later that same morning (at 3:30a.m.)—when she repeated her story in detail in front of prosecutor Mignini (which she signed at 5:45a.m.)—was also expunged and held as inadmissible, because she had no lawyer present.

Third decision: However, Knox's statement—legally defined as "Spontaneous" (voluntary)—written just after 5:45a.m., on that morning and her memoir written on 7 November 2007, were both admissible and could be used against Knox and others during the trial. This decision was a devastating blow to the defense! The second decision (not to allow Knox's statement because a lawyer was not present) was a big inconsistency with the assessment made on the first day of the trial (to allow Sollecito's statement, although he did not have a lawyer present). It seems Bongiorno posed a legitimate argument for her client after the second decision was made on day two; which certainly should be noted for appeal purposes.

In any event, with a major battle won by the prosecution it was time for them to call their first witness. But wait! Someone wants to say something. Suddenly Bongiorno makes an announcement that Raffaele Sollecito would like to make a *spontaneous statement* to the court. In Italian law defendants are allowed to make statements or ask questions at any time during the trial. Sollecito wanted to exercise that right. An emotional Sollecito—wearing a white turtleneck shirt—stood up and addressed the court in a tremulous voice.

"I find it difficult to understand how I have ended up in this situation. I have been in jail for one year and three months and I have nothing to do with all of this. I am not a violent person and the thought of hurting somebody has never crossed my mind. Anyone who knows me can tell you that I find it difficult to hurt a fly."

Sollecito then makes an interesting comment; he claims that he never met Rudy Guede before the murder. This is a statement that will later be tested; and if proven a lie, could debilitate his defense. Sollecito then backs up the statements made by Bongiorno on the previous day that he only met Knox on October 25th. Pleading with the court, Sollecito asks, "I humbly ask you to examine everything with extreme attention, to ascertain the truth. I feel I am the victim of a judicial mistake."

With his statement noted its time for the first witness of the trial to take the stand. In order to chronologically reconstruct the events of November 2nd, the prosecution called witnesses in the order that they arrived at the cottage that day. However, the prosecution does not start out with Knox and Sollecito. Prosecutor Manuela Comodi explained to the court the reasoning behind this. "Until now, under questioning the accused have only tried to divert the investigation; therefore, we do not believe that it is useful to hear them in order to make a proper reconstruction."

Each witness and each piece of evidence will have five to seven passes over:

1. Prosecution witness-examination
2. Defense #1 cross-examination
3. Defense #2 cross-examination
4. Defense #1 witness-examination
5. Prosecution cross-examination
6. Defense #2 witness-examination
7. Prosecution cross-examination

When defense witnesses take the stand the other defense can cross-examine them as well, so this could cause a total of nine passes in those instances.

With that being said, the first witness, Chief police inspector Michele Battistelli[1], took the stand. The first to testify will be Postal Police officials and agents who on 2 November 2007, arrived at the cottage at Via Della Pergola 7 to return Meredith's mobile phones and instead found her murdered. "There was quite a lot of blood," Battistelli said. "I saw (Kercher's) foot sticking out from the duvet, and given the color and the fact that she didn't move, I thought I'd call the emergency sanitary service." Battistelli testified that he did not enter the room, but later testimony from others would conflict this statement. Battistelli also testified that Knox and Sollecito appeared "surprised" by their arrival.

The second to testify was Fabio Marzi[2], the other officer who arrived at the cottage with Battistelli. Marzi testified that Knox had shown him small traces of blood in the bathroom next to Meredith's room. Acting almost as his own lawyer Sollecito interjected, stating that Knox was "very shocked, cold, silent, and staring into space," during that time. During their testimony both officers maintained that when they had first arrived the couple had told them that they had already called the carabinieri. Sollecito was also adamant that he called the carabinieri before the postal police had arrived. The prosecutions main focus regarding the officers' testimonies was to establish an exact timeline as to prove that Sollecito's phone call to the carabinieri came after the postal police had arrived. Both officers established that their arrival time at the cottage was 12:30p.m. The prosecution would try to corroborate their statements by showing CCTV footage from the car park across the street from the cottage that showed a black Fiat Punto (the same driven by the postal police) arriving at that time. Both officers also testified that the washing machine was running when they arrived; they could hear the noise of the centrifuge.

Next to take the stand was the Elisabetta family; the ones who had found Meredith's two cell phones in their yard. These three family members were called to substantiate the prosecutions timeline. One thing is certain: Sollecito's first call to the carabinieri was at 12:51p.m. Lana Elisabetta[4] testified that on the evening of the murder she was getting ready for bed. She walked into her bathroom and at that very moment she received a call from a stranger who tells her that there is a bomb under her toilet. She then calls the police who respond and check the house and the rest of her property; most likely the victim of an untimely practical joke. Lana goes to bed soundly that night. The next morning, at sometime after 10:30a.m., Lana's son, Alessandro Elisabetta[5], finds a Motorola cellular phone in the middle of Lana's garden, about 15-20 meters (approx. 60ft.) from the street. The phone had been turned off. Thinking possibly that the police might have left it there the night before when checking the garden, Lana called them at 10:58p.m. Filippo Bartolozzi[3], head of the Umbrian postal police, searched the Vodafone database and found that the phone belonged to Filomena Romanelli. Inspector Bartolozzi makes a record of his find at 11:31p.m., and then he radios two officers [Battistelli & Marzi] at approximately 12:00p.m., to head to Via Della Pergola 7.

Here is where the timeline gets tricky. Lana claims that she went shopping at around this time. However, her daughter, Giannetta Elisabetta[6], found an Erickson cellular phone in the bushes, about 5-6 meters (approx. 17ft.) from the street. The phone was ringing and the call was later confirmed to have been coming from Amanda Knox. Inspector Bartolozzi is notified and checks who the phone is registered to, but he has no luck this time, because the SIM is foreign. Lana claims that she was standing in front of her home with the two cell phones at 12:46p.m.; the same time that inspector Bartolozzi makes his second record of the incident. In this record, Bartolozzi writes that the patrol left after retrieving the two cell phones. This would mean that the police had arrived after 1:00p.m., which would mean that Sollecito was telling the truth when he said that he called the carabinieri before the postal police had arrived. However, Bartolozzi explains later that he made a mistake in the written record, and that the patrol was sent out around 12:00p.m., rather than after 12:46p.m. Plus we will need to wait until day 3 of the trial to get a more solid view of the timeline here, with help from Filomena and friends.

This day would only get worse for the defense as inspector Bartolozzi, whose agency oversees internet activity in Italy, said "an examination of Sollecito's computer indicated that there had been no activity on it between 9:10p.m., and 5:32a.m., on the night of the murder." This was another devastating blow, because Sollecito had claimed that he was on his computer during most of that time.

Meredith Kercher Trial Day 3 – (February 7, 2009)

Day three is a continuation of day two; which the main objective is to nail-down the time that the postal police arrived at the cottage. If they can prove that they arrived before 12:51p.m., then this means that Raffaele Sollecito had lied about calling the carabinieri before the postal police had arrived. On this day it would be left to Filomena Romanelli[7] and Paola Grande[8] to help clear-up this mystery. The second half of day there will be a showdown between Luca Altieri[9] and officer Battistelli, whose versions of events slightly contradict each others.

Filomena had spent the night of November 1st at her boyfriend's house, Marco Zaroli. The twenty-nine year old student who worked as an apprentice in a Perugia law firm testified that on the morning of 2 November 2007, she received a bizarre call from Knox while she was driving to a fair with Paola Grande. "There's something strange at the house," she quoted Knox as saying. "I go, 'Ciao, Amanda, What's happened? In what sense?" Filomena asked. "I arrived and the door was open," Knox replied. Knox explained that she spent the night at Raffaele's flat and that she had come home to a house that was an unusual mess. "But Amanda, I don't understand," Romanelli said to Knox. "Explain to me, because there's something odd. The door's open. You take a shower. There's blood. But where's Meredith?"

"Eh, I don't know," she recalled Knox saying. Romanelli told her to check the house again, call the police, and get back to her. Then Filomena called her boyfriend Marco Zaroli who lived closer to the cottage than where Filomena was physically located at the time and he could get there quicker than she could. Marco then calls his buddy Luca Altieri, and tells him that his girlfriend's place had been robbed and asks him for a ride over to the cottage. Not realizing at the time that this chance phone call was leading him directly into a hellish scene, Altieri accepts and rushes over to get Zaroli.

We know that Altieri and Zaroli arrived at the cottage before Filomena. When they arrived the postal police were already at the scene. Filomena arrived at the cottage around or just before 1:00p.m.

Car-park video shows the carabinieri car in front of the house at 1:22p.m. The timeline reconstruction certainly did not favor Knox and Sollecito's versions of events.

Then Filomena had some more daggers to throw in the direction of Knox. Her testimony would pose some real problems for the defense.

- Filomena testified that after she arrived at the cottage she noticed that the washing machine was "still warm" and she identified several of the clothes inside the machine as belonging Meredith. It was just another small piece of a puzzle that when completed would show a series of cover-up attempts made by the couple. The prosecution believed that these cover-up attempts would overwhelming prove the two had something to hide.
- Filomena helped police establish the staged break-in. She stated that when she returned home her room was a disaster; with clothes all over the floor and the cupboard was open, but no jewelry or anything was missing. "I remember that in lifting my laptop off of the floor I realized that I was picking up bits of glass because there were bits of glass on top and it was all covered with glass." The laptop was located on the floor on top of a bunch of clothes that had been scattered around the room.
- Filomena described Knox and Kercher's relationship by saying that they bonded immediately when they first met, but the relationship had deteriorated.
- Filomena examined the knife found in Sollecito's apartment that had Knox's DNA on the handle and Kercher's DNA on the tip. Filomena stated that she had never seen the knife nor was she aware of any occasion in which Kercher attended dinner at Sollecito's flat.
- Filomena testified that she witnessed Knox and Sollecito exchanging a note at the police station.
- Filomena tells the judge about what she thinks about Knox's actions after returning home on the morning of November 2nd. "The door's open. I go in. There's blood. I take a shower. I don't know about you, but I really don't think that that's normal."

- Then Filomena testified that Knox said to her, "I had a shower but there's blood everywhere. I'm going to get Raff. Meredith is nowhere to be seen. Oh God, maybe something's happened to her, something tragic."
- Filomena testified that Knox assured them that it was normal for Meredith to lock the door, even when she went for a shower. However, Filomena disputed this, saying "Meredith only locked her door when she left the house."
- In regard to the shutters on her window, Filomena testified, "I almost closed the shutters when I left" (Police would later testify that they "found the shutters almost closed").

Paola Grand's testimony added just a bit to the prosecutions' case overall, but there was one shinning moment for the prosecution in her account. Paola testified that she saw Knox and Sollecito emerge from Knox's bedroom just before 1:00p.m. Why is this important? Well, this is important because phone records indicate that Knox and Sollecito went into Knox's bedroom and made four phone calls beginning at 12:47p.m.

The first call was to Knox's mother, Edda Mellas, the second to Vanessa (Sollecito's sister), and the third and fourth calls were made to police (211-emergency). There also appears to have been haste exhibited by the couple during this time, because all four calls from beginning to end took a total of nine-minutes. In other words, while Luca and Marco were talking to the postal police, Amanda and Sollecito slipped into her bedroom where Knox then phoned her mother, Sollecito phoned his sister, and two calls were made to police. Knox claimed that she didn't remember making the call to her mother, because there were too many things going on. As to not skip too far ahead, Edda and Amanda will both testify about the call in the days to come, which will be detailed extensively. However, it should be noted that this was an important piece of testimony by Paola that will have further repercussions.

Meredith Kercher Trial Day 4 – (February 13, 2009)

Day four of the trial was another chance for the prosecution to character-bash Amanda Knox. This time, they would use seven of Meredith's close friends from Perugia, including the three who were with Meredith last on that fatal evening. All seven of Meredith's friends—Robyn Butterworth[10], Amy Frost[11], Sophie Purton[12], Nathalie Hayward[13], Jade Bidwell[14], Samantha Rodenhurst[15], and Hellen Power[16]—flew in from Britain to testify for the prosecution, who paid all expenses for the girls. Robyn Butterworth from Northampton was the first to the stand on this day. Almost immediately Robyn began discussing Amanda's frivolities at the police station.

Robyn Butterworth's testimony:

- "I remember something which upset me," Robyn told the court about Knox's behavior at the police station just hours after the body was discovered. "Natalie said I hope she [Meredith] wasn't in too much pain, and asked Amanda: what do you think?" Filomena then asks the court if she could use a swear word, and permission was granted. Filomena then claimed that Knox said, "What do you think, they cut her throat, she fucking bled to death!" This statement was corroborated by other witnesses present, including Amy Frost.
- "I found Amanda's behavior very strange, and I found it quite difficult to be around her," Robyn stated. "Everybody was upset and she didn't seem to show any emotions."
- Robyn overheard Knox on her mobile phone at the police station bragging to the caller about finding the body. "How do you think I feel? I was the first to find her, it could have been me."
- With her testimony being translated from English to Italian Robyn said, "I remember Amanda sticking her tongue out at Raffaele. They were talking and joking, kissing and cuddling."
- "Amanda kept saying 'I found her, how do you think I feel?'" Robyn said. "She seemed proud to have found the body. I heard her say that Meredith was in the closet with a blanket over her."

- Butterworth testified that Meredith was wearing *Puma* shoes on the day she was killed.

Amanda Knox was tense as Robyn stepped down from the stand. As if she had had enough and could not take another word against her, Knox stood and made her first public statement since her fourth preliminary hearing back in October 2008. In fluent English, Knox addressed the court. "I am innocent, and I'm confident that everything will come out and that everything will work out."

Next it was Amy Frost to the stand. Again attention shifted to the topic of Knox's odd behavior at the police station just hours after the murder. Amy corroborated Robyn's assertions, claiming that Knox was "making faces…such as crossing her eyes and sticking her tongue out." Amy testified that "In that moment [at the police station] I thought she was going crazy, that she was really crazy." Amy also said, "Almost everybody cried apart from Amanda and Raffaele. I never saw them cry." Amy then told a story to the court of a conversation that she had with Meredith. Amy said that Meredith told her that Amanda had a boyfriend back in America that had gone to study in China. Amy said that a few weeks before the murder one of the housemates informed Meredith that a boy living on the first floor of the cottage, Giacomo Silenzi, was interested in her. When Meredith relayed the information to Knox, she replied, "I like him [Giacomo] too, but you can have him!" Knox's reply seemed to anger Meredith, according to Amy.

Amanda and her American boyfriend, David Johnsrud (a.k.a. D.J.), had decided to have an open relationship due to the fact that they were living so far apart. Apparently this whole conversation about Knox, between Amy and Meredith, was gossiping and talking bad about Knox's perceived immorality with men, sexually. Amy explained that the conversation between her and Meredith shifted to a clear beauty-bag that Amanda kept in their bathroom that contained a pink vibrator. Meredith expressed to Amy how odd she thought that was. Knox again sprung up and asserted, "It was a joke," Knox told the court. "It was a present from a friend before I came to Italy," she said. She gestured with her hands, indicating the size of the toy. Judge Massei gave his estimation to the court, from Knox's hand gesture, that the vibrator was about 10 centimeters (4 inches) long.

Amy explained that Meredith believed that Knox idolized flatmate, Laura Mazzetti. She liked Laura's look and her many piercings. Knox decided to emulate Laura, according to Amy's testimony, and she pierced her ear five times on each side. Amy, Meredith, and Amanda went out together only twice: once for pizza and another time to *The Red Zone* (a nightclub known for techno music and synthetic drugs). It was at *The Red Zone* where Meredith first kissed her boyfriend Giacomo. Meredith also told Amy that one of Giacomo's flat mates, Daniel De Luna (21, from Rome), liked Amanda. It was known that Daniel had herpes on his mouth, which Amy claimed made him attractive to Knox, "because she [Knox] said if he had herpes it meant he's good in bed."

Daniel and Amanda also kissed that night at *The Red Zone*, and would have intercourse that night. According to Amy, Meredith smoked marijuana sporadically, but she was very upset when Giacomo asked her to water the Marijuana plants in his apartment. Meredith finally agreed, however, but she wasn't happy about it. Meredith also complained that Amanda wouldn't flush the toilet and would also bring strange men into the house on occasion. Meredith told Amy of a time when she was in the kitchen and saw a strange man come strolling out of Amada's room, which made her feel very uncomfortable. Among all these complaints, Meredith complained as well that Amanda was always playing the same chord on the guitar; a complaint that would also be made of her by her prison mates.

Next was the woman who walked Meredith home that fateful night, Sophie Purton from Essex. "I didn't know Raffaele but I knew Amanda," Sophie began. The prosecution would attempt and succeed at extracting as much information as possible about Knox's behavior at the police station. "As soon as I saw her at the police station I went to hug her," Sophie testified, "but she didn't reciprocate my hug. She wouldn't move her arms; she remained cold, and kept her hands at her side. I thought it was very strange." Sophie then broke down and started crying on the stand as she claimed to have asked Knox if she knew anything about how Meredith had died. "What do you want to know, because I know everything," Knox had replied. Knox told Sophie that "Meredith was found in the wardrobe covered by a blanket, with a foot hanging out and her throat cut." Meredith had voiced her disapproval several times to Sophie and others about Knox's wild sex-life and bringing strange men into the house. "This was something that we didn't do," said Sophie. "But Amanda was quite open about her sex life."

"She didn't show any sadness. She wasn't crying. She seemed quite angry and a bit frustrated and sometimes happy," said Natalie Hayward. Natalie told the court that she remembered Knox saying: "They slit her throat, Natalie; she would have died slowly and in a lot of pain." All of the girls claimed that Raffaele was quiet at the police station, but Amanda was overwhelmingly talkative and her behavior was bizarre. None of the girls claimed to have ever met Rudy Guede, nor did Meredith claim to have gone to meet him or anyone else on the last night of her life. Moreover, the three girls who were with Meredith at the bar on Halloween (Sophie, Robyn, and Amy) claim that they never saw Meredith talking to Rudy or any other black guy that night. The long day of testimonies was finally over. The day would certainly have taken its toll on the young American, who was blasted non-stop all day for her erratic behavior, immorality, and sexual exploits.

In a separate development, that night; Italian police arrested Albanian super-witness for the prosecution, Hekuran Kokomani, in Perugia, the ANSA news agency and local media reported. He was picked up on drug charges and cocaine had been found in his apartment, the reports said. Kokomani has told prosecutors that he saw Knox, Sollecito, and Guede together the night before the slaying in front of Knox's apartment. He had already given testimony during a preliminary hearing and had been scheduled to appear in court in upcoming hearings.

Just hours after leaving the court, Knox somehow managed to pass a letter to Sollecito in which she wished him a "Happy Valentine's Day." In the letter, Knox talks about the testimony of the British girls and even insinuates that Sollecito was trying to send her secret messages with his facial glances and mouthing words to her.

> "We got to exchange a few more glances than usual, though, I have to admit, I'm not good at reading the subtle messages that one passes through the features of the face, nor can I read lips. I must admit that I didn't pick up exactly 'word for word' what you may have wanted to transmit my way. And on my end, essentially what I was trying to tell you through the

various waggling of my eyebrows was essentially: 'Wow! These girls made up their minds to hate me really quick.' To tell the truth, for all the trash talk that made this day especially awkward for me, I don't feel bad about it. Honestly. I don't know why they think they can make judges about me or my relationship with Meredith by merely exaggerating a few instances that took place while we were still trying to settle in."

Meredith Kercher Trial Day 5 – (February 14, 2009)

The prior day's testimonies were undeniably damaging to Knox's fragile psyche, and it showed in her demeanor and appearance on this day. Knox entered the courtroom wearing a long, white t-shirt with the words *"All you need is love"* emblazoned across the front in large pink letters. Smaller letters were scrawled on the bottom right with the clothing brand *JJ Authentic*. The shirt went down past her hips, appearing as if it could double as a short skit. Underneath that shirt she wore a grey t-shirt with a green sweater closing out the upper body gear. With no makeup, her hair in a ponytail, and a cold sore on her lip, Knox entered the courtroom with a bizarre smirk on her face looking relaxed, almost sedated. This day would be much less pressing for Knox, but would still pack at least one punch to an already weakened chin. That blow would come in the form of Knox's other flat mate, Laura Mezzetti[17].

Amanda Knox's idol while in Perugia, Laura Mezzetti, entered the courtroom wearing a striped shirt, chocolate-colored sweater and khaki jeans. Amanda looked up to Laura, because she liked her style. Also, Laura was twenty-seven years old at the time of the murder, and was not a student, but worked as a legal assistant. Laura took the stand and reaffirmed previous testimonies. She claimed that Knox and Meredith had grown apart, and that Meredith had the same problems with Amanda as earlier described (not cleaning, strange men, etc.). Laura stated Knox and Sollecito were always together, a relationship that she defined as "obsessive and annoying." Nevertheless, Laura was not called in by the prosecution to repeat what was already said; she had a special purpose. "Amanda had a wound [a scratch] to her neck and I noticed it because it was known that Meredith had been killed by a wound to her neck," Laura said. She had noticed it while they were all waiting to be questioned at the police station.

"I was afraid that Amanda, too, might have been wounded. I was worried and I looked at it really intensely." Laura declared that she did not see the scratch on Halloween (night before the murder) when she saw Knox at the cottage that morning at breakfast. Laura did not see Knox until two days later at the police station. Laura described the wound as "vertical, less than 1-centimeter thick, and red in color." Knox's lawyer suggested the mark may have been a love bite or "probably a hickey." But Laura disputed this, saying that the scratch was different from a love bite or hickey, as those would be "purple and more-round," she stated. Laura had failed to mention to police that she noticed the scratch until her sixth or seventh interview with them—more than ten-months after the crime had been committed. When asked about this while on the stand, Laura said, "I thought everybody else would have noticed it."

Interestingly enough, Laura explained that back in September of 2008, she was driving on a road to Montefiascone, a town in the province of Viterbo, Italy. She happened to be on the phone with Stefano Bonassi[19] discussing Meredith's death, when the topic of the scratch on Knox's neck came up. Laura explained to Stefano what she saw and informed him that the bruise could be seen in a particular picture of Knox online. However, it wasn't until three weeks later, when Stefano had arrived to testify at the pre–trial hearing that he asked police about the scratch on Knox's neck. Having not heard this previously, police were undoubtedly interested in this juicy detail. It was then that Laura was contacted by police and confirmed the mark.

Next it's time for three of the four boys who lived on the first floor of the cottage, below the girls, to take the stand—Giacomo Silenzi[18], Stefano Bonassi[19], and Marco Marzan[20]. All three boys were on the train on their way back to Perugia when Giacomo got a call from Filomena Romanelli. During the call Stefano and Marco watched their friend turn pale while receiving Filomena's news. After the call had ended, the soft spoken Giacomo said to the others, "It was Filomena, Meredith is dead; she's been murdered." Giacomo spoke about the first time that he kissed Meredith, at the nightclub *The Red Zone*. Prosecutors, however, were more concerned about

Amanda and Daniel getting together that night. Daniel was a friend of the boys and had met Amanda on a previous occasion. The boys testified that after *The Red Zone*, they returned to the cottage; where Meredith and Giacomo went into Giacomo's room and Amanda and Daniel went into Amanda's room for the evening.

Prosecutor Comodi pressed the boys about what Knox and Daniel did on that evening. "They probably made love," Giacomo told her. "They had sexual intercourse," Stefano testified, claiming that Daniel had told him this after the encounter. The encounter between Knox and Daniel was a one night stand, the boys said. On the other hand, Meredith and Giacomo started dating, although Giacomo describes to the court that it was just a sexual relationship. "There was no jealousy between us," he said. "We didn't ask anything about each others previous relationships, we didn't want to know." There were no calls between the two on the days that Giacomo was away. He did not send an 'I miss you,' or a 'can't wait to see you when I get back.' The only message Giacomo sent Meredith was, "Can you take the sheets off the line?" It would be the last communication that he would have with her.

The boys defined Knox and Kercher's relationship as "normal." They also were not aware of any other men that Kercher had been involved with during her stay in Perugia. Giacomo was the only one out of the boys who testified that Kercher had expressed her anger over Knox not doing any cleaning in the cottage. All the boys claimed that they knew Rudy Guede and that they saw him frequently at the basketball court at Piazza Grimana near the cottage. They all described one evening in which they and the four girls (flat-mates who lived upstairs) were all standing outside a bar when Rudy joined them. They all went back to the cottage to smoke some joints. Back at the house, Giacomo testified that, "Rudy asked one of us if Amanda had a boyfriend," and they replied that she did not. This is just prior to Knox meeting Sollecito.

On 21 October 2007, Rudy made a second visit to the cottage, showing up drunk and uninvited to watch the seventeen Grand Prix motor racing championship. However, he made no mention of Knox on this occasion. According to Stefano, Rudy stumbles into the bathroom at some point and defecates without even closing the door; where he falls asleep while on the bowl. Coincidentally, he forgets to flush on this occasion as well as on the night of the murder. In the morning they find him passed-out on the couch. He soon woke up and left. The boys described Guede as not aggressive and an easy speaking person while drunk.

A few days later Stefano meets Sollecito, who introduced himself as Knox's boyfriend. Giacomo did not meet Sollecito until they were all at the police station, where Sollecito again introduced himself as Knox's boyfriend. All of the boys also expressed observing strange behavior exhibited by Knox at the police station, just as Meredith's British friends had done. Back in mid-October a friend of the boys, Giorgio, expressed his concern; claiming that he saw a shadowy figure hiding in the cottage garden at 9:30p.m. About a week later, Meredith informed Giacomo that she had seen the same thing, and that she was afraid. Giacomo, however, makes the assumption that the house was relatively safe; although Meredith was murdered on the first night she was alone in the house. After the boys had finished their testimonies, it was time to hear Raffaele Sollecito's call to 112. His defense team notices and makes statements that he was talking normally and did not appear to be keeping his voice down so that the postal police would not hear him.

At the end of the hearing Knox decided that she would address the court. Noticeably overwhelmed by the testimony a day earlier; Knox felt compelled to straighten-up her relationship with the girls, particularly her relationship with Meredith. Perhaps emboldened by the statements of Marco and Stefano—claiming that Knox and Kercher's relationship was normal—Knox nervously rose to her feet to make a "spontaneous declaration" to the court.

"I just wanted to say that I am very sorry to hear that after all this time there are all these things underlying," Knox said." I always had good relationships with the girls, because it really wasn't like this." The testimonies of the British girls—holding Knox as an eccentric outcast of sorts—really seemed to get to her, and shocked and drained her to say the least. "I am unhappy to hear, after all this time, extremely exaggerated things presented about the cleaning," Knox promulgated in Italian. "I spoke to the girls about it, but it was never a reason for conflict, never. And I always had a good relationship with the people; so I am really saddened about it."

Chapter 6 - The Trial of the Century

Black Mass

The house at Via Della Pergola 7 has become a tourist attraction in the hilltop city of Perugia. The house, much like the house in Amityville, NY, has become the new house of horrors, attracting all kinds who want to get a glimpse of its mystique. In fact, many Italians are calling it *"casa degli orrori"* ("house of horrors"). On 18 February 2009, it was found that the cottage suffered another unsettling event. Police had been guarding the property for weeks after the murder, but it had been abandoned by authorities for some time. Police tape had remained around the property and it had been sealed off as an ongoing crime scene, but police had not visited the crime scene since January. This didn't stop intruders, however, from entering the home and ransacking it. Police were investigating the house the next night as they reported that there was a possibility that a devil-worshiping ritual had taken place there sometime in the past few weeks. Police said that the room that had belonged to Meredith had drips of candle wax stuck to the floor. Four knives were positioned in the kitchen in ritualistic fashion and a candle was also found in another room. Devil worship and occult activity is a widespread phenomenon in Italy; and although police claimed that this is what occurred, they were unable to confirm it for sure. Police said that the intruders gained entry to the abandoned cottage through the second-floor kitchen window, which is the floor where the girls lived.

Speculation immediately spread that this demonstrated how easy it was to break-into the house. Sollecito's lawyer, Marco Brusco, used this opportunity to reaffirm his position that the murder was part of a similar break-in. "This break-in just shows that anyone could get into the house," Brusco said. "It proves how easy it is to get into the house and it proves what we have always said, that a thief broke into the house and murdered poor Meredith Kercher." Although his statement on the matter appears to make sense, a closer look at the situation proves that this had nothing to do with the original claims of a break-in.

Police did not reveal the details of the recent break-in—only that a flower pot, positioned on the outside balcony—was used to break the window. After a brief look at the entry point, nonetheless, it is clear how the intruders gained easy access. The kitchen window is located in the back of the cottage on the second floor. The intruders could have casually walked on the grass towards the rear of the property via Sant' Antonio. Once they reached the back of the house they would be eye-level with the fist-floor window. Just to the right of the window there are iron bars that could have been used as a ladder. These bars were pictured hanging awkwardly out of position, perfect for climbing to the next level. From there they could have reached up to the iron balcony handrail to thrust themselves up onto the balcony. Once on the balcony, out of site from any onlookers, the intruder could have taken all night breaking into the house. The likelihood that any random passer-by would be able to see the balcony is very slim.

The kitchen window, however, was not reported as damaged during the murder investigation, and no seals were ever broken on the window guard. Filomena's window, located near the entrance of the home, would be much harder to break-into without being spotted by people passing by in their cars; her window is just a few yards from the roadway, and in clear view. Furthermore, that side of the cottage is illuminated at night by the car-park across the street, which posses another big problem in this theory. So, it is relatively easy to break into the cottage the way that the recent intruders demonstrated, but not through Filomena's window.

Meredith Kercher Trial Day 6 – (February 27, 2009)

Scheduled on this day were three of the chief officers involved in the investigation. The prosecution would attempt to reconstruct the investigation from its initial stages, with the officers detailing their probe that led to the arrest of Knox, Sollecito, and Guede. We will also get to hear about DNA evidence for the first time; as DNA evidence that prosecutors say points to Knox and Sollecito was listed with the court. Prosecutor's claim that Knox's DNA was found on the handle of a knife that they believe was the murder weapon and Kercher's DNA was found on the tip of the same blade. The knife was found at Sollecito's house. The prosecution also listed that Sollecito's DNA had been found on a bra clasp that belonged to Meredith. The defense teams both contend that the evidence might have been inadvertently contaminated during the investigation and evidence collection process. Nonetheless, since those testifying on this day are not DNA specialists, we will have to wait for further testimony to legitimize these findings. Also, Knox and Sollecito's phone records will be brought into question, the first of many testimonies on these key pieces of evidence. Escorted into the courtroom by two security officers, Knox appeared more stressed than on Valentine's Day. Led to her seat, she sent a smile over to her father Curt, who was seated in the third row.

The first to testify was Domenico Giacinto Profazio[21], the former head of the Perugia police detective squad (who managed the Mobile Squad until they sent him to Rome). Profazio testified that both Knox and Sollecito had "strange attitudes" at the police station during the initial questioning. He confirmed that Knox sat on Sollecito's lap and he (Profazio) told them this was inappropriate. During the 6 November 2007, interrogation of Sollecito, Profazio claimed that Knox was noisy and mischievous while Sollecito was being questioned. "It was reported to me that in the police station she turned a cartwheel and did the splits," Profazio testified. However, during the early hours of questioning the following morning Profazio testified that Knox had cried after admitting she was at the house during Meredith's murder.

Most of Chief Superintendent Profazio's three hour (plus) testimony was spent explaining the details of the investigation and defending himself against the defense council's repeated attempts to establish that vital forensic evidence in the case was contaminated by investigators. Profazio testified that he avoided entering the cottage when he had first arrived, because he had just had his hair cut. He did not want loose hair that had just been cut to fall into samples collected by his forensic team. All investigators were completely covered from head-to-toe with protective gear, as witnessed by the forensic video. However, Profazio admitted that he and others wore only gloves and overshoes during early inspections. Moreover, Profazio also admitted that he did not change gloves each time that he had moved an object at the scene.

By far the most poignant testimony from Profazio was when he told the court that both Knox or Sollecito's turned off their mobile phones at around 8:30p.m., on the night of the murder until 6:00a.m., the next morning; making their whereabouts untraceable. Their phones had been turned off at about the same time, showing the possibility of a coordinated effort.

The next to testify was Commissioner Marco Chiacchiera[22], the city's chief investigator (vice director of Mobile Squad and manager of the Criminality Sector). Chiacchiera testified that no record was found of a call that Sollecito claims he had received from his father via his landline phone at 11:00p.m., on the night of the murder. In actuality, his father had sent him a text message at 11:14p.m., that night, but it was not received until 6:02 a.m., when Raffaele turned on his mobile phone. Kercher's family lawyer, Francesco Maresca, told reporters that the cell phone details were "highly significant;" claiming that "The phones were always on, and were switched off exactly that night, from the evening to the next day."

Monica Napoleoni[23], who heads Perugia police's homicide squad, was the next to testify. Since Napoleoni was Knox's main interrogator, she faced questions whether Knox was beaten or battered during her questioning and subsequent arrest. Napoleoni denied such wrong doing, claiming that "We gave her drinks, chamomile tea; we took her to have breakfast at the cafeteria. Amanda was treated well." Napoleoni recalled feeling that Sollecito and Knox appeared "indifferent to everything" when they were at the police station for questioning. "They would make faces, kiss each other, while there was the body of a friend in those conditions," she said.

All three officers testified that they immediately ruled upon arriving at the scene that the break-in was staged. The glass was on top of the clothes, indicating that the window was broken after the clothes in the room had been thrown around. The location of the rock in the room—which was used to break the window—was too close to the window to be thrown from outside. Even if it was thrown from outside, their testimony shows that they believe that it was strategically placed under the chair by the window in Filomena's room.

The testifying officers told the court that they immediately began verifying alibis of all house mates and friends of Meredith—ringing every doorbell, and following every possible lead. The first two officers were only on this case part-time, so many of the investigative details were fuzzy to them. It was Napoleoni who had been on this case since day one. All three of the officers said that they were always under the assumption that the killer(s) was someone Meredith was familiar with or that she knew. Another case rumor was also put to rest when they informed the court that they broke into the apartment below the murder and found nothing significant. This means that earlier rumors—that the killer(s) broke into the apartment downstairs and smeared blood on the walls—were unfounded. Since the first two testimonies ran long, officer Napoleoni's testimony would be cut short, and she would need to come back the following day to complete her questioning.

Meredith Kercher Trial Day 7 – (February 28, 2009)

Day seven of the trial began with the continued testimony of Officer Monica Napoleoni, the head of Perugia's homicide squad, which had been halted the day before. Recalling the state of Meredith's body when she first saw her, Napoleoni said, "Her eyes were opened. She had been massacred." She testified that Meredith's body had been cut-up so violently that it was very hard for her to even look at the wounds. About the investigation, Napoleoni pointed out that shoe covers and gloves were worn by everyone present. The shoe print that was found on the pillow under Meredith's body was also brought into questioning. Napoleoni testified that forensic experts determined the shoe's size ranged from 36-Euro size to 38-Euro size (U.S. female size 6 to 7 ½). Knox wears a 37-Euro size

(U.S. female size 6 ½); While Kercher wears 38.5-Euro size (U.S. female size 8).

Next to testify was Rita Ficarra[24], officer in charge of the Perugia Flying Squad. Ficarra was the officer who questioned Knox leading to her arrest. Ficarra testified that only "Sollecito had been requested to be interviewed, and she [Knox] had accompanied him." Ficarra said that Knox "was not required to stay, and could have gone home any time." Her first encounter with the aloof American came in the waiting room of the police station that evening. "I saw her in the waiting room doing splits, cartwheels and bridges. She was showing off her gymnastic capabilities." Ficarra testified that after uncovering the text message from Lumumba in Knox's mobile phone—reading, "*Certo. Ci vediamo più tardi. Buona serata.*" ("*Certenly. See you later. Good evening*")—Knox "started crying and wrapping her hands around her head, she started shaking it, and then she said: 'it was him…Patrick killed her.'" Regarding questions of mistreatment, Ficarra stated, "Amanda was never mistreated…she had a chance to rest, go the bathroom, and eat."

Ficarra also told the court about what she perceived as inappropriate behavior exhibited by Knox and Sollecito. "Everybody else was terrified except for Amanda and Raffaele, who seemed indifferent, were smirking, and kept on French kissing." Regarding the voluntary statement given by Knox, Ficarra said, "When Knox was notified of her arrest she asked for a pen and paper, saying: 'I'll give you a present.'" Ficarra added, "Knox asked me to read what she was going to write before she was taken to jail, because she wanted me to have a clear idea about what had happened." Ficarra upheld that Knox had never been subjected to any threats of violence and that she was treated firmly, but cordially. Ficarra told the court that Knox grew "bothered and tired" by police questioning. "I told her off," Ficarra said, when speaking of Knox's intolerance of the questioning. "And I asked her: 'Don't you realize we're talking about the murder of a friend of yours?'"

Knox made a brief statement to the court in Italian: "They did offer me drinks and food, but they started treating me as a person only after I made those declarations." Sollecito's address to the court, on the other hand, took a bit longer. Sollecito told the court that during his interrogation he asked to call his father, but was denied. He then asked permission to call a lawyer and was denied that request as well. The prosecution and the police maintained that when Sollecito asked for a lawyer he was not yet a suspect, but his status was still that of witness. Although Sollecito made these assertions, he has never reported any physical or psychological abuse by police, except that police had taken off his shoes "without giving a reason" and "left me barefoot all night." Clearly the reason was that police wanted to see if the shoes he was wearing were connected to the crime, as they had suspected.

Homicide squad officer, Lorena Zugarini[25]—also present during Knox's questioning—denied that Knox was beaten or mistreated during questioning and said drinks were provided even before Knox started making statements. Zugarini—who is built like an East German swimmer—also informed the court that she was ordered by PM Giuliano Mignini to break down the door to the downstairs flat after they saw traces of blood just outside the door. The blood was later found, however, to be from the wounded ear of the cat that had been owned by the boys who lived down there. No useful clues were recovered from the first-floor flat.

Armando Finzi[26], an assistant in the Perugia police department's organized crimes unit, took the stand next. Finzi explained to the court that he was present during the initial search of Sollecito's flat. He testified that upon entering he immediately noticed the "strong smell of bleach." He entered the kitchen, opened a drawer and saw a "very shiny and clean" knife lying on top of the silverware tray. "It was the first knife I saw," he told the court. Upon cross-examination, Finzi said his "investigative intuition" led him to believe it was the murder weapon because it was compatible with the wounds as they had been described to him. With gloves on his hands, Finzi testified that he "placed the knife in a new police envelope, taped it shut with Scotch tape, and then placed it inside a folder."

Following Finzi, homicide unit captain, Stefano Gubbiotti[27], took the stand. He testified that after receiving the knife from Finzi back at police headquarters, "he took the knife out of the envelope [also while wearing gloves] and placed it in a cardboard box" that he had in his office and it was soon sent to Rome for forensic analysis.

Meredith Kercher Trial Day 8 – (March 13, 2009)

After nearly a two week break, the trial resumed. Up to this point the testimony had primarily focused on Knox's strange behavior exhibited after the murder and the arrival time of the postal police. This day would be no different, with one shining moment for Knox that actually made her seem human and frail. The most intriguing event scheduled for this day was the presentation of car-park video—located across the street from the cottage—which had allegedly captured Meredith walking past on her way home, and possibly an image of the killer walking towards the house minutes later.

Knox entered the courtroom in a multi-colored stripped jumper. She smiled at Sollecito and nodded to her stepfather before taking her seat. Three more police officers and two of Knox's interpreters were scheduled for this day. The prosecution would continue along the same lines: trying to prove that Knox's behavior was viewed as bizarre by everyone, as well as trying to prove that she was not abused during questioning. They would also attempt to prove the postal police's arrival time, by examining a video capturing the events from across the street from the cottage. It would also benefit the prosecution on this day that three of the witnesses are English speaking. These witnesses were present at the questioning and witnessed Knox's behavior—and using their testimonies to corroborate the statements of all other witnesses, would also help prove that Knox's words and behavior were not just being "lost in translation."

Fabio D'Astolto[28], an English-speaking police officer in Perugia (who also interpreted for Knox), testified that Knox's behavior worried him on the day that Meredith's body was discovered. He told the court that he had been asked to go to the police station on 2 November 2007, to assist in the questioning of Amanda Knox. D'Astolto testified that when he arrived at the station Knox "seemed calm, as if nothing had happened, while everyone else was crying." When Officer D'Astolto later brought Knox to be fingerprinted, he stated that Knox "was nervously walking up and down bringing both hands to her head and hitting it." He mimicked the gesture for the court.

Ada Colantone[29] described Knox's behavior two days after the murder when Amanda, Laura, and Filomena (other roommates) were taken back to the scene of the crime. According to Colantone, when the girls were taken into the kitchen to confirm that the knives found in the drawer belonged there, Knox began "shaking." Colantone said that Knox "was shaking so hard that the coroner went over to her." Knox was so "visibly upset" that she was instructed to lie down for a few minutes to collect her-self.

Colantone then substantiates the statements of Laura Mezzetti regarding the mark on Knox's neck. "We had just gotten back from a search of the house and she [Knox] was trembling and then she started crying. Then I saw her in a side room; she looked very pale, her eyes were closed. Her throat was bare, she was wearing a blue zip-up track suit top, and I was struck by her extraordinarily pale color; from which the red mark leapt out...she had a red mark on her neck."

Colantone had also been asked to translate some 600 letters written by Knox while she was in Capanne Prison. "Nothing really came of them," Colantone said about the letters. Knox then turned to her lawyer, Luciano Ghirga, and handed him a note written in perfect Italian: "Is it not relevant that all those letters show that I am innocent?" Colantone claimed that she was under the impression that Knox knew that her letters were being intercepted.

Anna Donnino[30] was the interpreter for the Perugia police department who was called to translate for Knox on 6 November 2007, arriving just after midnight. Knox was calm during the first part of the questioning, Donnino recounted. However, she went into "emotional shock" when she was shown the text message from Patrick Lumumba. "She brought her hands to her head, and shook it," Donnino told the court. Donnino asserted that Knox continued putting her hands on her head, which she was shaking and saying, "It was him, he did it, I can feel it—he's bad, he's bad," referring to Lumumba. Donnino testified that Knox said that she was in the kitchen and had covered her ears while Lumumba was killing Meredith. Donnino was repeatedly asked whether Knox had been abused mentally or physically during her interrogation, which she adamantly responded, "Absolutely not!"

Detective Daniele Moscatelli[31] was called to the stand to recount Sollecito's behavior while being interrogated. Officer

Moscatelli said that Sollecito was "quite confused and nervous" during questioning in the hours following the murder. Officer Moscatelli told jurors that Sollecito was searched that night and they found a long knife in his pocket. Sollecito told Moscatelli that he was "a fan of weapons and knives." The knife had since been ruled out as the murder weapon. Officer Moscatelli was the one who removed Sollecito's shoes. He informed that court that he did so to compare them to the prints found at the murder scene.

It was then time for the prosecution to reveal video that showed the postal police arriving at the scene. Police inspector, Mauro Barbadori[32], had been assigned to retrieve and inspect the video from the car-park across the street from the cottage on 1 November 2007. Barbadori showed the jury a series of grainy black and white images taken by a CCTV camera at the car park above the cottage. The photographs show a female figure walking down the slope to the cottage at 8:41p.m., on the night of the murder. Barbadori testified that, "From the time on the film and the fact it is a female figure—the belief is that it is Meredith, but it is very poor quality and we cannot say for sure."

The testimony of Mauro Barbadori—a witness for the prosecution—appeared to help the defense, in that his testimony of a girl wearing jeans and a dark colored jacket passing the car-park at 8:41p.m., contradicted the earlier testimony of the girls that were with Meredith earlier that evening. The testimony seemed to cause more confusion than anything else. If the CCTV cameras were behind some seventeen-minutes, then they, in effect, help the defense by casting doubt about the arrival time of the postal police. The chain reaction from this possible error in time could then mean that the postal police did arrive sometime after Sollecito made the call to the Carabinieri. This would certainly change the complection of the case.

Raffaele Sollecito again stood and addressed the court:

> "Mr. President, ladies and gentlemen of the jury. I just wish to repeat, about what I've heard that I would have stayed a very short time barefoot at the police station and that I was asked if I wanted to call a lawyer—that it's absolutely not true. I couldn't call a

lawyer and not even my father. They took my shoes away right before the vision of the minutes and I was barefoot until I arrived home; where they gave me a pair of my shoes that were there. I walked barefoot at the police station and in the street. That's all, thank you to the jury, Mr. President."

After Raffaele had finished, Amanda decides to address the court as well. In a respectful but insistent tone, Amanda stands and addresses the court in a well-spoken Italian voice:

"Good evening! Thank you Mr. President and everybody. I just wanted to insist that witnesses are not saying the truth about the night between the 5th and 6th of November. I wanted to clarify on some events that for me are very important. There are hours and hours, before Raffaele would have said that I wasn't with him. There were hours and hours that they don't talk about, during which I confirmed my story and there was an aggressive insistence on the text message to Patrick. They were very, very aggressive with me. They called me a liar. Donnino told me of the trauma she received and that would have been the same for me too. Then there are these *scappellotti* (cuffs or open handed strikes) that I really received on my head. Thank you Mr. President."

Mignini did not look pleased with Knox's allegations, and sent a note over to prosecutor Comodi of what surely was a reminder to add her last statement onto the slander charge that they already had against her. Knox had previously claimed that she was called a "dirty bitch," which in this statement had been changed to "a liar." It was not the fact that she mixed up the words just a bit that was the problem, but just another inconsistency added to her already exorbitant list.

Meredith Kercher Trial Day 9 – (March 14, 2009)

A relatively slow day as far as from the witness stand; this day would be all about forensics. Raffaele Sollecito has always maintained that he spent the entire night at his apartment on the computer on the night that Meredith was murdered. This is of course aside from what he claimed in his first public interview just a few days after the murder, when he said he and Amanda were at a party that night. On the contrary, it was determined that he was not at a party and he has never made a comment or alluded to that so called "party" since.

The prosecution dealt a devastating blow to the alibi of Raffaele Sollecito when Marco Trotta[33], a police computer expert, testified that after a close examination of Sollecito's laptop, the film *Amelie*—which Knox and Sollecito claimed to watch—was run from that computer at around 6:30p.m. As Mr. Trotta showed the court videos detailing technical simulations that he and his team had performed; he concluded that "there was no human interaction between 9:10p.m., on 1 November 2007, and 5:32a.m., on 2 November 2007." Oreste Volturno[34], the police officer who led the search of Sollecito's apartment, testified that he had been struck by "the powerful smell of bleach" while in the Sollecito's flat. The prosecution remains firm that the murder weapon, which was found in Sollecito's flat that day, had been scrubbed clean with bleach in an attempt to erase blood and DNA traces.

Antonella Negri[35] was the final witness to take the stand on this day. Negri, Knox's Italian professor in Perugia, told the court that as an exercise she instructed her class to write a letter to their parents at home in Italian, which included Knox. "In it she said she [Amanda] was worried and confused and she wanted her mother to travel to Perugia so she could distract herself and they could go shopping together," Ms. Negri testified. One of Sollecito's lawyers, Luca Maori, told reporters after the session had ended that the defense will challenge the computer findings and insisted that his client "stayed at home" on the night Kercher was killed. Although, Maori did not give any details of how they intended to contend Mr. Trotta's findings.

Meredith Kercher Trial Day 10 – (March 20, 2009)

The cottage where Knox and Kercher had resided was once again broken into the night before day 10 of the trial. This was second time in a month that the scene had been intruded upon, although police had the premises sealed-off. Police noticed the break-in after a routine inspection. They noticed that a window had been broken and that things had been moved around; yet, neither prosecutors, police, nor the court would say whether anything had been taken or not. It was only after Meredith's lawyer, Francesco Maresca, confirmed that there were items stolen during the break-in that it was made pubic. Maresca and journalist, Giornale dell'Umbria, confirmed that the intruder(s) took Meredith's mattress, a suitcase belonging to Knox (which had cutlery inside), as well as a knife and some pillows. The court refused a police request to put metal bars on some windows in the house.

Raffaele Sollecito entered the courtroom appearing particularly cheerful as he took his seat. Knox entered wearing a blue v-neck sweater with a white t-shirt underneath that was barely peeking-out above the v-neck intersection. As the American media reported the mistreatment of Knox during her interrogation/arrest—and allegations from her step-father, Chris Mellas, that she was "beaten by police" and that Knox's alleged bizarre behavior in the days after the murder was irrelevant—the trial was once again underway. On this day there would be more destructive testimony to the defense. This time, however, it would come in the form of cell phone records.

Police inspector Letterio Latella[36] took the stand, giving a lengthy testimony using PowerPoint slides to point out the cell phone activity of the two defendants on the night of the murder. Latella's analysis and testimony revealed a few destructive blows to both defense teams. Latella informed the court that both Knox and Sollecito's cell phones were turned off almost simultaneously.

- Sollecito's phone was inactive from 8:42p.m., on Nov. 1st until 6:02a.m., the following day—at which point he received the text message that his father had sent him the prior evening (at 11:14p.m.).

- Knox's phone was shut down from 8:35p.m., on Nov. 1st and didn't show any activity until 12:07p.m., the next day—at which time she placed a call to Kercher's phone.

This was an unusual pattern for the couple, according to inspector Latella, because cell phone printouts of each day of October show cell phone activity until late evening for both Knox and Sollecito.

Sollecito and his team continued to maintain that he was at his flat the entire evening and had received a call from his father at 11:00p.m., on the night of the murder. However, phone records indicated that no such call was received. The last call from Meredith's Erickson cellular phone was at 10:00p.m., to her bank in England. It was speculated by Latella that it may have been an accident, because Meredith had her bank programmed as the first number in her phone. Likewise, inspector Latella also revealed that there was a data connection (GPRS) on Kercher's English registered (Erickson cellular) phone at 10:13p.m., again, to her English bank on the night of the murder, and again he claimed that it may have been unintentional, because it could have been a "messy touching of the phone keys."

It was undetermined where the phone was located at the time of this brief connection. However, Judge Micheli noted in his 106 page report that tabulations of previous days showed that there was a normal bounce between the two surrounding cell towers, and that the connections from Meredith's phone at 10:00p.m., and 10:13p.m., most likely originated from the Via Della Pergola zone. Moreover, Micheli stated that unless considering outside logic, that the girls in the cottage took a walk toward Via Sperandio every time they placed a call to their family members, the calls came from the cottage. Inspector Latella also testified that later, at 12:10a.m., that same phone received a call that was intercepted at Via Sperandio, meaning that it was no longer at Via Della Pergola, but was in Lana's garden about a mile away from the cottage where it would be found the next morning by Giannetta Elisabetta.

Raffaele's father sends him a text message later that night at 11:14p.m., and it is not received until the next morning, because his phone is already turned off. Inspector Latella told the court that there were no reported glitches in the network that night. Giulia

Bongiorno contended that the cell phone data was inconclusive, sighting that the communications company's records did register attempted calls. Bongiorno contested that Kercher's cell phone showed three attempted calls on 1 November 2007, which were not detected by the company's registries.

Simone Tacconi[37], head of the forensics for the Postal Police, analyzed the printouts from Knox's text messages. Tacconi testified that Knox received a text message from Patrick Lumumba at 8:18p.m., on the night of the murder, but it was not readable (Lumumba deleted the message sometime soon after receiving it). He then said that Knox responded to Lumumba at 8:35p.m., by text, writing, "*Certo. Ci vediamo piu` tardi. Buona serata!*" ("*Certainly. See you later. Good evening!*"). Knox's phone registered in the vicinity of Sollecito's flat. Knox and Lumumba both turned their cell phones off almost simultaneously right after this message. Although he was already exonerated at this time, at 8:38p.m., on the night of the murder Patrick Lumumba's cell phone signal was captured in the area of the cottage, for what its worth.

Meredith Kercher Trial Day 11 – (March 21, 2009)

Five witnesses were scheduled for this day. One of the witnesses, however, would steel the show, and would pose a serious problem for the defense. That would have to wait for the moment as first to the stand was Jovana Popovic[38] who was a friend of Sollecito. Nothing real significant came from her testimony, though. Popovic, a Serbian medical student studying in Perugia, claimed that she met Sollecito through mutual friends some months before the murder, but they weren't that close. Popovic testified that she went to Sollecito's flat at around 5:30-5:45p.m., on November 1st to ask Sollecito for a ride to the bus station where she had to pick up a suitcase that would be arriving from Milan. Popovic arrived at sollecito's door, greeted over the intercom by Knox, and was then buzzed-up.

She claimed that Sollecito was acting a bit cold and unusual, relative to his normal fun-loving nature, but nothing to make a big deal about. Sollecito agreed to take her to the bus station at around midnight, planning that they would meet back at Sollecito's later that night. She only stayed for about ten-minutes; because she had an appointment at 6:00p.m. During her meeting she was informed that the suitcase would not be arriving that night after all. When her meeting ended (at around 8:00p.m.) she decided to walk by Sollecito's flat and inform him that she no longer needed his assistance. When she arrived she was again greeted by Knox, who came down stairs and told her that Raffaele was upstairs, and Knox invited her up. Popovic gracefully declined, and told Knox to thank Raffaele, but she didn't need a ride any longer. Popovic testified that she said goodbye to Knox at about 8:40p.m. That was the extent of her testimony, but it proved that Knox was at Sollecito's apartment until at least that time.

The next witness to take the stand was Alessandra Formica[39] who originally told police that her and her boyfriend had run into a "person of color" by the house that seemed to be running away in a hurry on the night of the murder. Formica testified that she and her boyfriend parked their car in the car-park across the street from the cottage at around 8:00p.m., on November 1st. They walked out of the garage, past the house, up across the square, and traveled through the Etruscan arch to have dinner. There was a long wait at the restaurant, about 45 minutes, so they didn't finish dinner until around 9:30p.m. They left shortly after and decided to take a short walk through the center of the old city before heading back to their car. To get back to their car from that location they had to take the route that Meredith had taken just hours earlier.

So once they reached the infamous basketball court (at Piazza Grimana) on Via Pinturicchio, they went down the long and steep stairs that led to the car park and ultimately Via Della Pergola. Towards the bottom of the stairs Formica noticed a black-man with a dark puffy jacket, walking in a hurry with his head down in their direction. The man bumped into her rudely, she described, to which she replied "excuse me," but got no response. She claimed that he rushed off in a hurry. Police estimate that this man was Rudy Guede, but Formica could not say for sure. This occurred, by her estimation, at sometime between 10:00-10:30p.m. This time was also corroborated by the car park ticket (time of paying and exiting the garage).

Formica also testified that immediately after the incident, she remembered seeing a station wagon in front of the cottage with a guy outside of it on his mobile phone. She also recalls seeing a woman in the back seat and possibly a baby, but she could not confirm whether there was a baby or not. The station wagon in front of the cottage posses some significant testimony to come in the weeks that follow. Also, recall the phone call from Meredith's phone at 10:00p.m., and the data connection 10:13p.m. Formica has provided key testimony that may help tie all of this together later. Formica's testimony, for the moment, seems to help Knox and Sollecito; as it makes perfect sense that Guede could have carried the phones away from the house at this time. Yet, drawing conclusions now would be a bit premature with nearly nine-months to go in the trial. Moreover, a bombshell of a testimony waits on this day alone.

Next to take the stand was Sollecito's former Ecuadorian cleaning lady, Rosa Natalia Guman Fernendez de Calle[40]. Rosa worked for Sollecito for about two-months, cleaning his flat every Monday between 2:00p.m, and 4:00p.m. Her presence on the stand was basically to discuss if she ever used or saw any bleach in Sollecito's apartment. Rosa testified that she cleaned Sollecito's flat for the last time on 5 November 2007, the day he and Knox were arrested. Rosa said that she never used bleach to clean his apartment; she never saw any bleach there, nor was she aware whether or not he had kept any bleech there. She told the court that she only used Lysoform to clean his apartment. On her last day, Rosa went under the sink to get the cleaning products and noticed a bucket of water with wet mop rags in it. When she asked Sollecito why the bucket was there he replied, "There was a leak." When asked about the type of water in the bucket, Rosa told the court that it was clear.

Many surprises lay ahead in this trial, and on this day one of the prosecution's aces-in-the-whole would be publicly revealed. Amanda Knox has maintained that she spent the evening of 1 November 2007, at Raffaele Sollecito's flat. Knox has always insisted that she did not leave his flat until after 10:00a.m., the next morning. However, Marco Quintavalle[41]—owner of the *Conad Store,* a supermarket located on Via Garibaldi (the street that Sollecito lived on)—testified that Amanda Knox entered his store at 7:45a.m., on 2 November 2007, and purchased cleaning products. Mr Quintavalle had two female cashiers on duty that morning, and they both had arrived at 7:30a.m. Mr. Quintavalle said that he went to open the store's security gate, as it was just about opening time for the store, when he noticed that a young lady was waiting for him to open.

Mr Quintavalle told the court:

> "I was inside and I opened the shutters of my supermarket at 7:45a.m. Outside I saw a girl waiting to come inside; she came in and I was struck by how pale she looked and also by her clear blue eyes. She had a hat, jeans, and a scarf on with a grey & white jacket. But what struck me was how pale she looked and the colour of her blue eyes; I can still see them in front of me now. She was young, around twenty or twenty-one-years old. She came in, I said 'buon giorno,' but she did not say anything in response, and she went to the section at the back of the supermarket on the left where there are the cleaning products. I can't remember if she bought anything. A few hours later I heard about the murder, and then a few days later I saw Amanda's picture in the newspaper and I recognised her as the same girl. The shape of the face was the same, as was the nose; she was pretty. For me the girl in the newspapers was the same girl who had come into my supermarket at 7:45a.m., in the morning."

Quintavalle also testified that when the woman who appeared to be Knox left the store, she travelled in the direction of the cottage. Quintavalle claims that he was at the cash register when she arrived, but was not when she left—which is why he did not see if she purchased anything. On the other hand, here is where his testimony becomes conflicting. Mr. Quintavalle told the court that a few hours after allegedly seeing Knox he heard about the murder and recognized Knox on the news. However, under cross-examination, he said that when police first questioned him on 15 November 2007, he told them nothing. Police left him that day, saying he could call them if he remembered anything, but he never did. Quintavalle told the court that he didn't want to get involved in the case. It wasn't until about nine-months later (August 2008)—after the urging of a journalist friend—that Quintavalle actually contacted police and informed them that Knox was in his store on the day that Kercher's body was found.

It was quite a climactic scene as the entire courtroom braced-themselves when the prosecutor asked Quintavalle to identify the person he saw that morning in his store. Quintavalle looked at Knox in the courtroom, stared directly into her eyes, pointed at her and said, "Era lei, era Knox" ("It was her, it was Knox") "she was the person I saw that morning." Knox remained restrained during Quintavalle's testimony and showed no outward reaction to his assertions. The defense, particularly Carlo Dalla Vedova, was outspoken regarding their belief that Quintavalle is an unreliable witness. They claimed that too much time had gone by for him to remember everything that he was claiming and with such certainly that it seemed to be a feet of super-human memory. They asked him if he could give an estimate on the height and eye colour of Raffaele. He was close on the height estimation, but claimed that he did not know his eye colour. Many believe that his testimony was almost too precise, and his memory almost too good to remember such details as he disclosed. However, there is no plausible motive for him to lie, unless he was getting paid to do so or good PR to promote his store (none of which have been confirmed).

Quintavalle remembers Sollecito, as he was a frequent customer and lived just down the block. Quintavalle had no other known connection with anyone else involved. In any event, his testimony was surely the most damaging blow to Knox's defense thus far. An eye witness testimony that had no doubt that it was Amanda Knox who was in his store at 7:45a.m., the morning after the murder; hence, disproving that Knox had awoken at 10:00a.m., as she claimed; added yet another possible lie to her already long list.

Fabrizio Angeluce[42], owner of the Laundromat and dry cleaners also located on Via Garibaldi, was the last to take the stand on this day. Angeluce testified that Sollecito came into his store on either Friday (November 2nd) or Monday (November 5th)—he could not remember the exact date, but said it was one of the two—and dropped off a *Jean Paul Gaultier* shirt that needed to be dry cleaned. He claimed that Sollecito asked him to clean it "as soon as possible," because he needed it right away for an upcoming graduation ceremony. Angeluce told the court that the shirt had appeared to him as if it had already been washed.

Meredith Kercher Trial Day 12 – (March 27, 2009)

The media was still buzzing over the testimony of Mr. Quintavalle. To make matters worse they had nearly a week to ponder and stew over his testimony. Yet, that time had past and there was plenty more testimony to come. Knox and Sollecito appeared relaxed as they entered the courtroom and greeted their lawyers. One day earlier, Knox had sent Sollecito a card commemorating his 25th birthday. The two even appeared chummy, smiling and gesturing at each other during a pause in the trial. The prosecution would attempt to establish the time of the murder, using witnesses who heard a gut-wrenching scream coming from the house. Seven witnesses in total were scheduled to testify on this day.

First up was Nara Capezzalli[43], a 69 year-old widow who lived with her daughter across the street from the cottage, directly above the car-park. Looking out her window, Nara can only see the roof of the cottage. Nara explained that she normally goes to bed at about 9:30p.m., and she did so as well on 1 November 2007. Nara said that she woke up at around 11:00–11:30p.m., that night to go to the bathroom, which she normally does, as she takes a diuretic pill that takes about two hours or so to take effect. Nara testified that it is common for her to be awakened by noise, because the nearby street is relatively noisy. But the scream she heard that night, however, she claimed was distinct and unusual. Nara testified that she was on her way to the bathroom that night; she made it only as far as her living room when she heard a scream that stopped her in her tracks. "It was a prolonged woman's scream," Nara told the court. "It was not a normal scream," said Capezzali; "it made my skin crawl." She imitated the scream softly and said that the only time she'd ever heard one like it was at the movies. The scream was so unusual and frightening that she looked out the window, but saw no one. A few minutes later Nara claimed that she heard what sounded like a few people running in different directions. "I heard someone running on the metal stairs and someone else on the leaves and gravel in front of the house across the way," Capezzali said.

Nara testified that the scream was so horrible that she could not fall back asleep, because it kept running through her head. Eventually she slept after making herself some chamomile tea; she awoke the next morning between 7:30a.m.-8:00a.m. She then went to the news stand next to the basketball court at Piazza Grimana, at about 11:00a.m., where she was alerted by a few patrons of the grisly murder that took place the previous night at Via Della Pergola 7. Her timing, here, clearly does not match the time that the body was discovered; the body was found by police no earlier than 1:00p.m. That's not counting how long that it would take for this news to circulate to the general public and become water-cooler conversation. In any event, Nara said that she returned home and watched the cottage from her window for the remainder of the day— as police, CSI, and others arrived to investigate.

During cross-examination Bongiorno pressed Nara about why she waited twenty-days to report the scream to police and why she had not informed police that she had a chamomile tea in her written testimony. Nara also said that she couldn't remember the exact date that she heard the scream. However, this tactic by Bongiorno seemed to backfire as she read Nara's previous testimony aloud and Nara began sobbing. She appeared flustered by the tragedy and recalling the scream, and possibly over the fact that she did not call police immediately after hearing it. Overall, however, her testimony appeared sincere and made a big impression on the court. Even many advocates for Knox and Sollecito's innocence called her testimony genuine. Although her somewhat poor timing posed a problem; she remained a very strong witness for the prosecution.

Maria Luisa Dramis[44] was next to take the stand. Maria is a young woman who also lives above the car-park. Maria's bedroom window faces Via Del Melo, where her front door is located and the back of her apartment faces north over Via Della Pergola. She can see the roof of the house and the top part of the doorway of the cottage. Maria testified that on the night of 1 November 2007, she went to the movies with a friend and returned home around 11:00p.m. Shortly after going to bed that night, at around 11:30p.m., she told the court that she was awoken by someone running up or down her street just under her window. Her testimony seems to coincide precisely with Nara's, and she was positive of the date that this occurred. Her testimony bolstered Nara's testimony. She said that it only struck a cord with her because she heard about Kercher's death the next morning.

Antonella Monacchia[45] took the stand next; a young woman who lives with her parents on Via Pinturicchio, which is the street behind the car-park. Her house is on a higher slope, overlooking Maria and Nara's apartments. From her window she can clearly see the roof, terrace, window, doors, and driveway of the cottage. Antonella testified that at about 10:00p.m., on 1 November 2007, she heard people arguing loudly, and she thought it sounded like a man and woman. She claimed that she looked out her window, but didn't see anyone. She said that she wasn't sure if it was coming from the cottage itself, but she was sure that it was coming from Via Della Pergola. She also pointed out that when she looked at the cottage she noticed that it looked dark. When pressed by the defense why it took her one-year to come forward to police, she said that she didn't think that it was relevant until she was persuaded to come forward by a journalist friend who had been following the case.

Giampaolo Lombardi[46] was a tow truck driver who was called to Via Della Pergola on the night of 1 November 2007, to help with a car that needed assistance. The car was the station wagon which was seen by witness number 37 (Alessandra Formica) that night, as she had described in earlier testimony. Giampaolo testified that he received the distress call around 10:30-10:40p.m., and it took him about 15-20 minutes to get there. When he arrived he noticed that the car was parked on the opposite side of the cottage, just a few meters from the front door. Two couples awaited him (two men, two women); both of whom told him that that they were from Rome and vacationing in Perugia. The car was located just before the car-park entrance/exit so he had a clear view of the entrance to the house, as he was working practically across the street from the gate. As he prepared to tow the car, he noticed that a small, dark-colored car was parked in front of the driveway gate of the cottage. He also noticed that the gate was slightly open. He could not identify the type or color of car for sure, only that it was there and it was a dark color. This is significant for the prosecution, because Raffaele Sollecito drove a dark colored Audi at the time.

Francesco Tavernese[47], Leonardo Fazio[48], and Antonio Galizzi[49] all testified for the defense as character witnesses for

Raffaele Sollecito. Tavernese is the director of the men's ONAOSI student center for university students in Perugia where Sollecito was housed from 2003 through 2005. Tavernese described Sollecito as introverted, shy, and often blushing. He also claimed that Sollecito "was into strange movies," such as horrors, and was once caught with a porn movie. Fazio is a young man about Sollecito's age who became friends with him during his time at ONAOSI. He described Sollecito as an introverted and calm gentleman who liked to go to the gym and work out. Fazio also testified that he had seen Sollecito and Knox in the days following the murder acting normally as if nothing had happened. Galizzi is the captain of the carabinieri station in Giovinazzo, a town just up the coast from Bari, where Sollecito grew up. He testified that Sollecito and some friends were arrested in 2003 in Southern Italy for possession of 2.657 grams of hashish. He also told the court that he remembered Sollecito in grammar school as a normal student who never got in trouble and was calm.

Meredith Kercher Trial Day 13 – (March 28, 2009)

March madness would come to a close with this day of the trial. Some very revealing testimony has been uncovered thus far. Today will be no different, as more prosecution witnesses will blast both Knox and Sollecito's alibis. Knox entered the courtroom wearing a lilac jumper and blue jeans. She exchanged several glances with Raffaele throughout the day, including smiling and joking with those guarding her.

The first witness called to the stand was a fifty-two-year-old homeless man by the name of Antonio Curatolo[50]. He explained to the court that he has spent most of his time for the past 8 or 9 years around Corso Garibaldi (the street where Sollecito lived) and Piazza Grimana (the piazza in front of the School for Foreigners where the basketball court is located). Dirty and dressed in an old jacket and winter knit hat, Curatolo was helped into the courtroom by court assistants. He testified that he was in Piazza Grimani around 9:30-10:00p.m., on the night of the murder and he witnessed a couple across the piazza sitting next to each other. He called them a couple because of the way they were acting. Curatolo stated that he observed Knox and Sollecito go over to the railing several times to look down towards the cottage on Via Della Pergola (which is in view from that location).

When asked to describe the couple he turned to Knox and calmly said "it was her," while pointing at her. He then turned to Sollecito and said "and him," while pointing at him. This was the first time that he had seen them together he stated, but he was sure that it was them. Curatolo stated that he saw Knox and Sollecito "around five times" between 9:30p.m., and midnight, and that the last time that he saw them was when they returned just before midnight. At about that time he left and went to go sleep in the park. Under cross-examination Bongiorno asked Curatolo, "How could you possibly know it was 9:30?" Curatolo responded by saying, "Because the sign next to the piazza has a digital clock. I look at it often to check the time. When I sat on the bench to read [L'Espresso weekly magazine] I looked at my watch and it was just before 9:30...and I saw them shortly afterwards." Although homeless, Curatolo spoke very clearly and was certain of what he had seen. Even under cross-examination Curatolo's testimony remained strikingly consistent. Curatolo's testimony was also key because Knox had claimed in her written statement to police that she saw herself in a vision at the basketball court (at Piazza Grimana) with Patrick Lumumba.

Fabrizio Gioffredi[51] was next to take the stand. He testified that that on 30 October 2007, he had parked his car at the junction where Via Della Pergola begins and the street leads up to piazza Grimana, which he described precisely as being across from the pub "Contropunto." He said that this was around 5:00p.m. At this time he claims that he saw four people coming from the driveway of the cottage walking onto the road. He testified that these four people were Amanda, Raffaele, Meredith, and he was 99 percent sure that Rudy was trailing just behind them. Gioffredi said that he remembers them so distinctly that he could even state what they were wearing.

He said that Meredith was wearing jeans, a dark coat, and high heels; Amanda had on a red coat with large 60's style buttons and jeans; and Raffaele had on a long dark jacket and dark pants. He also said that he could not tell what Rudy was wearing because he was behind the rest of the group, but he could see his face clearly. When asked to point out whom he had seen that night, Gioffredi pointed to Knox and Sollecito and said, "Him and her." Gioffredi said that he was sure of the date because he had nicked the car in front of his on the way out. He claimed that he left a note for the driver of the other car and wrote down the information car's (license plate etc.) as well as the date and time.

After a short break Sollecito made another spontaneous statement to the court that was sparked by the previous testimony. Sollecito stood and said that he had never met Rudy Guede so it was impossible that Mr. Gioffredi could have seen them together. He added that he had also never seen Knox wearing a red jacket, as Mr. Gioffredi's testimony also indicated.

Next to the stand was Antonio Aiello[52] (a lawyer and close personal friend of Hekuran Kokomani, who was scheduled to testify next). There were serious doubts about the credibility of the prosecution's previous super-witness, Hekuran Kokomani, who was being held in jail at the time for beating his girlfriend, and also facing drugs charges after eight-grams of cocaine were found in his house. Mr. Aiello was there to testify as a character witness for Hekuran Kokomani. Mr. Aiello described Kokomani as a "decent person" despite the trouble he was in at the time. Aiello explained to the court that Kokomani had contacted him shortly after the murder and wanted to talk to him. Aiello explained that he was very busy and asked Kokomani if it could wait until he returned from Albania. Upon Kokomani's return, he told Aiello everything that he knew about his encounter with Knox, Sollecito, and Guede. Kokomani wanted Aiello's advice and also wanted him to be there with him during police questioning.

Hekuran Kokomani[53] was touted as the prosecution's "super-witness," because he is the one who confirms that Knox, Sollecito, and Guede were all together on the night of the murder. However, his testimony was hard to understand and at times contradictory and hard to watch. Kokomani is an Albanian born man who had spent the last 15 or 16 years in Italy. Conversely, his Italian is not good, so the court appointed an interpreter. Kokomani testified that he was driving along Via della Pergola on his way to a bar when he saw what looked like a large black sack in the middle of the road. He stopped the car and realized that it was actually Knox and Sollecito lying on the ground (in the middle of the road).

Kokomani then said that Sollecito came to his driver's side window and the two got into a fist fight. He then claimed that Knox went to the passenger window, pulled out a knife (the same one that was used in the murder—he said he recognized it in the newspaper), raised it above her head with both hands, holding both the handle and blade, and began to curse at, and threaten, him in Italian. To combat this, Kokomani said that he threw olives and his old Nokia cell phone at Knox. He also said that he took a picture of Knox and Sollecito with his Ericsson cell phone, but later deleted it. As this was occurring, Kokomani claimed that Rudy Guede walked out the front door of the cottage and stopped at the top of the driveway. Kokomani said that he could hear one person yelling or moaning and these strange sounds were coming from the cottage. He asked Guede what the origin of the noise was and Guede told him that it was music and that the Knife that Knox was holding was just used to cut a cake at a birthday party. He looked at the cottage, saw a light on, and went on his way.

Mr. Kokomani's testimony was very hard to watch, because it was all over the place. A lot of the questions that he answered only left us with more questions and scratching our heads. There were many examples of this during his testimony. For instance, when asked, "What color is your car" he responded, "black/blue." When asked again he said, "I paid only two hundred Euros for it." When asked, "At what time do you usually eat dinner," he said "when I get hungry." When asked, "What color are Amanda's eyes" he says, "occhi bianchi" ("white eyes"). When asked, "How did you know the time when you were on the street" he said, "I have a clock on my dashboard." When asked what time it said, he responded, "it does not work." When asked if he had spoken to reporters he said, "No," then "maybe," then "I don't think so." The defense then showed him being interviewed by a reporter, and his final answer was "yes."

Adding to his list of fumbles, Kokomani claimed that he had seen Knox and Sollecito together back in August or September of 2007, having lunch. However, the couple hadn't met yet at that time. Another big question mark remains about his testimony. Kokomani claims that he worked on the day he had this encounter with the three suspects and he also stated that it was raining. Since November 1st is an Italian holiday and it wasn't raining, he probably meant October 31st. In any event, Kokomani originally reported seeing the tow-truck in front of the house, and his cell phone was pinged in the vicinity of the cottage on both the night of the 31st October and the 1st of November. No one is sure what to make of his testimony. Mr. Kokomani was escorted away in handcuffs once he had finished testifying.

After Mr. Kokomani's testimony at the second pretrial hearing on 26 September 2008, some sources reported that he was held as discredited, because of all of his inconsistencies; however, this was not the case. In Judge Micheli's report—released on 26 January 2009—Micheli wrote that despite the fact that his testimony was garbled and that his dates make no sense; the details that he provided regarding the broken-down car, the tow truck, and the people involved weren't known by anyone else. According to Micheli, Mr. Kokomani was credible, at least, in implicating Knox, Sollecito, and Guede as accomplices.

Meredith Kercher Trial Day 14 – (April 3, 2009)

Only two witnesses scheduled for the day, and each would reiterate versions that had already been widely reported in the media for almost a year; still, the day would have its moments. April starts off with the first decision to shut down cameras, as graphic crime scene photos will be shown for the first time. The courtroom waited in anticipation to see Knox and Sollecito's reactions to the violent nature of the photos. Francesco Maresca asked for the media to be excluded from the hearing in order to "preserve Meredith's memory and dignity." Maresca told the court that the images shown by Police pathologist, Dr Luca Lalli[54], would be "very traumatic" for the Kercher family. Maresca also informed the court that he had no objection to journalists hearing the proceedings, but just without video. However, judge Massei ruled that neither the images nor the sound would be provided to the press or the public. Some journalists mocked the decision as the pictures and video footage had already been displayed on the Italian television station *Telenorba* earlier in the year. In contrast, Maresca said that the images that had been broadcast earlier by *Telenorba* had already upset the family, and there was no reason to have them go through that again.

At the conclusion of the ruling Dr. Lalli took the stand, armed with pictures and video footage of the post modems conducted on the victim. Dr. Lalli testified that there were a total of 23 cuts and bruises located on Kercher's hands, face, neck, and legs. Three of the cuts were stab wounds to Kercher's neck, according to Lalli. He said that there was no "biological evidence of a sexual attack." However, he did say that due to the amount of bruises it is likely that a sexual attack occurred. Still he offered that he could not provide proof that she was sexually assaulted. Not much new from the good doctor, only things that have already been reported in detail prior to his testimony. The actual cause of death, according to Dr. Lalli (asphyxia) was that Meredith choked on her own blood. Amanda Knox did not look, not even a peek, at the photos or video footage shown by Dr. Lalli. Instead, she kept her head down on the desk, covering her head with her arms. Meanwhile, Raffaele Sollecito glimpsed sporadically at the images.

Carlo Maria Scotto di Rinaldi[55] took the stand next. Mr. Rinaldi was the owner of the trendy clothing store *Bubble*, which was located on Via Calderini in Perugia. Rinaldi testified that the couple had come into his shop the day after the murder, as captured on CCTV footage, to purchase clothes. Rinaldi said, "They were kissing and hugging. They were acting like young lovers. They were speaking in English and I picked up a few words. I heard Raffaele say that they would have *hot sex*, good sex." According to Rinaldi, Knox held up a pair of G-string underwear and replied, "I can put this on and have *wild sex* with you." It seems another lost-in-translation moment occurred after Rinaldi's testimony. A debate in the courtroom broke-out over whether their sex was *hot* or *wild*, as in Italy the word *wild* means violent (wild=selvaggio=savage).

In any case, Knox reportedly purchased a sweater, a loincloth, and that fateful G-string from *Bubble* that day. Knox's lawyers contend that she was locked out of the cottage and had no clothes, which was the reason that she needed to go shopping. The purpose of Mr. Rinaldi's testimony was clear: the prosecution continued to build the case that Knox was cold and unemotional in the hours and days following the murder.

Meredith Kercher Trial Day 15 – (April 4, 2009)

Today would be the last day of the trial before the Easter break. Again, most of this day's proceeding would be held behind closed doors as a continuation from the prior day's decision. Knox entered the courtroom dressed in jeans and a purple top, while Sollecito entered dressed in a red coat and jeans. A medical examiner and a gynecologist were scheduled to testify for the prosecution in another closed-door session. This day would not be like the day before, as today's testimonies would not be rehashed news. The evidence presented by these two experts would do irreparable damage to the defense, as these witnesses were adding corroborating expert testimony that there had been more than one attacker. Because the session was being held behind closed doors the media would not feel the real impact of the two expert witnesses, but the courtroom would.

Medical Examiner (Police coroner from Rome), Dr Vincenza Liviero[56], told the court, "In my opinion there were signs of more than one person being involved and there was also evidence of sexual violence." Gynecologist, Mauro Marchionni[57], testified that in his experience he had not seen such wounds before on a person who had consented to sexual intercourse. Marchionni also told the court that in his opinion there was more than one attacker because of the number of bruises and knife wounds on Kercher's body. The only difference in the testimony of Dr. Lalli and these two witnesses—in regard to the sexual assault—was that Lalli could not say for sure that sexual assault occurred, while these witnesses believed that there was enough proof to say conclusively that a sexual assault took place. Francesco Maresca played theatrics outside the courthouse, telling the media that "The medical experts confirmed to the court the cruel signs of the wounds Miss Kercher suffered, and the fact that more than one person was involved." Maresca even used sarcasm as if gloating over the experts testimonies today when he said, "If it was only one person then that person had more than two hands."

Rudy Guede[58] entered the courtroom in handcuffs, escorted by police. Guede was called as a prosecution witness to testify against Knox and Sollecito. He was expected to explain the story that he had told police; that while in the house on the night of the murder, an Italian man (possibly Sollecito) threatened him with a knife. He had also claimed that he heard a female voice that sounded like Knox's voice. Guede took the stand and was eyed only briefly by Knox and Sollecito, but did not even look their way for a moment. Guede confirmed his name, age, and place of birth. Under Title IV, Articles 61 and 64 of the Code of Criminal Procedure ("CCP") of Italian law, the accused has the right to silence and silence cannot be taken as a basis for any negative conclusions about the accused. This right extends to not answering questions posed by the prosecution, the criminal investigation of police, and or the examining judge.

Rudy Guede had decided to exercise this right; telling the judge that he would not speak, because he had already been found guilty. Guede was also awaiting his appeal and it is very likely that he did not want anything that he might say to be used against him in the appellate court. Guede was escorted back to Viterbo Prison to await his appeal. The prosecution then requested that the transcripts from Guede's earlier police interrogation be admitted as evidence. The defense objected and the judge denied the motion, making the interrogation transcripts inadmissible. Guede's lawyer, Walter Biscotti offered-up an explanation behind Guede's silence: "The prosecution has always insisted that Guede is a liar and now they have called him as a witness in this trial; that is why he chose not to speak." Guede would wait until his appeal to give his testimony. Later that day Guede faxed a letter to Biscotti asking that "*Those who have harmed Meredith and myself*" to finally confess.

Chapter 7 - The Trial of the Century

Meredith Kercher Trial Day 16 – (April 17, 2009) – The Inspection

After a two week Easter-break layoff, the trial resumed. The first half of the day's preceding would take place in the courtroom, and the second half would be a field trip to inspect the crime scene at the cottage. The morning session, however, would again be behind closed doors as the fourth and final medical consultant would give his expertise regarding the cuts and bruises on Kercher's body. Pathologist, Dr. Mauro Bacci[59], took the stand and told the court that it was his opinion that an attempt had first been made to strangle Kercher before she was stabbed in the throat; possibly with two different knives. He also testified that there was evidence of non-consensual sex, and that the knife found in Sollecito's apartment was compatible with the larger wound found on Kercher's neck. Under cross-examination, Dr. Bacci admitted it was possible that the wounds could have been caused by smaller knives.

After a recess, the two judges, six jurors (and their substitutes), the prosecutors, and the defense attorneys all went to inspect the crime scene. This session was closed to the media, but a crowd of journalists and photographers—and some hangers-on—all gathered on the road just above the cottage. Knox and Sollecito attended the morning session, but exercised their right not to attend the afternoon activities. The group prodded around together for about two-hours. They started by thoroughly examining the exterior of the cottage. Together they inspected the broken window outside

131

of Filomen's room. Once they had thoroughly examined the exterior, they moved inside the cottage to view the interior. Before they did so, police activated a generator, as the electricity in the cottage had been turned off. The group spent a lot of time in Kercher's room discussing the position of her body and other things. They finally had a chance to see for themselves if more than one attacker could have been in the room at the time of the murder. The house was a total mess according to all involved; the fact that there had been two recent break-ins did not help the state of the cottage. Inside, they also examined Filomen's room and the placement of the rock that was supposedly used to break the window from the outside.

Meredith Kercher Trial Day 17 – (April 24, 2009)

The cottage was unsealed and the court lifted the confiscation order, releasing it back to its female owner. She claimed that she would immediately change the locks and put it up for rent. More evidence and expert testimony was scheduled for this day. The prosecution's main event of the day was the testimony of Claudio Cantagalli[59], the head of forensics for the Perugia police. Claudio video taped the scene just hours after Kercher's body was discovered. His testimony on this day would be accompanied by that very video, which contained a walk-through of all evidence recorded. The first forensic witness to the stand, however, was Alberto Intini[60], the Director of Italy's National Forensic Police. Although Mr. Intini did not take part in the two forensic inspections, he did oversee the operations and was there testifying on behalf of the forensic team. Intini told the court that the "best resources and manpower in every required field" were involved in the investigation.

The defense lawyers' all alleged that evidence was contaminated. They showed Intini photos of the crime scene, showing some objects (such as the doors of Kercher's wardrobe and Meredith's bra clasp—which had Sollecito's DNA on it) were moved between the first and subsequent inspections. Intini repeatedly stressed that the crime scene was not contaminated in any way. "DNA doesn't fly, like pollen or hair, or get thrown upon things here and there," Intini insisted. "Even if in theory contamination can never be ruled out, it is not easy for it to happen, and there must be direct contact." He also stated the same point another way. "Biological contamination in an entirely abstract is possible, but unless it can be proven that it occurred then there has been none."

Next Claudio Cantagalli[61] took the stand, armed with the video footage of the forensic investigation. As the police video began, with a view of the outside of the cottage, Knox and Sollecito exchanged grins. Both were chewing gum and Knox mouthed a message to Sollecito, who was sitting some distance away, in the same row. The video was silent, and that silence was intermittently broken by Claudio's interpretation of the events shown on the screen. The camera moved from the cottage's entrance to the kitchen, the living room area, then into Filomena's room; where the camera picked up some images of the staged break-in. Both Knox and Sollecito watched intently as the camera moved through the cottage. The camera also focused-in-on the large stone under the desk in Filomena's bedroom. This stone was allegedly the object that was used to break the window from the outside. There was about a three-foot space between the window and a grassy area where the stone would have been thrown from. The three-foot gap in between has a large drop-off below that leads down to the first floor. One would have to be remarkably athletic to then jump from the grassy area, across the gap, to the window. That person would then need to hang-on, hoist himself/herself up and climb through a broken window, avoiding the broken glass when entering. Or, after breaking the window, that person would have had to walk around to the first floor and then scale the bars of the window below; while avoiding falling, being seen, or being cut by the broken glass as the person then tried climb in the window.

Before the next segment, the judge ordered that the following be in private, because of the graphic nature of what was to follow. As the camera moved into Meredith Kercher's room Knox turned somber and again buried her head in her hands. Sollecito, on the other hand, continued to watch attentively with no expression. The camera moved in on the victim, showing her bloodied-face with her eyes open, and her barefoot sticking out from the duvet that was covering her while she lay on the bloodstained floor. The camera spent a significant amount of time in Kercher's room, showing forensic scientists examining bloody footprints and fingerprints, and a handprint in blood on the wall (which was later identified as belonging to Rudy Guede).

Forensic photographer, Gioia Brocci[62], took the stand next. Brocci photographed every room inside the cottage in detail and was also in charge of taking all the blood and other forensic evidence in the small bathroom closest to Kercher's room. She told the court that traces of blood were found on the light switch and the bathroom rug as well as on the wall behind the toilet. She also testified that multiple drops of blood mixed with water were found in the sink and the bidet of the same bathroom. Brocci admitted under cross-examination that she used the same piece of absorbent paper to wipe up the different blood stains on the sink, and then a different piece of paper to collect the bloodstains on the bidet. Her reasoning for using the same absorbent to collect the blood on the sink, as she explained, was because to her it was clear at that time that the blood was from the same source.

Brocci was also present when Knox was brought back to the cottage. Brocci testified that Knox had been visibly shaken when she was taken into the kitchen and shown knives in the drawer after the murder. "A drawer with cutlery in it was opened and I remember that Knox started to tremble; she closed her eyes and put her hands over her ears…She reacted in such a way that she had to be escorted out of the room and taken into the corridor by the officers from the Perugia Flying Squad who were with her."

In the afternoon two fingerprint specialists involved in the investigation were called to the stand to give their analysis of what they found. Agatino Giunta[63] and Antonino Francaviglia[64] testified that There were a total of 108 papillar fragmented prints listed by police; of those, only 61 were usable and 48 certain: 17 of the prints belonged to Kercher, 1 to Guede (bloody hand print), 5 to Sollecito, 5 to Romanelli, 5 to Mezzetti, 4 to Silenzi (Meredith's boyfriend), and 13 were unidentifiable (Of the 13 unidentifiable prints found, four were found in the victim's room). Of those only one, found on a glass in the kitchen, was attributable to Knox even though she admitted to being in the house on the morning of 2 November 2007, when Kercher's body was discovered.

One of the five fingerprints found belonging to Sollecito was located on the gold door handle on the outside of Kercher's room. "The choice of the objects to analyze inside the villa, how was this decision made?" asked Knox's lawyer Carlo Dalla Vedova. "It is me and the officer responsible for the inspection who decides what should be analyzed, based on our investigative experience," Mr. Francaviglia responded. Both the judge and the defense lawyers all asked whether it was strange that only one of Knox's prints was found in a place that she had lived for two-months. Both responded that it was not odd. Both also testified that there were many prints that could not be identified because they were smudged. Both witnesses defined finding 97 prints as a relatively high number. All the objects in Knox's room were analyzed (only nine prints were found, and none were usable) as well as all the silverware. There are more than 16 characteristic points that have to be present to determine that a print is a match. There are many reasons why no useful prints may have been found: perhaps they were only partially defined or there was not enough pressure, humidity, or the surface wasn't right; or there could have been a clean-up initiated as well.

Meredith Kercher Trial Day 18 – (May 8, 2009)

A relatively uneventful day, as police print expert, Giuseppe Privitera[65], reiterated the fingerprint findings of the others experts. Privitera did clarify that the lone print belonging to Guede was a bloody palm-print (Kercher's blood) found on a pillow underneath Kercher's body. The court had originally scheduled this day to hear details of how DNA was found on a knife and bloodied bra strap. This information was to be provided by the Chief of the Italian Scientific Police Unit in Rome, Patrizia Stefanoni. However, after a defense motion to postpone the crucial testimony after the prosecution mentioned another crime-scene video that the defence hadn't seen yet; the video had previously been corrupted, but had been recently restored; the judge granted the request and postponed Stefanoni's and other forensic DNA testimony until 22 May 2007.

Just prior to this motion, the prosecution showed the jury video footage of the forensic investigation that took place on 18 December 2007, more than six-weeks after the murder. It was at this time (during the forth forensic investigation) that the notorious bra-clasp of Kercher's—which had Sollecito's DNA on it—was collected. This video footage of the investigation—as the defendants watched closely—showed the cottage in complete disarray.

As the trial resumed, prosecutor Comodi spent several minutes trying to get her laptop to work and could be heard muttering under her breath as her repeated attempts failed. Fellow prosecutor Mignini stepped in to try and help but he was unable to resolve the problem; the video CD of the crime scene wouldn't play. Things became surreal as Sollecito offered to help, pointing out he was a computer studies graduate. They allowed him to fiddle with the computer and figure out what the problem was. He was quickly able to establish that the prosecution's laptop did not have the correct program to play the DVD with the evidence and offered his own—not before spending several minutes clicking through the files on the screen. And since it may have contained evidence that would incriminate him, one couldn't help wondering whether Sollecito might be tempted to wipe the hard drive clean, or at least start deleting files.

Meredith Kercher Trial Day 19 – (May 9, 2009)

The nineteenth-day of the trial heard from two footprint experts called in by the prosecution. The first, Dr. Lorenzo Rinaldi[66], testified for nearly five-hours. His testimony was crucial because he stated, "You can see clearly that this bloody footprint on the rug does not belong to Mr. Guede, but you can see that it is compatible with Sollecito." Dr. Rinaldi—director of the print-identity division of Italy's scientific police (the Italian equivalent of the FBI)—said, "All the elements are compatible with Mr. Sollecito's foot," as he pointed a red laser to a PowerPoint presentation containing the prints, which were projected onto a big-screen in the courtroom. Rinaldi showed a variety of comparisons between Knox, Sollecito, and Guede's footprints and those left at the crime scene.

Rinaldi also testified that yet another bare footprint highlighted by luminol (found in the hallway) was positively identified as compatible with Sollecito's foot, and two latent bare footprints—also highlighted by luminol—are compatible with Knox's foot. Dr. Rinaldi pointed out that of the two prints compatible with Knox's right foot, one was in the hallway outside Kercher's door, facing toward the room; the other was found exiting Knox's bedroom. During his stunningly damaging (to the defense) testimony, Dr. Rinaldi explained to the court how microscopic point-to-point measurements such as "heel to toe" or "toe and arch width" were used to identify the prints. He described methods of image analysis, metric and grid measurements as well as particular characteristics of the footprints.

There were also two footprints left on the pillow that was found half under Meredith's pelvis. Dr. Rinaldi identified the larger print as being attributed to the right shoe-print of Rudy Guede; while the second, smaller print as unidentifiable because the specific kind of shoe could not be determined. However, Judge Massei asked Dr. Rinaldi what size the shoe-print was. Rinaldi answered "Between 36 – 38 euro size shoe." Judge Massei then asked Rinaldi what size shoe Knox wears. Rinaldi responded, "The Sketcher shoe we sequestered belonging to Amanda Knox corresponds with size 37." This would bring the total of Knox's footprints found in blood at the scene up to three. During his cross-examination, Rinaldi admitted that "Luminol reacts to rust, bleach, and various types of fruit juices [because of the iron they contain], but in forensics we generally use it to find traces of blood." When asked what substance the footprints were made in, Dr. Rinaldi said that he only does image analysis and such a determination would have to be made by a forensic biologist (Dr. Patrizia Stefanoni is scheduled next session).

After lunch Sollecito made a spontaneous statement to the court in which he said, "Those bare footprints cannot be mine." Sollecito also reminded the court of the bloody shoeprint in Kercher's room that was originally (wrongly) attributed to him, that is now identified as Guede's. He told the court how much stress that incident caused him. In any event the next footprint expert who took the stand, Pietro Boemia[67], also testified that the bare footprint in blood on the bathmat—which only shows the top half of the foot— "matches the precise characteristics of Sollecito's foot." Boemia was Dr. Rinaldi's assistant, but a print specialist nonetheless.

Meredith Kercher Trial Day 20 – (May 22, 2009)

Knox entered the courtroom dressed in a purple top and beige trouser, and appeared to be in a cheerful mood. Little did she know that the twentieth-day of the trial would quite possibly become the day that handed her a life-sentence for the murder of Meredith Kercher. Today, hard forensic evidence would be presented by

forensic biologist and Chief of the Italian Scientific Police Unit in
Rome, Dr. Patrizia Stefanoni[68]. This testimony was rescheduled
from earlier in the month by a defense motion, but the delay was
now over. This day would be all about Dr. Stefanoni, as she would
spend more than nine-hours on the stand explaining the biological
evidence found at the cottage and on the knife recovered from
Sollecito's flat. Dr. Stefanoni took the stand and presented slides and
graphs describing the complicated science behind DNA analysis.

Dr. Stefanoni explained that of the six crime scene
inspections conducted they found 228 pieces of evidence and 460
traces of genetic material. The only good news for Knox on this day
would be that no traces of her DNA were found in Kercher's room.
However, the rest of the news was completely damning. According
to Dr. Stefanoni, there were five spots in the cottage where they
found a mix of Knox and Kercher's DNA.

Dr. Stefanoni testified that in the bathroom next to Kercher's room
three spots of blood revealed the genetic profiles of both Knox and
Kercher:

- On the drain of the bidet
- On the Q-tip box located at the ledge of the sink
- On the edge of the sink

Dr. Stefanoni said that these bloodstains were "of diluted blood,
blood presumably mixed with water." Also in that bathroom, a drop
of Knox's blood was found on the sink faucet. Kercher's blood was
also found on the toilet lid, on the upper part of the bathroom light
switch (which Dr. Stefanoni explained indicated that it was left when
the light was turned on, not off), and on the bathmat.

Stefanoni also testified that a mixture of Knox and Kercher's DNA
was also found:

- In a luminol-enhanced bare footprint in the hallway outside
  Kercher's room
- In a luminol-enhanced spot found in Filomena Romanelli's
  room

Dr. Stefanoni also told the court that the 20-inch knife retrieved by police from Sollecito's flat—which consisted of one of the three wounds on Kercher's neck—had Knox's DNA in a small scratch on the knife's black handle and Kercher's DNA on the sharp tip. Dr. Stefanoni said that they noticed "particular diagonal scrapes on the side of the blade that suggests someone had vigorously rubbed the knife, conceivably to clean it." Dr. Stefanoni told the court that in her opinion the positioning of Kercher's genetic material found on the blade indicated that it "was used to pierce and not to cut."

At some point during her testimony, the analysis focused on the bra-clasp recovered from Kercher's room more than 40-days after the murder. Dr. Stefanoni said that the clasp contained Sollecito's DNA, and that it was not contaminated in any way. This was key evidence, because it puts Sollecito in the room at sometime during or after the murder; particularly that his DNA was located on the bra-clasp that had been violently ripped, or meticulously cut, from the helpless victim. The defense maintained that all of this evidence was a result of contamination, but they gave no reasonable explanation of how exactly this could have occurred. Dr. Stefanoni contended that her team used gloves, shoe covers, tweezers, and evidence bags at all times.

Perhaps understanding the precariousness of her client's situation, Sollecito's lawyer, Bongiorno, was particularly animated during her cross-examination. As the big-screen rolled video footage of the forensic evidence collection, she insisted that one of the officers used the same collection swab to swipe two different blood samples (pointing it out on the screen). Dr. Stefanoni quickly stepped in and said, "If the same cloth was used to collect two samples of different blood it would be evident in the data analysis. These samples match Knox and the victim."

Dr. Stefanoni also testified that in Kercher's room they found DNA traces of Rudy Guede:

- On Kercher's purse
- On her sweatshirt and bra
- And traces of his cells were found on a vaginal swab of the victim (which contained no semen).

Further explaining the science behind her conclusions, Dr. Stefanoni explained that trace *A of Exhibit 36* (handle of knife) corresponded with the genetic profile of Knox (from a cotton swab) and on trace *B of Exhibit 36* (tip of knife) corresponded with the genetic profile of Meredith Kercher (swab taken from her neck wound). Dr Stefanoni stated that "a small quantity of DNA is a quantity of DNA that does not always produce a complete genetic profile for all 16 gene points; accordingly, it does not always produce a peak height that is greater than 50 RFU. In the case of Exhibit 36 (the knife) the height was observable and it was quite low. In the first locus, D8, ,we have the allele pairs 13-41 and 16-28; allele 14 and allele 18 are, respectively 47 [RFU] and 32. Some alleles are also 51 and 75 [RFU]; it depends a bit on the gene locus. So, D18 is 75 and 39; D5 is 113 and 36; and therefore they are not well balanced, and, above all, many have a low RFU level."

In regard to the mixed DNA of Knox and Kercher, the RFU counts were very high. Dr. Stefononi's results showed that Knox "has the alleles 11 and 12, which are the first two; the peaks ... are in the order of 2000, beyond 2000 RFU; the other pair ... it is in fact the pair 13 – 16 because it has quite homogeneous peaks; one peak is 931, the 13, and the other peak is 752, are a little uneven, but all in all quite homogeneous. In this case, but also in other cases...there is a compatibility [which is], one could say [*come dire*], a little stronger...because it would not be plausible to pair the 11 with the 13 and the 12 with the 16, because their heights are too dissimilar." From this, Dr. Stefononi concluded that, "Specimens can be more easily attributed when in the presence of quite unequal mixtures in which each one has contributed a different quantity of DNA."

Upon further questioning by Knox's defense regarding Exhibit 36, Dr. Stefanoni explained that "any machine which uses fluorescence as analytical data, whatever kind of fluorescence and for whatever kind of analysis it is used for, the analysis will unavoidably be accompanied by background noise...false peaks which are very, very low with respect to those which belong to the true analytical data." In practice, it is thus "possible to have background noise in an electropherogram, and in any analysis, since this is unavoidable, it is inherent in all genetic analysis of this type," Dr. Stefanoni clarified. Such results are produced by the machine in the laboratory, and subsequently evaluated by the geneticist, she explained.

Dr. Stefanoni indicated that the pillow found underneath Meredith's body was not analyzed, because it was considered more useful to use it for print analysis, whether of shoeprints or handprints. Dr. Stefanoni also testified that the traces present on the door handle of the victim's room; they had been identified as being from Kercher; only blood of the victim was found; this is aside from the fingerprint found on the handle as well, testified to by fingerprint experts as being attributed to Sollecito.

Meredith Kercher Trial Day 21 – (May 23, 2009)

Although each defense team appeared hopeful in front of the media outside the courtroom (downplaying Dr. Stefanoni's testimony), they were certainly reeling from the previous day's testimony. And after a grueling day of testimony, Dr. Stefanoni was back for more cross-examination. Dr. Stefanoni stressed that normative protocols were followed while collecting evidence and a stringent piece-by-piece analysis of evidence with impeccable handling occurred. She also told the court, "In seven years of work, I have never had any accidental contamination." To further explain the plausibility or implausibility of the question of contamination, Dr. Stefanoni said:

> *"Each biological trace is treated and examined on its own and it is absolutely impossible to end up mixing DNA in one trace with another or to mix them up with each other or with those belonging to other cases...Contamination of specimens is absolutely impossible. In the laboratory, we apply all necessary precautions, with a view to the end that any specimen does not end up being mixed with any other. Checks are done in each work session" and, during the course of work in the lab, single-use material is utilized. The victim's DNA was extracted, sampled and subsequently also used for comparison with that found on the knife seized from Sollecito's house and held by the prosecution to be the murder weapon."*

Francesco Camana[69], a blood pattern analyst in Rome's criminal forensic division and physicist, would provide the remainder of Saturday's testimony. Knox and Sollecito appeared tenser on this day, listening intently to testimony, taking notes, and strategizing with their lawyers. Dr. Camana presented the court with bloody photos, suggesting that the trajectory of blood splatters showed that Kercher was most likely killed while on her knees facing her wardrobe and close to the ground. "When she was struck with a knife, in what would turn out to be the mortal blow, Meredith's neck was approximately 40cm from the floor in front of a wing of the wardrobe in her room," Camana said.

Camana discussed various possibilities concerning the victim's position, but he did provide a possible scenario that, from his experience, he believed was the most plausible: "She was kneeling down in front of the wardrobe, her face was pressed almost to the floor; she was on her knees with her chest pushed forward and her legs behind her." Camana also stated that "the three who were at work in that spot had the whole space of the room at their disposal" His completed analysis on the positioning of Kercher's body while she was being stabbed was, "40cm from the ground, 30cm in front of the wardrobe and 33cm from the wall of the bedroom."

Meredith Kercher Trial Day 22 – (May 29, 2009)

Although the trial up to this point must have felt like forever for the defendants, for the rest it felt as though it had just started. With that being said, the prosecution was getting ready to wrap-up their case with three final witnesses: two today and one on day 23. After months of character assassination and damning evidence, the trial was getting ready to shift gears, and Knox and Sollecito (and their lawyers) had the daunting task of trying to reverse the course of the seemingly inevitable. Tension clearly began mounting as the focus of the trial was soon expected to take a sharp turn, and Knox was expected to take the stand in the near sessions. Even Knox's mother and the Kercher family were scheduled to testify. Much of the media took trial days 22 and 23 off; with clearly nothing important occurring they began looking ahead with anxiety. The prosecution would send a few more forensic experts to reiterate and help validate previous forensic testimony. The climax of the prosecutions' case came with the testimony of Dr. Stefanoni.

Most of the media and onlookers were focused on the "love triangle" scene that had played out on this day. Knox's former boyfriend and former fiancé from Seattle— David Johnsrud (a.k.a. DJ)—had flown in to catch the last day of the prosecutions' case. DJ was Knox's real love, and Raffaele a mere fling. The only real resemblance between Sollecito and DJ was that they both seemed reserved and had much less charisma than the 'queen bee,' Knox. DJ sat in the hall with Knox's father, Curt, and seemed very reserved and on guard. Mr. Knox, DJ, and his friend (John) took their seats in the courtroom; sitting just a few feet behind Amanda. DJ and Sollecito exchanged a smile and a greeting gesture as he entered the courtroom. Later DJ was approached by journalists, but kept his guard up, saying, "No comment."

The testimony of the day focused on a 3-D (three-dimensional) reconstruction/simulation of the crime administered by the 'Violent Crime Unit'. It was a complete walkthrough of the crime based on previous forensic testimony to give the jury a visualization of how the prosecution believes that the crime occurred. The conclusion was that four people (the victim and three others) were in Kercher's room during the murder and three perpetrators committed the crime. The simulation also focused on the broken window in Filomena's room, which is totally incompatible with the possibility of climbing 3 meters and 78 centimeters (Aprrox. 13 feet high), and that they found the glass above the stone and other traces of tampering. Also, they pointed out that the large stone weighed 3 kilos and 990 grams (Approx 9 pounds). It was also determined that Meredith struggled to free herself from her assailants before she died, and she brought her left hand to her neck, covering the fatal knife attack. The evidence proved this, according to experts, by the blood found on her hand and, in particular, the index finger.

Forensic scientist, Edgardo Giobbi[70], added the last piece of evidence against Knox's odd behaviour in the hours after the murder. According to Giobbi, just hours after the murder he handed Knox a pair of shoe covers to prevent contaminating the evidence. "As she put them on she swivelled her hips, pulled a face and said 'opla'—I thought it was very unusual behaviour and my suspicions against her were raised," Giobbi testified. At the end of the day the prosecution was done, but the Kercher family's lawyers still had a few tricks up their sleeve.

Meredith Kercher Trial Day 23 – (June 5, 2009)

Just when we thought that the assault on the defendants was over, more expert witnesses took the stand. This time, however, the witnesses would be called by Kercher family lawyers, Francesco Maresca and Serena Perna. Also expected to be in the courtroom were some members of the Kercher family; although when the first witness took the stand they had not arrived yet. All of this was part of the civil lawsuit filed by the Kercher family; in Italy, civil lawsuits can be attached to criminal trials. Knox entered the courtroom wearing a white patterned top with white trousers; she turned occasionally throughout the day and gave her father a smile. Sollecito, who was dressed in a red shirt, appeared anxious as he bit his nails and awaited the fist witness.

Forensic expert and professor, Dr. Gianaristide Norelli[73], was the first person called to the stand. Dr. Norelli told the court that there were multiple lesions on Kercher's body, which he indicated was consistent with being held and attacked by more than one person. Dr. Norelli also testified that the bruises on the Kercher's hips were consistent with a sexually violent approach, which was the first time during the trial that an expert has made this determination. Graphic pictures were again displayed in order for him to show a visualization of his results. This again meant that those parts of the session would be closed-off to media and the public, which incorporated most of his testimony.

From his experience, Dr. Norelli broke-down the exact cause of death during his reconstruction. He testified that the stab wounds on Kercher's neck were indicative of having been inflicted as threats during the struggle and that the main cause of death was suffocation. The prosecution and court documents state that the cause of death was suffocation caused by the hemorrhaging following the neck wounds. However, Dr. Norelli claimed that the suffocation was also aided "manually" by forcing the victim's mouth and nose shut and by strangling her. Dr. Norelli also told the court that while the neck wounds may have been inflicted to scare Kercher, the strangulation showed a clear intent to kill. Dr. Norelli concluded that the knife found in Sollecito's flat was compatible with the wounds on Kercher's neck. Interestingly enough, Dr. Norelli said that Kercher's own movement may have inadvertently contributed to making the stab wounds deeper.

DNA expert and Professor, Francesca Torricelli[74], took the stand next. Suddenly, the Kercher family entered the hallway and proceeded toward the courtroom to hear Torricelli's testimony. Kercher's mother (Arline) and father (John) walked past reporters without commenting. Meredith's sister, Stephanie Kercher, commented that she felt "anxious" about going inside, as they continued in and took their seats. "I have no doubt the traces are compatible," Professor Torricelli told the court; referring to the findings that Knox's DNA was on the handle and Kercher's DNA on the tip of the alleged murder weapon. Professor Torricelli also told testified that she believed that the samples of Sollecito's DNA found on Kercher's bra-clasp were a significant enough amount that it was unlikely to have been left by contamination. Oddly enough, Amanda Knox stared intently at the Kercher family for most of the session. One witness later told reporters that "It was very unusual. I'm not sure if she was looking for sympathy or trying to offer it, but Meredith's parents never looked at her."

After the session, Maresca told reporters outside that "They [the Kercher family] were rather emotional, I think that's inevitable. Everything contributes to their remembering inevitably their daughter and sister. They came to Perugia not out of hatred; but to obtain justice."

Meredith Kercher Trial Day 24 – (June 6, 2009)

Today the Kercher family would close their civil arguments personally, with testimony provided by three of the family members. Quiet and somber would be the pervasive mood in the courtroom throughout as Meredith's loss would be no more evident than through the words of her family. Surprisingly the American media was noticeably absent from today's proceedings; as oddly reported by ABC News. The Kercher family were very dignified in the courtroom and while giving testimony. Meredith's mother, Arline Kercher[75], took the stand first and spoke gut-wrenchingly about how the loss of her daughter has personally affected her. "Her death was unreal in many ways," she said, "and still is. I still look for her...We will never, never get over this. It's such a shock to send your child to school and not have her come back." Kercher family lawyers would try to show that Amanda and Meredith's relationship was a strained one.

When asked about Meredith's relationship with Knox, Arline testified that she recalled Meredith telling her that she had invited Knox to lunch with her other English friends and Meredith told her mother that, "she [Amanda] didn't want to socialize with English people, she wanted to socialize with Italians" in order to learn the language better. Meredith's older sister, Stephanie Kercher[76], testified that Meredith had told her that Knox had a habit of singing loudly all the time and that it was extremely annoying. These sentiments were echoed while Knox was incarcerated, as some of her fellow inmates had complained to guards about Knox's loud signing. Meredith's father, John Kercher[77], told the court, "She [Meredith] spoke to me about her [Knox], about the fact that she was surprised how soon Amanda had gotten a boyfriend. When she arrived in Perugia she told me, a couple of weeks before she died, that she was upset that Amanda never seemed to flush the toilet."

Kercher's lawyers also tried to show, through the family, that Meredith was a fighter and would have defended herself—possibly to show that there was more than one attacker. When asked if Meredith would have fought-off her attacker(s), Stephanie responded, "Absolutely, 110 percent! Mez had a strong personality, and physically she was very strong. She was very passionate about things that were important to her—family, friends, coming to Italy. She fought for her place here, and she would have fought to the end." John Kercher also gave similar remarks when he said, "She was a very strong person, and when she was about 17, she studied karate for a year. I think she would have put up quite a fight." Later, Francesco Maresca told reporters, "This confirms that the attack [on Kercher] was strong, and repeated, and carried out by more than one person."

All-and-all Knox appeared very somber in the courtroom. She occasionally glanced back at the Kercher family, who were seated behind her. Knox left the courtroom with her eyes to the ground looking atypically unanimated. On the other hand, as

Sollecito left the courtroom he turned to journalists and said, "I await justice, just like they do." The trial would now shift to the defense, leading-off with the long anticipated testimony of Amanda Knox, beginning next session. Predictions surfaced regarding record-amounts of journalists that will be on hand on June 12th as Knox is scheduled to take the stand in her own defense. One of Knox's lawyers, Luciano Ghirga, told reporters after the session that Knox cannot wait to give her point of view and that she will answer all questions posed by the prosecution.

Chapter 8 - The Trial of the Century

Meredith Kercher Trial Day 25 – (June 12, 2009) Knox Speaks

Unlike Sollecito, who has exercised his right to silence, Amanda Knox had volunteered to take the stand. As we have seen, the Italian justice system has several differences from that of the United States Justice system. One of those differences is that in an Italian trial witnesses must swear to tell the truth, however, defendants do not. Defendants can also interrupt the questioning at anytime or even choose not to answer certain questions, in theory of course, but in practice it would be a bad move (incriminating) if a defendant chose not to answer. One of Knox's lawyers, Luciano Ghirga, told reporters a week earlier that Knox would be answering all of the prosecution's questions.

Knox's defense team, however, would offer-up objection after objection on even just the simplest questions, and this came on the day that was scheduled just for defense questioning (aside from Patrick Lumumba's lawyer). Every time Knox was caught in a contradiction, a fight would break-out between defense and prosecution. Knox's vague answers along with her lawyer's objections distracted lawyers and made it very hard for them to extract anything substantial out of her. It was apparent early on that this was going to be a long drawn-out examination with nothing substantial provided toward her defense. Not only was Knox vague, but she seemed annoyed and not necessarily eager to tell her story; even using sarcasm on a few occasions and snapping at prosecutors. In the end, her testimony hurt her more than it helped her, because it did not help clear up her whereabouts at the time of the murder, and it lent to the notion that she was lying.

Morning Session

The schedule for the day was going to be questioning from her-own defense team, along with questioning from Patrick Lumumba's lawyer, Carlo Pacelli. Knox entered the courtroom with a her hair tied back with a light-blue scrunchy, a white short sleeve collared top, pale trousers, and what appeared to be a large cold sore on her upper lip. She looked tired and pale as she took her seat, and looked around nervously as reporters jockeyed for position at the back of the courtroom. The beginning of the session was held up a bit as Judge Massei discussed with lawyers whether to allow cameras in the courtroom. The final decision was to exclude cameras, allowing cameras to roll during only the first 20 minutes of Knox's testimony. Questioning began with Carlo Pacelli, who would get the first crack at Knox as part of Lumumba's civil lawsuit. Seated immediately to Knox's left was a heavy-set, brunette interpreter. Knox understood most questions that were thrown at her and the interpreter mostly translated to the court what Knox was saying as opposed to what Knox was being asked by Italian litigators.

Mr. Pacelli started by asking Knox if she knew Rudy Guede. Knox admitted meeting Guede before the murder, claiming that she met him while she was mingling with the boys that lived in the apartment underneath her. Knox said that they were in the center, near the church when the boys introduced her to Guede. On that occasion, Knox says that she spent most of her time with Meredith, as they all (including Guede) went back to the cottage and had a party on the first floor. This party apparently took place in mid-October of 2007, a little more than a month before the murder. Knox also admitted seeing Guede at Le Chic (Lumumba's restaurant) at least once. Knox said that at the party she and others smoked a "*spinello*" ("marijuana joint"). Pacelli then focused on Knox's relationship with Lumumba. Knox testified that Lumumba never mistreated her, always treated her with respect, there relationship was good, and that she was not scared of him. Mr. Pacelli then brought Knox back to the night of the murder, asking her if she knew what time it was when Lumumba sent her the first text message on 1 November 2007. Knox said "around 8:15-8:30p.m."

When asked, "When you answered Patrick's message, where were you?"

Knox replied, "In the apartment of Raffaele, I think, yes." Pacelli indicated that Knox answered the message 25 minutes later from another location. "It seems from cell pings that you were out of the house when you answered, in the center. Where were you?" asked Pacelli. This question was met by a stream of objections and a heated discussion between defense and prosecution. When the dust cleared Knox stated that she was at Sollecito's apartment when she responded to the message.

Knox had deleted all received text messages on her cell phone at some point after receiving the last message from Lumumba. Knox claimed that this was because she had limited space on her cell. When asked why she did not delete the text messages that she sent, she answered very sarcastically, "I'm not a technical genius, so I only know how to delete the ones that I receive when I get them." Knox told the court that she didn't have an appointment to meet Lumumba at the basketball court on the night of the murder. When asked why she wrote in her statement to police that she met him at the court that night, Knox responded, "It was a complicated situation. I can explain it if you want me to go into it." Knox then proceeded to explain her version of what occurred and why she wrote what she did in the spontaneous letter to police after her arrest. She proceeded to explain what she claimed was a long grueling interrogation where police began asking the same questions over and over.

Then, in a long, drawn-out, drab tone that only an American could understand (due to the prosodic—rhythmic, intonational aspect of human speech—nature of the tone), Knox said that they kept asking her questions such as "w-h-o k-i-l-l-e-d M-e-r-e-d-i-t-h," that sounded as if she was down-playing the question, because she had heard it so many times. Knox began to show several glimpses into the bizarre behavior that was previously testified to by others. Although it may sound trivial, the response was strange; and coupled with the multiple accounts her of odd behavior, it only added to the quandary. During this monologue, Knox stated that police called her a "stupid liar," several times when she asserted that she had been at Sollecito's flat all night. Knox then quoted her interpreter during the interrogation, claiming that she had said that Knox was "traumatized and couldn't remember the truth."

Knox then continued with her confusing explanation of what happened during her interrogation/arrest:

> "So what ended up happening was that they told me to try to remember what I apparently, according to them, had forgotten. Under the amount of pressure of everyone yelling at me, and having them tell me that they were going to put me in prison for protecting somebody, that I wasn't protecting, that I couldn't remember, I tried to imagine that in some way they must have had, it was very difficult, because when I was there, at a certain point, I just, I couldn't understand why they were so sure that I was the one who knew everything. And so, in my confusion, I started to imagine that maybe I was traumatized, like what they said. They continued to say that I had met somebody, and they continued to put so much emphasis on this message that I had received from Patrick, and so I almost was convinced that I had met him. But I was confused."

The next few questions were met with objections by Knox's lawyer, Carlo Dalla Vedova, and banter between he, the judge, and Pacelli. More objections came when Pacelli asked Knox why she claimed to hear Meredith scream, with now several different lawyers arguing and trying to plead to the judge their reasons why the question should or should not be answered. The argument centered on what was and was not admissible according to the Supreme Court decision at the beginning of trial. Judge Massei then declared that they would take a short recess and he would consult with the lawyers in private on the matter. When they returned, Judge Massei overruled the objections and stated that the question is permitted because it comes from Knox's spontaneous statement, which was ruled as admissible during the first week of trial. Knox then switched to speaking Italian upon Judge Massei's approval. Finally, Knox was able to answer the question, which she replied, "No," I did not hear Meredith scream.

The following sequence occurred next:

Carlo Pacelli: In the interrogation of November 6, 2007, at 5:45, you declared that before she died, you heard Meredith scream. How could you know that Meredith screamed before she was killed? Who told you?

Knox: So when I was with the police, they asked if I heard Meredith's scream. I said no. They said "But if you were there, how could you not hear her scream? If you were there?" I said "Look, I don't know, maybe I had my ears covered." So they said "Fine, we'll write that down. Fine."

Carlo Pacelli: [louder] But I can tell you that on November 6, the police did not know that Meredith screamed before she died, so why would they suggest it to you?

Knox: I imagine that maybe they were imagining how it might have been.

Knox asserted that police were not telling her what to say but suggesting paths of thought. "I kept following their suggestions," Knox stated. "They asked me if I was in her room when she was killed. I said no. They said but where were you? I said I don't know. They said, maybe you were in the kitchen. I said, fine."

Knox testified that she went to the police station with Sollecito the night that they were arrested because she was scared and didn't want to be alone. She verified that she was not called-into the station that night. Knox also confirmed that the spontaneous statement that she made was her idea, and not the result of pressure from police. Knox said that she asked for a piece of paper and a pen, and that she wrote it to explain her confusion to the police.

Knox then said several times that while at the police station after her arrest she "really wasn't sure" what had happened on the night of Kercher's murder. Knox told the court that she gave the written statement to the police freely, voluntarily, and that police did not suggest the content nor pressure her into writing the statement.

The following sequence occurred next:

Carlo Pacelli: Listen, in this memorandum, you say that you confirm the declarations you made the night before about what might have happened at your house with Patrick. Why did you freely and spontaneously confirm these declarations?

Knox: Because I was no longer sure what was my imagination and what was real. So I wanted to say that I was confused, and that I couldn't know. But at the same time, I knew I had signed those declarations. So I wanted to say that I knew I had made those declarations, but I was confused and not sure.

Carlo Pacelli: But in fact, you were sure that Patrick was innocent?

Knox: No, I wasn't sure.

Carlo Pacelli: Why?

Knox: Because I was confused! I imagined that it might have happened. I was confused.

Then the questioning turned to when Knox realized that Patrick Lumumba was innocent. Several fights and objections broke out over this line of questioning. The defense seemed to know that Pacelli was onto something and they were trying at all ends to block him or throw him off. Pacelli explained that in Knox's 7 November 2007, memorandum, Knox wrote, "I didn't lie when I said the murderer might be Patrick." However, Pacelli said that during a phone call with her mother on November 10th (three days later) Knox stated that she felt horrible because she (Knox) got him [Lumumba] put in prison and she knew he was innocent. Knox, then speaking like a politician, led Pacelli—and even the judge—around in circles; not giving a straight answer to the question: when did you inform police that Patrick Lumumba was not the killer?

Pacelli was trying to show that Knox had written that Lumumba was the killer on the 7th, told her mother that Lumumba was innocent on the 10th, but never informed the police at anytime after the 10th that Lumumba was innocent. He was subsequently released three weeks after his arrest, and at no time during the three weeks did Knox inform police that she falsely accused Lumumba. Knox's final reply on the matter was, "I had explained the situation to my lawyers, and I had told them what I knew, which was that I didn't know who the murderer was." So, Knox never really did answer the question why she never informed anyone—besides her mother on November 10th—that Patrick Lumumba was not the murderer. This was important because Pacelli already knew what Knox's mother had told investigators about the call and what the basis of her testimony would be. Pacelli knew that her mother's testimony was coming up the following week, and he wanted to get Amanda's version on the record knowing that her mother would clarify and contradict—or at least not help—her (Amanda's) story. Knox also revealed that she never actually said she was sorry to Patrick for her false accusations that put him behind bars for three weeks. With that, Carlo Pacelli ended his questioning. Judge Massei then announced a break in the action and that the court would reconvene at 1:30p.m.

Afternoon Session

The afternoon session began at exactly 1:38p.m., as declared by the presiding judge, Giancarlo Massei, who called Knox's defense team for further examination. Knox took the stand again as her lawyer, Luciano Ghirga, stepped forward to begin his questioning. Mr. Ghirga began by asking Knox the last time that she saw Meredith alive. Knox began by reiterating her previous version: which began around noon on November 1st, just before Meredith went to Robyn Butterworth's apartment. This time, her answers were clear and concise. Knox further explained her first meeting with Raffaele Sollecito, the configuration of the living arrangements at the cottage (including who lived there with her and Meredith), and how the rent was paid.

Ghirga then began discussing Knox's relationship with Meredith, trying to establish that there was no problem between them. Knox claimed that she and Meredith were close friends, but she did mention briefly that Meredith had expressed her discontent over her [Knox's] cleaning habits; although she made excuses and downplayed the discussion. Knox snickered a bit and claimed that she "wasn't the cleanest person in the house," speaking of herself.

Going further into the night of the murder, Knox testified that she and Sollecito read a bit of the book *Harry Potter*, listened to music, watched the movie *Amelie*, and then ate a fish dinner around 9:30-10:00p.m. After dinner Knox told the court that Sollecito began doing the dishes. It was then that Knox claims that the sink began leaking water all over the floor. Sollecito was "displeased" she said, because he had recently had the sink fixed. Sollecito didn't have a mop, so they found some rags and let the water soak-in and Knox told him that she would go and get the mop she had at the cottage in the morning and bring it back to his place to clean the mess. Once that was determined, Knox says that they went into his room and smoked a joint (marijuana cigarette). After that she said that they had sex then fell asleep.

From there Ghirga stepped back a few hours to the text message from Lumumba. Knox said that she received his message "just before or right after" the movie had started. Knox claimed that she was so excited that she didn't have to go into work that night that she jumped into Sollecito's arms and screamed, "Woo!" Knox then reiterated her previous version; which she woke up the next morning around 10:00-10:30a.m., etc. (similar version in her November 4, 2007, email to family and friends).

Knox claims that they had plans to go to Gubbio, so she left his flat, went home to take a shower, and return to Raffaele's so that they could go to Gubbio. After noticing the blood in the bathroom and taking a shower, she returned to Sollecito's flat. There, Knox claims that they cleaned the floor in his apartment with the mop she retrieved from the cottage, and then ate breakfast and had coffee at Sollecito's apartment. Knox then proceeded to testify that she called Meredith's phone first then she called Filomena, both from Sollecito's apartment. This varies from her 4 November 2007, email to family and friends, because in that email she wrote that she called Filomena first, and then Meredith. Also during her testimony, Knox never mentions running outside and banging on a neighbors door, which she writes in her November 4th email.

Before breaking the door down to Meredith's room, Knox testified, "Yes, because I told them, look, the door is locked, and Filomena was going 'Mamma Mia, it's never locked, it's never locked,' and I said no, it's not true that it's never locked, but it is strange." Knox testified that when Meredith's door was broken down she was near the entrance. Yet, in her 4 November 2007, email to family and friends she claimed that she was "in the kitchen, having really done my part for the situation." It also contradicts all other versions of those who were there at the time who claim that Knox was in the kitchen when the door was kicked-in. Knox also claims that while in the car with Paola and her boyfriend, on the way to the police station, they informed her and Sollecito that Meredith's throat had been cut. This statement is suspect, however, as Paola testified that because of the *"penumbra"* (or "lack of light") in the room, only a foot could be seen, no blood or anything else. Knox claims that after she was told that Meredith's throat was cut she cried. According to Luca and Paola's testimony, Knox did cry in the car, and they also testified that they told Sollecito and Knox what they knew about how Meredith had died before they had gotten to the police station.

The questioning then switched to the 4 November 2007, questioning when Knox was brought back to the crime scene. Knox explained that the police requested her presence at the police station. Knox testified that she had requested to meet them at the cottage, but police asked her to meet them at the station first. She was driven there by Sollecito and the police then took her over to the cottage. To her surprise, her other roommates, Laura and Filomena, were there; but they arrived without a police escort. Knox then briefly discussed her mental breakdown at the cottage when she was shown the knives. She claimed that she was very scared when shown the knives and that she was in shock; she claimed that she was just beginning to understand what exactly had happened there.

Luciano Ghirga then shifted questioning to what Knox had told police on November 4th about a man nicknamed "Shaky." On that date police had asked Knox to remember if there were any males who had visited the cottage that seemed like they could be dangerous. She could only think of one man who had made a bad impression on her since she had been in Perugia and his name was

Shaky. Knox said that they called him Shaky because of the way he danced.

> **Amanda Knox**: one time I had a, he [Shaky] went for example to the place where I worked, at the time when I was supposed to go home, it was very late, and he offered me a ride home on his motorbike. But during the ride, he insisted that I go have some dessert with him, and I said, "Look, I really want to go home," and he said "No, look, I'm giving you a ride, a bit of dessert is nothing," and he took me to have it, and then he took me to his house, which to me...I kept telling him again and again, "Look, I really want to go home, it's really late, I'm really tired," and he kept saying "No, no, relax, relax, come on, sit down on my bed, relax, make yourself comfortable." I said "No, look, take me home." So he finally brought me home, and that was it, but it left me with an ugly impression because I thought he wanted to somehow try something, and he was the only person that had made an impression of strangeness on me, like he had intentions that were different from what I wanted. So he made that impression on me, but that's all, because everybody else I met was nice.

Mr. Ghirga then switched question back to the November 4th, when police brought Knox to the cottage. Mr. Ghirga asked Knox what conversations were had between her, Laura, and Filomena. Knox said that they discussed how stunned they were about what had happened, why nothing was stolen during the break-in, and the overall situation that had transpired thus far. Knox said that they also discussed future living arrangements, as the girls were staying with friends and Knox was staying with Sollecito. On that day the three girls were talking about possibly moving-in together at a different location. Mr. Ghirga then said that he wanted to ask Knox about the evenings of the 5th and 6th, but he was cut-short by judge Massei, who suspended the proceedings. The time was 2:30p.m., and judge

Massei announced that they would have a break in the action and reconvene at 3:00p.m.

The trial picked-up again at 3:00p.m. Judge Massei called for silence and Luciano Ghirga resumed questioning. As Ghirga began to speak crowd noise could still be heard. Judge Massei again called for silence and Ghirga repeated his question, asking Knox about when she first came to Italy. Amanda Knox had first moved into the cottage in Perugia in late September of 2007. She had previously been in Germany at her aunt's house with her sister Deanna, and both Amanda and Deanna had gone straight to Italy afterwards. Ghirga then asked Knox how many piercings that she had in her ear, as he pointed out that he counted eight on the left ear and four on the right ear; Knox agreed. It had appeared as though Mr. Ghirga was going to try and establish that the blood found at the scene of the crime that belonged to Knox came from the piercings. Yet, without warning, Ghirga said that he had exhausted the topic and went back to Knox's interrogation on 5 November 2007.

Mr. Ghirga then asked Knox about her allegations that she was struck in the head by police:

Amanda Knox: So, during the interrogation, people were standing all around me, in front of me, behind me, one person was screaming at me from here [she points in front of her], another person was shouting 'No no no, maybe you just don't remember' from over there [points to her left], other people were yelling other things, and a policewoman behind me did this to me [Knox mimics the sound of two whacks to the back of her head].

Luciano Ghirga: Once, twice?

Amanda Knox: Twice. The first time she did this, I turned around to her, and she did it again.

Luciano Ghirga: I wanted to know this precise detail.

Amanda Knox: Yes.

Luciano Ghirga: After all that, that whole conversation, that you told us about, and you had a crying crisis, did they bring you some tea, coffee, some cakes, something? When was that exactly?

Amanda Knox: They brought me things only after I had made some declarations. So, I was there, they were all screaming at me, I only wanted to leave because I was thinking that my mother was arriving, and I said look, can I have my telephone, because I want to call my mom. They said no, and there was this big mess with them shouting at me, threatening me, and it was only after I made declarations that they started saying "No, no, don't worry, we'll protect you," and that's how it happened.

Ironically, just moths earlier—at Rudy Guede's trial—Luciano Ghirga undermined and contradict his own client's (Knox) story when he said, "There were pressures from the police but we never said she was hit." Knox then recalls being brought several papers to sign: arrest warrant, declarations, etc. She claimed that she wasn't sure what the papers were, and that just signed everything because she wanted to go home. However, these papers were brought to her after she had been informed that she was under arrest, which she doesn't make reference to during this exchange. After repeated questioning about her unpleasant interrogation—in an effort to show that she made the confessions out of exhaustion, intimidation, and miscommunication—Knox claimed to have asked for a piece of paper and a pen so that police could be sure that they understood her. "Look, I'll give you a present," Knox claims to have told police, as she lets out a small laugh. Knox then speaks about the second letter which she wrote when she was first taken to jail.

Amanda Knox: So in prison I again asked for paper, because that's how I'm used to expressing myself, the way I succeed best, also to organize my thoughts, I needed to write them down. I needed to reorganize all my thoughts, because at that point I was still confused, I still had these images in my memory that finally I understood were a mixture of real images in my memory from other days mixed with imagination. So I needed those pieces of paper, so I could take everything and put it in order.

Knox's answer even seemed to confuse Ghirga, who responded by saying, "All right, I've finished the subject of the night in the Questura." Knox testified that she lost track of the hours and was unsure of any of the times involved, which is quite common when a suspect is initially confined. There had been some confusion after the murder why Knox did not leave the country when she had the chance. Knox claims that she had worked hard to get to Perugia and that she wanted to stay and finish her studies. However, she also said that she asked police if she could leave the country and they said "No." Mr. Ghirga then attempted to clear-up the statement made by Knox (on November 17th of 2007), which she made to her mother and father. The calls were from prison and were recorded by police. There was a long pause as Ghirga flipped through the transcript of the calls and found the quote on page eight. Once he found the page, he read Knox's comments aloud to the court. Knox said to her mother and father, "I was there. I can't lie about this. I'm not scared of the truth. It would be stupid to lie about this because I know I was there." Knox responded by claiming that when she said, "I was there," she meant that she was at Sollecito's flat during the murder, not at the cottage.

Mr. Ghirga then pulled out a letter that was written by Knox on 9 November 2007, which was addressed to him; Ghirga claimed to have received it on November 12th. In the letter Knox writes in English that she "felt upset about mentioning Patrick Lumumba's name." The letter was not known at the time by any other party and that along with the fact that it was written in English and transcribed into Italian by Knox's other lawyer, Carlo Dalla Vedova, brought an objection by prosecutor, Manuela Comodi. A small argument ensued over the translation of the letter from English to Italian. Prosecutor Comodi stated that she did not trust that the translation was accurate. Judge Massei settled the argument by letting the interpreter, who was there translating for Knox, translate the two lines in the letter that Mr. Ghirga was referring to.

After Ghirga had established that Knox had informed him that she was upset about falsely accusing Patrick Lumumba—which slightly clarified an earlier question posed by Lumumba's lawyer—he then switched questioning to the morning after the murder. Mr. Ghirga wanted to establish that Knox was not at the *Conad Store* on Sollecito's street at 7:45a.m., the morning after the murder. These statements were made earlier in the trial by Mr. Quintavalle, who owned the store and had testified that Knox was in his store at that time. Knox denied being at the store at that time or on that day. She did admit to being in the store a couple of times on other occasions, but with Sollecito—never alone. Knox also denied ever owning a red coat or anything resembling a red coat, which Mr. Gioffredi had testified that she was wearing when he saw her.

The last questions from Mr. Ghirga were regarding the scratch (or bruise) on Knox's neck, which was clearly visible in a picture of Knox outside the cottage just after Kercher's body was discovered. As indicated by prior testimony, the scratch was also seen by two others who had testified to its presence. Knox told the court that it was a hicky from Sollecito. In the background, Kercher family lawyer, Francesco Maresca, shouted, "Is it a scratch from Meredith?" Knox responded, "A hickey from Raffaele." With that, Mr. Ghirga said, "For now, I've finished," and he took his seat.

Carlo Dalla Vedova

Knox's other defense lawyer, Carlo Dalla Vedova, then took the floor to question Knox. Before questioning began, Mr. Dalla Vedova and Judge Massei asked Knox if she was too tired to continue. Knox stated that she was "ok to proceed." Judge Massei advised Knox that being fresh and lucid is important while on the stand and that if at any time she feels tired and wants to stop to say "*Basta*" and the court will take a short recess. Knox thanked the judge and the questioning resumed. Mr. Dalla Vedova began with a puzzling line of questioning that didn't seem to have a purpose, but somehow he connected the questioning to Knox's prison diaries and how she was told that she may have had AIDS—a ploy claimed to be a plot to extract from Knox how many sexual partners that she'd had. Dalla Vedova began by asking Knox about her family and why she decided to come to Perugia. They then began discussing a particular writing course that she had taken at Washington State University. It was unclear, at this point, where Dalla Vedova was leading with this line of questioning; yet, prosecutors made no objections as the questioning was virtually irrelevant to the case and was not helping her defense anyway. One would assume that prosecutors would let this continue all day.

Mr. Dalla Vedova led the questioning to Knox's writing, which she described as a way of expressing herself. Knox claimed that she often kept a diary, even back home, as a way to "let off steam" and to "understand herself." While in prison, Knox kept a diary up until 29 December 2007, which at that time was confiscated by prison officials and held in her dossier. Knox testified that she was faced with the choices of surrendering her diary willfully to prison officials or they would come retrieve it with a warrant; Knox gave it wittingly. The 'confiscated diary' was at one point analyzed by one of Britain's top criminal psychologists, Dr. David Wilson. In the diary Knox describes that when she first arrived in prison, blood was taken from her. Later, prison officials explained to her that the results of the blood test indicated that she may have AIDS, but she was told "not to worry" as it "could be a mistake." In the diary she then appeared to write down—freely and without being previously instructed—all of the men that she had slept with up to that point, which totaled "seven men." Knox explained to the court that for two weeks she was made to think that she had AIDS.

Also in that diary, Knox turned on Sollecito for the first time, speculating that he could have killed Meredith and framed her. "This could have happened: Raffaele went to Meredith's house, raped her and killed her and then, having come back home, pressed my fingerprints—I was asleep—onto the knife," Knox wrote. Seeing how Mr. Dalla Vedova's questioning was leading them nowhere, the more skilled Luciano Ghirga took over the questioning. Ghirga takes Knox back to her arrival in Perugia. They briefly discuss how well her Italian has gotten since she first arrived and what languages she spoke with some of her friends and roommates in Perugia. Knox claimed that she had been spending most of her time in prison studying, which is why her Italian has improved so much over the last two years. Knox claimed that she was currently reading *Hadrian's Memoirs* by Marguerite Yourcenar; a French writer, but she was reading the Italian version.

Mr. Ghirga then asked Knox to describe her relationship with her three female roommates. Knox stated that Laura was a lawyer during the day and a free-spirited guitar player at night. They often played guitar together—Knox borrowing Laura's second guitar—and practiced yoga. With Meredith, Knox testified that they would often discuss literature, because Meredith was always reading.

Ghirga spent the next several minutes establishing the relationship between Knox and Kercher. At some point the discussion turned to Meredith's English friends who had testified on day four of the trial.

Luciano Ghirga: Did you also get together with Meredith's English friends?

Amanda Knox: Yes, but not much. [Laughs] Not much, because in the end, after I got a job with Patrick, we didn't get together much, because they didn't go to my university, they went to Meredith's university. So we didn't meet there, and then I wasn't going around having fun any more, I was going to work. But that was fine.

Luciano Ghirga: But you preferred to be with Italians or foreigners?

Amanda Knox: I preferred to be with Italians, because I wanted to feel Italian, I didn't come to Italy to feel English.

Mr. Ghirga then asked Knox what she thought about the assertions of Meredith's English friends. The question was intercepted by Judge Massei who wanted Ghirga to be more specific with his question: the reason for this is, as Italian law prescribes, the witness (Knox in this case) is not permitted to give his or her impressions on the testimony of others. After a brief discussion Ghirga clarified, asking Knox what she thought of the assertions of the girls that there was friction between Knox and Kercher towards the end. Knox disagreed with these assertions, claiming that for her there was no friction in the house. According to Knox, the reason why she hadn't been hanging around with Meredith towards the end was because she was working at *Le Chic* and had no time to go out and socialize. Ghirga asked Knox if she had been aware of any "candeggina" ("bleach") in the cottage at the time of the murder. "I didn't know if there was any there, in the house," Knox replied.

Knox stated in her testimony (which was confirmed by her cell phone records) that she had asked Meredith via text messaging to meet up with her on Halloween night; oddly enough, Knox testified that she had met a male friend (not Sollecito) at Merlin's Pub, but she did not go inside the pub. Meredith was at this pub with friends and Knox met the boy outside as he exited the pub, but she did not go inside to speak to Meredith. Knox alluded that she did not know that Meredith was inside the bar, and that she only knew that Meredith had gone to dinner with friends. This may have been because Meredith had not replied to the last two text messages sent by Knox. Maybe there was a reason why Meredith did not want Knox to know where she was going for the evening? In any event, it was well known that Merlin's Pub was Meredith's favorite bar in the area and that she often frequented that establishment.

Mr. Ghirga then takes Knox back to the night of 1 November 2007. There was nothing new that came out of this questioning, just reiteration of information that has already been said. One can wonder what the good lawyer was trying to accomplish by this line of questioning. In fact, Ghirga was trying to go through the day of November 1st with Knox, but she could not remember the times that any of the events had occurred. As Ghirga prodded into the days events, he made several suggestions—leading the witness. This was met by a few objections from Francesco Maresca. There was, however, one interesting piece of testimony to come out of this exchange; one that did not necessarily help the defense. Ghirga asked Knox if she usually turned her phone off at night. Knox responded, "Not usually, because I use it as a clock, an alarm clock, so usually I don't, but on that night I did." Ghirga wisely left that response alone and moved on to November 2nd, but again nothing new or helpful to her defense. At several points during Ghirga's questioning of Knox, it seemed as if he hadn't ever met with her before. Usually in criminal cases such as this, the suspect's lawyer will rehearse the questions with the defendant or at least ask questions that he is aware that his client can answer. Yet, as the questioning continued it became evident that this was not a well thought-out interview.

Mr. Ghirga then requested the judge's permission to play the court an audio tapped conversation between Amanda and Filomena on 5 November 2007, at 10:29p.m. The call—which originated from Knox's phone—was intercepted by police. The two spoke mostly in Italian, then at one point Filomena switched to speaking English. Her English was horrible and hard to understand. Ghirga stopped the tape periodically to ask Knox a question or two then restarted the tape. At the time of the call Knox was in the police station.

Knox had arranged to meet Sollecito at the police station and she was waiting by the elevators for him to arrive. During the call Filomena asks Knox her whereabouts. Knox responds, "At the police station." Filomena seems surprised and asks, "So you're there again today?" The reason for the call was apparently to discuss where they were going to live. The remaining roommates (Laura and Filomena) were trying to get out of the contract with the agency that they had rented the cottage from and find another place. Filomena informed Knox that she had an appointment the following day (November 6th) with that agency to discuss the situation. Again, the purpose of Ghirga playing the call was unclear, other than to show that Knox's main preoccupation was where she was going to be living-out the rest of her days in Perugia. Following the ending of the conversation, Ghirga discusses why neither Knox nor her family were concerned about the continued questioning by police.

Luciano Ghirga: I see. So, in all these days, following the discovery of the body, did you ever think about turning to the American Embassy, or to a lawyer?

Amanda Knox: No.

Luciano Ghirga: Because they were calling you every day to the Questura.

Amanda Knox: No, no. More than anything, I thought they wanted to talk to me so much because I was the closest person to Meredith in the house. And then, I was the person who went back to the house and found the mess. I never thought I needed a lawyer or to talk to the Ambassador, because I thought, okay, I'll just answer a couple of questions, and then I can get on with my life, I don't know. And I still had to orient myself in the world around me; I never even thought of contacting someone like a lawyer.

Luciano Ghirga: And the fact that you were being called every day to the Questura, didn't that worry you and your family?

Amanda Knox: [Sigh] For me, I didn't understand why, but I really never, never thought that they suspected me; never.

Luciano Ghirga: When they arrested you, did they tell you why? When they put the handcuffs on your wrists, on the morning of the 6th?

Amanda Knox: If they told me, I didn't understand it. Because in the end, when I found myself—

Luciano Ghirga: And what did you think, when they put the handcuffs on you?

Amanda Knox: I was surprised. I thought -- they told me "Come on, it's just for a couple of days, because we're protecting you," so I said "All right, fine, but actually, you're not even listening to me." And then in those following days, when I was like ah -- when I was alone in the cell, in those days, I was suddenly brought in front of the judge, with two lawyers, and they said "Ah, you are accused of murdering Meredith," and I just stood there with my mouth open with everybody staring at me like "Hmmm."

Luciano Ghirga: On the morning of the 6th, you didn't understand why they were arresting you.

Amanda Knox: No. No. I -- they -- I thought that, as I had understood from them, that it was a formality that they had to do because there was some testimony that I had been near the scene of the crime or something like that.

Luciano Ghirga: But in the days that you spent in prison before that, before you met the undersigned lawyer Ghirga, what were you thinking during those days? What did you think was happening?

Amanda Knox: In those days, I only wanted to clarify the things that I hadn't understood before, those images that I had imagined, that contradicted the reality that I remembered. This was my main preoccupation. For me, those days were a big moment of crying and confusion, and fear, and cold. Really, it was freezing.

Mr. Ghirga then requests that the remainder of the defenses' questioning be suspended until the following day because he sensed that Knox was getting tired. Judge Massei denied the request, citing that the following days proceedings were scheduled for cross-examination by the prosecution. Knox's defense had squandered precious time on irrelevant issues, and now they were feeling the pressure. Perhaps it was just that Knox didn't really have much to offer in the way of her defense. A discussion ensued, and Judge Massei conceded that he would allot time the next day—only in the morning—for the defense to continue if need be. In the meantime, Judge Massei ordered a ten-minute break.

The questioning recommenced at 5:16p.m., with Carlo Dalla Vedova again taking the floor. Dalla Vedova began with brining Knox back to the 17 December 2007, interrogation. Conducting the seven hour interrogation was the public prosecutor, Giuliano Mignini. Knox recalls that she had an interpreter—Australian born Giulia Clemish. Knox explained that she was quite frustrated with her because she was not a very good interpreter and this led to much confusion. Dalla Vedova pointed out that they had to get a different interpreter to translate the translator. Dalla Vedova then asks about how she got the nickname "Foxy Knoxy." Knox explains that the nickname came out of the fact that she was a defender in soccer and that it also rhymed with her name, "fox," "Knox." Alessandro Clericuzzio, the interpreter responsible for retranslating the whole December 17th interrogation, translated "Foxy Knoxy" to "Mean Fox." Mr. Dalla Vedova was clearly trying to demonstrate how the phrase "Lost in translation" had applied to this situation, which then shows that this could have applied to things Knox had said during other interrogations.

Knox was asked if she knew that Meredith had taken out money prior to her death. Knox said she did not, and then she corrected herself. "Wait, one time she told this thing to Filomena that she could already give her the money and Filomena said no, let's wait a little, but I didn't know if she carried it around in her wallet or left it at home." As Knox indicated in earlier testimony, this conversation was in regard to the rent for November 2007, so Knox did have prior Knowledge to the fact that Kercher had already taken out money to pay the rent.

The final discussion of the day centered around Knox's cell phone discussions with Filomena on the day that Meredith's body was discovered. The final discussion also touched upon the time between when Knox first arrived at the cottage and when the first officers arrived. Judge Massei took over the questioning at one point on the matter to get clarification on Knox's story. His questioning continued for several minutes. Judge Massei asked Knox whether she knew if anyone was home the first time she claimed to arrive at the cottage on the morning of 2 November 2007 (allegedly after leaving Sollecito's flat in the morning and returning to the cottage). Knox told the court that she had called out the names, Filomena and Meredith, thinking that maybe they were home. She said that she knew Filomena was going to a party the previous night and she wasn't sure if she had returned home by then or not. The brief segment that followed was just a reiteration of prior testimony, with Carlo Dalla Vedova retaking command of the floor.

At the conclusion of the defenses' questioning of the witness, Judge Massei asked the prosecution if they wanted to begin their cross-examination. The prosecution seemed eager to get to questioning with Manuela Comodi saying, "We can start now or we can start tomorrow." Judge Massei asked Knox if she could continue, but Knox asked if questioning could be suspended for the day as she was tired. There was no doubt that the day had been long, drawn-out, and grueling for all present—particularly Knox. Realizing this, Judge Massei suspended the proceedings, announcing that they would continue the following morning at 9:00a.m.

Chapter 9 - The Trial of the Century

Meredith Kercher Trial Day 26 – (June 13, 2009)

The 26th day of the trial would be a public court spectacle like the world has never seen. The highly anticipated showdown between Knox, her lawyers, and prosecutors—which many had been looking forward-to for more than a year-and-a-half—had finally arrived. There would be more arguments and objections in the first few hours than in a full year of courtroom activity. To compare the calamity that occurred on this day would be a mix of a WWE wrestling show meets Barnum & Bailey circus with the animals running loose in the crowd. There would be interruption after interruption, objection after objection; Knox's own defense would even object once at the conclusion of one of Knox's own statements.

Judge Massei summed it up when he adamantly stated several times, "It is impossible to continue on this way!" The rabblerousing came mostly from the defense as the head prosecutor Giuliano Mignini fought desperately to ask questions and actually get them answered. It didn't help that Knox answered vaguely and remembered only certain details, but not others. If this was in an American court, Carlo Dalla Vedova would have spent more time in jail for contempt of court than Joe Pesci in the movie *My Cousin Vinnie*. Not to make light of the situation, but it really was a circus while Mignini had the floor.

Morning Session

Knox walked into the small, frescoed courtroom escorted by a female security guard holding her left arm. Wearing jeans, a white halter top with pink spots, a loose black necklace, and her hair tied back with a pink hair-clip; she was led to her seat next to her lawyers. The tense courtroom scene began with the judge addressing all lawyers. He asked them not to repeat questions that have already been answered and to keep the background noise to a minimum. At the end of the discussion Giulia Bongiorno brings up the subject of the presence of television cameras and photographers in the courtroom. After a ten-minute discussion on the subject, it was determined that there would be no video or photographs taken during the questioning. However, cameras flashed and video rolled (allowed by the judge) very briefly as Knox and her interpreter took the stand.

With all of this out of the way it was time for Knox to take the stand. Judge Giancarlo Massei began the proceedings by asking the general public in the courtroom to politely cease the noise and comments; he was trying to set the tone for what was sure to be a conflict-filled day. Judge Massei recalls "trial of Amanda Knox and Raffaele Sollecito," and lists all of the lawyers involved, including the civil plaintiffs. With that, he asks Knox to state her name, etc., for the second time in two days. "Amanda Knox, born July 9, 1987, in Seattle, Washington, USA," she proclaims. When she is done, Judge Massei gives the "go-ahead" to the lead prosecutor Giuliano Mignini and the questioning begins.

The questioning began relatively slowly, with Mignini asking Knox about when she met Sollecito and what she did that day and evening. "It was at a concert at the *Universita per Stranieri* [University of Foreigners]," Knox responded. "I think it was on October 25th. She claimed that she met a friend (Spiros) for coffee in the town's center after the concert, but couldn't remember what she did after. On her own she then moved to the days events on Halloween, claiming that she first went to *Le Chic* then met with Spiros for a second time that day, outside of Merlin's Pub; Spiros then accompanied her to a nearby church where she met Sollecito (most likely the Santa Maria Nuova Church at the entrance of the Dei Tei Arch on Via Pinturicchio, which was close to Sollecito's flat). Mignini then asked Knox if she had ever made use of drugs.

Knox said, "Yes" and stated that she had smoked a joint with Sollecito that evening. Mignini asked Knox several questions regarding the text messages to and from Patrick Lumumba, which she reiterated all prior statements with consistency.

Mr. Mignini followed up the text questions with questions regarding Knox's cell phone activity just after her last text message from Lumumba. He pointed out that her cell phone activity stopped at 8:35p.m., and Sollecito's stopped just seven minutes later, at 8:42p.m. Knox replied that she turned off her phone because she didn't want to get another message from Patrick saying that she had to come into work. She explained that if the bar had gotten busy Patrick might have called her into work and she wanted to stay with Sollecito. This is consistent with what Knox had stated the previous day. Surprisingly, Mignini does not bring up the fact that Patrick had recently reduced her role at the bar. Instead, Mignini pulls out a transcript of Knox's 17 December 2007, interrogation—which Mignini had been present—and quoted her as saying, "I turned off my phone to save my battery." Mignini asked her if she recalled saying that. Knox replied smugly, "Well, if it's written there, it must be okay."

Mignini, trying to prove that Knox frequently changes her versions of events says, "Today you're saying one thing, in the interrogation you said another." Mignini's first test of Knox's character was met with murmuring from the crowd and defense lawyers. "Can you be more precise about the page?" one of Knox's defense lawyers calls out to Mignini in regards to the December 17th transcript. Mignini replies, "Page 40," and without pause he re-reads that portion of the transcript. Mignini then stops, appearing annoyed by the constant mumbling by the defense lawyers. Judge Massei intervenes and asks for silence. One lawyer, who was clearly the one mumbling, explains that they are not interrupting; just trying to find the page that Mignini is quoting. Now Judge Massei seems annoyed and says, "Please, please." Judge Massei says that it is either on page 39 or 40, and alludes to the page number as irrelevant as it is in the transcript somewhere; and he instructs Mignini to continue.

As the questioning continues, Mignini tries to pin Knox down on whether she turned off her phone so that she didn't have to go to work or that she wanted to save her battery—because it was low. Carlo Dalla Vedova stands and objects and several voices are again heard murmuring. Again Judge Massei seems annoyed and acknowledges that he heard the objection. Defense lawyers continue to try to get the judges attention and announce that in the interrogation Knox stated two reasons for turning her phone off that night. Judge Massei clarifies to the entire court that yesterday Knox said that she turned her phone off to guarantee her a free evening without being interrupted, But at the December 17th interrogation she said that it was both to save battery and also for this reason.

Still not satisfied, Dalla Vedova says, "The objection isn't about that. It's about..." Determined to keep order, Judge Massie cuts him off. "Excuse me, please. This is an analysis; let's return to the cross-examination by the pubblico ministero. The defense lawyers will have the final words. Everyone will hear what they have to say then." However, Dalla Vedova was even more determined to continue his interruptions. "My objection was because the introductory request...," he utters. "Please, please," Massei says, "Enough now." Yet Dalla Vedova spitefully continues. "My objection concerned the way the pubblico ministero presented his question." Dalla Vedova continues, reiterating what Judge Massei had already stated: that Knox had two reasons for turning off her phone that night. "Excuse me, fine, we heard," Massei responds. Again spitefully, Dalla Vedova says, "It wasn't an objection," despite the fact that he himself had called it *an objection* just seconds earlier. Judge Massei then explains again that the defense will have their time later to analyze and determine whether Mignini has contradicted or misquoted the text in any way. Mignini, who had patiently remained silent through the bickering says, "I would like not to be interrupted." Still appearing annoyed by Dalla Vedova's outburst, Judge Massei gives Mignini the go ahead.

Continuing, Mignini then asks Knox why she never mentioned Patrick Lumumba's name before the November 6th declarations. Knox replies that it was in that, and only that, interrogation that Patrick's name was suggested to her. Mignini appeared to have other questions for the subject ready at that time, but he says that he will get to them later. He then begins to challenge Knox on her definition of "suggestion," trying to capitalize on her last statement. He reminds Knox that she stated that the name Patrick was suggested to her and that she was hit and pressured. "Yes," Knox relies. "The name of Patrick didn't just pop up like a mushroom" Mignini said, and he asked Knox to explain step-by-step exactly how his name was suggested and who hit her. Knox appeared to be avoiding giving an answer. Judge Massei interrupts and says that the question is quite clear and asks Knox to recall exactly what was suggested to her and who the person was who hit her.

Instead of responding directly to the question, Knox started her story from the beginning; when she had first arrived at the police station on November 5th. As Mignini saw that she was going to give a long-winded version of the events, he cut her off. "Excuse me, excuse me" Mignini says. Knox replies by reprimanding Mignini sharply and coldly, "Can I tell the story?" Mignini responds politely, "Excuse me for interrupting you, otherwise we'll forget." However, this did not fly with Dalla Vedova; who obstinately objects. Dalla Vedova cited his reason for the objection, saying that if a question is asked all should wait for the answer. "It's impossible to go on like this, no, no," attested Mignini. A brief exchange ensued between Mignini and Massei, but this time Massei was not having it. "No, no, no! Interruptions are absolutely not allowed!" Massei replied. After restoring order, Judge Massei posed the questions again; this time asking for Knox to be more detailed in her answer, and he reiterated; no interruptions.

Knox explains that she understands the question and begins a five-minute or so explanation of the events. Just as anticipated, Knox gives a long-winded, confusing response that did not answer the two specific questions asked. Taking advantage of a slight pause in her speech, Judge Massei slipped in. "Excuse me, excuse me, the pubblico ministero wants to hear precise details about the suggestions about what to say, and also about the cuffs, who gave them to you." Knox told the court that police did not believe her story and that they continually called her a liar and threatened that if she did not tell them the truth that she would go to prison for 30 years. Knox continued on, claiming that the situation was a "continuous crescendo." Still, however, she was not answering the questions asked. Taking advantage of slight stammer from Knox, Judge Massei intervened. "Excuse me; okay, we understand that there was a continuous crescendo…But if we could now get to the questions of the pubblico minister…" Judge Massei again reiterates both questions to Knox. Judge Massei took over the questioning for a while as Knox had a hard time explaining the details of her interrogation. She also continued to explain, but avoided answering Mignini and Massei's questions.

After an even longer explanation by Knox, still not answering the questions, Judge Massei seemed irritated and said point blank, "So, the pubblico ministero asked you, and is still asking you, who is the person that gave you these two blows that you just showed us on yourself?" Knox replied, "It was a policewoman, but I didn't know their names." Seeing as how they were back on track, Judge Massei relinquished the floor back to Mignini. But the questions still would be avoided as bedlam broke out. "So, now, I asked you a question, and I did not get an answer. You...," Mignini stated, but was interrupted by an objection from Luciano Ghirga. However, Judge Massei was having none of it, and again warned the defense team to hold off on the interruptions. "But...," Ghirga said, but was cut off by Massei, who continued to restate; no interruptions. Judge Massei then reprimanded Mignini, asking him to please avoid analysis or personal evaluation of the answers.

Thus far, Knox had spoken of the interrogation as if she was not aware that she was a suspect or why the police were pressuring her. Mignini returned to questioning: "You must have understood that there was a murder, and this was a police station, and the investigation was hot; and what I am asking you is; who was actually conducting the interrogation?" Before Knox could answer, Judge Massei again took over questioning. Massei wanted Knox to answer the original questions, starting with a description of the person who hit her. Knox ignored the question and began describing the person who was doing the interrogation. Massei interrupted and informed her that she was starting with the second question, but advised her to continue. Knox explained that there were lots of people asking her questions, but the main interrogator was a policewoman with long, chestnut brown hair—Knox could not remember her name. Knox claimed that there were others circling her and she was unable to see who gave her the first blow because it came from behind her. Knox claims that after the blow, she turned and saw the women who had hit her. As she turned she told the court that the same women hit her again. Oddly enough, however, Knox stated that the same women she described as the lead interrogator (the policewoman with long, chestnut brown hair) was the same woman who struck her twice from behind. This is odd because the lead interrogator—the person asking most of the questions—would almost always be stationed in front of the suspect. Judge Massei again returned questioning to Mignini.

Prosecutor Mignini resumed, going back to the second question: who suggested Patrick Lumumba's name (as Knox indicated in prior testimony)? First, Mignini wanted to get Knox's definition of the word "suggestions," as he stated from Knox's description of the word that he didn't see any suggestion. Immediately Mignini's question was met with strong and loud objections. Judge Massei quickly tried to quell the defense.

Judge Massei: "Excuse me, excuse me, please, please, excuse me, excuse me! Listen, the pubblico ministero is asking you: 'suggestions.' You also mentioned words that were 'put in your mouth,' versions, things to say, circumstances to describe. The pubblico ministero is asking two things: who made the suggestions, and what exactly were you told to say?"

Amanda Knox: All right. It seems to me that the thoughts of the people standing around me, there were so many people, and they suggested things to me in the sense that they would ask questions like: "Okay, you met someone!" No, I didn't. They would say "Yes you did, because we have this telephone here that says that you wanted to meet someone. You wanted to meet him." No, I don't remember that. "Well, you'd better remember, because if not we'll put you in prison for 30 years." But I don't remember! "Maybe it was him that you met? Or him? You can't remember?" It was this kind of suggestion.

Judge Massei: When you say they said "Maybe you met him?" Did they specify names?

Amanda Knox: Well, the important fact was this message to Patrick; they were very excited about it. So they wanted to know if I had received a message from him –

Suddenly multiple voices began screaming out, unintelligible because they all spoke at the same time. "It's not possible to go on this way!" Dalla Vedova said aloud. Then Mignini yelled something to Dalla Vedova. Judge Massei tried to restore order. "Please, please, excuse me, excuse me!" Massie shouted. Then Mignini shouted, "I'm going to ask to suspend the audience! I demand a suspension of five minutes!" Both sides continue to argue as Judge Massei tries unsuccessfully to restore order. Judge Massei finally announces that the court will make the decision on whether to suspend or not. This leads to several moments of silence in which the two judges speak quietly to each other. Judge Massei then announces that there will be no suspension, and explains that the accused (Knox) has offered answers to every question thus far. He orders that the prosecution (indirectly) must refrain from asking the same questions over and over; and he further explains that the accused goes under different rules than the witness, and can at any time stop answering questions and exercise her right to silence (as Sollecito has done). Judge Massei asks Knox if she is ok to continue, and she says that she is fine. Judge Massie continues, again taking over the questioning.

Judge Massie actually proved to be a skilled questioner, and he managed to extract from Knox that her phone did not show Patrick's name, and that she was the one who first mentioned him, when asked about the message. Note: this was the message that Knox had sent to Patrick, because she had previously (prior to the interrogation) deleted the messages that she had received from him. Judge Massei then relinquished the questioning back to Mignini. Resuming his original question, Mignini points out that in the Italian language, the word "suggerimento" (Suggestion) means someone who 'suggests' a name, actually says the name, and the other person adopts it. Continuing, Mignini asks Knox if it was her or police who first mentioned the name Patrick, and if it was pronounced after having seen the text message or before the message was seen. Immediately Dalla Vedova called for an objection. Interestingly enough, after calling for the objection, Dalla Vedova actually says, "Before the objection, what was the question?" So, he objected to a question that he didn't hear or understand. In any case, Judge Massei reiterated Mignini's question.

Knox stated that police kept shoving the phone message in her face and calling her a 'stupid liar' because she claims that she kept telling them that she didn't remember writing the message. Knox says that they kept pressuring her to remember, and that is when she was struck on the back of the head. Then Judge Massei made an interesting and true statement of clarity. "Remember!" is not a suggestion. It is a strong solicitation of your memory." Knox appeared to try to cover her misuse of the word 'suggestion' by saying, "But it was always 'Remember' following this same idea, that..." Massei cut her off, "But they didn't literally say that it was him?" Knox finally conceded, but with an explanation. She claimed that they did not literally say his name, "but they said 'We know who it is, we know who it is. You were with him, you met him.'" This is standard police procedure—making suspects think they know more than they do—which Knox seemed to indicate was why she gave Patrick's name, fingering him as the killer. It certainly was a strong point made by Massei and the prosecution, which did not play well for Knox and her team. "So, these were the suggestions?" Massei asked for clarification. "Yes," Knox replied.

Judge Massei passes the questioning back to Mignini, who immediately objects based on the dynamics of Knox's answer; as he believes there to be a contrast with what she stated in the December 17th interrogation. Mignini instructs the court to page 95 of the interrogation and argues that the police could not have suggested. Cross-talking ensues as several lawyers complain that the page numbers are different in their versions. Judge Massei reminds the court that while Mignini is talking there should be no interruptions. Massei confirms that the page numbers are different on some versions held by different lawyers. Mignini begins reading Knox's answer during the interrogation in regards to when she first named Patrick: "The police were saying, 'We know that you were in the house. We know you were in the house.' And one moment before I said Patrick's name, someone was showing me the message I had sent him." With that Mignini placed his objection on the fact that Knox stated that she mentioned Patrick's name immediately after police showed her the text message she had sent him. He noted that this was the precise moment when Knox mentioned Patrick for the first time, after police were showing her the message, which at that time they didn't know who the message was from. His point was that police never suggested Patrick nor did they show her the text and continually state, "You were with him." This was significant, because it corroborated the testimony of all of the officers present at the interrogation, as well as Knox's original statement on December 17th.

More cross-talking and arguing broke out after Mignini's explanation of his objection. "Excuse me, excuse me...excuse me, excuse me," Judge Massei says furiously as to quell the arguing. Once everyone quiets down a bit, Judge Massei reiterates Mignini's objection to the court. "Do you confirm the declarations that the pubblico ministero read out?" Judge Massei asks Knox. "I explained it better now," she replies. Then Mignini asked Knox what happened next. Knox then goes into an explanation reminiscent of her 'spontaneous written statement,' where she speaks of her visions of what might have occurred at the cottage during the murder.

> **Amanda Knox**: Well, first I started to cry. And all the policemen, together, started saying to me, you have to tell us why, what happened? They wanted all these details that I couldn't tell them, because in the end, what happened was this: when I said the name of "Patrick," I suddenly started imagining a kind of scene, but always using this idea: images that didn't agree; that maybe could give some kind of explanation of the situation. I saw Patrick's face, then Piazza Grimana, then my house; then something green that they told me might be the sofa. Then, following this, they wanted details; they wanted to know everything I had done. But I didn't know how to say. So they started talking to me, saying, "Okay, so you went out of the house, okay, fine, so you met Patrick, where did you meet Patrick?" I don't know, maybe in Piazza Grimana, maybe near it; because I had this image of Piazza Grimana. "Okay, fine, so you went with him to your house. Okay, fine. How did you open the door?" Well, with my key. "So you opened the house." Okay, yes. "And what did you do then?" I don't know. "But was she already there?" I don't know. "Did she arrive or was she already there?" Okay. "Who was there with you?" I don't know. "Was it just Patrick, or was Raffaele there too?" I don't know. It was the same when the

pubblico ministero came, because he asked me: "Excuse me, I don't understand. Did you hear the sound of a scream?" No. "But how could you not have heard the scream?" I don't know, maybe my ears were covered. I kept on and on saying I don't know, maybe, imagining...

This statement from Knox certainly did not help her position. It appeared as if she was trying to reasonably explain this part of the interrogation as being the fault of the police, and not actually taking responsibility for the things that were coming out of her own mouth. Judge Massie actually cut her off and said, "Okay, okay. Go ahead, pubblico ministero." Before Mignini could start, Carlo Dalla Vedova stands and says, "I'd like to ask a question, I'd like to make an objection." This was a rare instance where a lawyer actually objects to a statement made from his own client. More cross talking begins and Mignini asks, "Is it a question or an objection?" Judge Massei again calls for no interruptions. "I said, I am asking a question and making an objection," Dalla Vedova answers. Realizing that Dalla Vedova was apparently objecting to his own clients answer, Judge Massie asks that Mignini be allowed to continue uninterrupted. Frustrated with the continued interruptions, Mignini says, "I appeal to the court that this is making the examination impossible." Judge Massei calls for Mignini to continue, but Dalla Vedova stands up again and interrupts Mignini before he can finish the first sentence of what he was about to say. Now more frustrated than ever, Judge Massei says (apparently to Dalla Vedova) "But it's not possible to hinder things this way, avvocato (Lawyer). Excuse me. Why?"

Possibly realizing that his client had just made some damaging statements in her last monologue, Dalla Vedova desperately announces, "The defense would like to formally ask for a break?" Judge Massei seems puzzled. "We haven't even heard what he [Mignini] is trying to say yet. You can't make preventive objections! I'm sorry, avvocato (Lawyer)." Della Vedova tries to stall for time. "I'm not making an objection," he says as he continues to talk loudly to others. Trying desperately to stop him from talking, Judge Massei pleads with Della Vedova to remain quiet. "Please, please avvocato, no no no no, the pubblico ministero is speaking!" Mignini has some words with Della Vedova. "Excuse me, excuse me," Judge Massei says again, but Della Vedova continues his tirade. At this point Judge Massei really needs a gavel to bang, but in the Italian Justice System they do not use Gavels. This segment in the trial would make a good argument that they certainly need one.

With the tirade far from over, Mignini again says a few unpleasant things to Della Vedova. "Please, pubblico ministero! Please! Now, excuse me," Judge Massei again pleads. Judge Massei finally gets the two to settle down for a moment and explains that the tone of the conversation between the two "has gotten bitter and loud." This gets them going once again, but only momentarily. Judge Massei explains "...but we are getting the impression that the objections are preventive." Judge Massei orders that while Mignini is speaking he should be afforded the same right to question as was the defense was the day before. Massei also orders that the tone should always remain cordial. Before he is able to finish his sentence, Della Vedova cannot help himself from interrupting again. "Yes, yes, no, no. But it's just that, I am asking that—" However, Judge Massei had finally had enough. "Please, avvocato (Lawyer). There's no reason!" Judge Massei somehow restores order and tries to reiterate to the court where they had left off before the ruckus. Judge Massei explains to the court what Knox meant by the prior statement ("She wasn't speaking of an effective memory of circumstances that had effectively occurred in her perception; that is the meaning of the response of the accused), to which Knox agrees.

Then Mignini quickly jumps in. "But you said that you remembered Piazza Grimana," Mignini asks. "I had an image of Piazza Grimana," Knox replies. Mignini takes her back to the December 17th interrogation and reads Knox's original answer to the question regarding the text message. Knox had simply stated that Patrick had sent her a text message not to come to work and she answered the question. Mignini then asked Knox why then didn't she just stick to that story and end her response on it. Instead, Mignini asserted—faced with the message, and the questions of the police—that Knox threw out this accusation, accusing Lumumba. "So I am asking you," Mignini said. "Why start accusing him [Patrick] when you could calmly explain the exchange of messages? Why did you think those things [images/visions] could be true?" Knox replied that she was confused. Mignini was not satisfied with

Knox's reply. He begins to press her story of confusion and images/visions in a very resourceful and reasonable fashion.

You have repeated that many times (in regards to being confused). But what does it mean? Either something is true, or it isn't true. Right now, for instance, you're here at the audience, you couldn't be somewhere else. You couldn't say "I am at the station." You are right here, right now." Knox replies, "Certainly," and some crowd noise begins. "The question is clear," Judge Massei declares. "Can I answer?" Knox asks quite rudely. The crowd reacts to Knox's rude retort.

Quelling the noise, Judge Massei says," Excuse me, excuse me!" Then he asks Knox to proceed. Knox explains that she changed her story because they called her and liar so many times—saying that she was at the murder—that she eventually became so confused that she didn't know what was real anymore. Then Knox claims that at one point she became convinced that she just might have forgotten and was at the cottage when Meredith was killed. "I didn't understand anything anymore. I was so scared and impressed by all this that at some point I thought, what the heck, maybe they're right, maybe I forgot." This is another damaging statement as Knox is actually trying to convince the court that in her confusion she thought that she could have been at the cottage during murder. This is also a contradiction from what she said a few minutes before (and in other testimony); that she only described the images because she wanted to give the police what they wanted to hear so that she could go home. In that version she is saying that she didn't actually believe that the statements could be true. However, in this explanation, Knox tells the court point blank, that she was so confused at that point, that she couldn't remember if she was present at the cottage at the time of a murder, which occurred only four days before these admissions.

The next part of Mignini's questioning went relatively smooth. It was Mignini's attempt at this time to try and get Knox to slip-up on her time table of the events on November 1st (Night of the murder) and 2nd (day body was discovered). However, it would be Knox's excuse of her memory loss that would try and stop that from happening. Knox testified that the water leak in Sollecito's apartment on November 1st occurred after dinner, but she couldn't remember the time. When pressed by Mignini (and after several 'I don't know' gestures), she estimated that they had eaten dinner around 10:30p.m., and it happened after that; so she claimed around 11:00p.m. When asked what time that she arrived back at Sollecito's flat the next morning to clean up the leak, Knox claimed that she "didn't look at the clock," but she estimated that she left his flat at around 10:30a.m., and must have returned before midday. She then clarified that it was probably around 11:30a.m., when she returned— and again she reiterated that she "didn't look at the clock."

Mignini made it a point to ask Knox where she was at the time that Meredith's door was broken down and her body discovered. He was attempting to prove that neither she nor anyone else was akin to the details of the murder at that time; yet that Knox somehow relayed the gory details to her friends at the police station on November 2nd. Knox admits that both she and Sollecito were near the entrance of the living room when the door was opened, and that neither she nor Sollecito had gotten a glimpse into Meredith's room. Mignini pointed out that Amy Frost and others testified that Knox and Sollecito had claimed to have seen Meredith's body in the closet. Knox replied, "All right, firstly, I think Frost made a little mistake, because I never said that I saw Meredith's body in the closet. I said that I had heard people around me saying that there was a body in the closet that was covered, with a foot sticking out." Knox testified that the group was largely speaking Italian, so Sollecito was the one who was asking the people around them (when the body was first discovered) what they had seen. As he retrieved information from others he relayed it back to Knox. Mignini turns to page 79 of the December 17th interrogation and reads what Knox asserted that Sollecito had told her in the garden outside the cottage. "Apparently there's a girl, there's the body of a girl in the closet, but the only thing you can see is her foot."

Mignini then moves to the November 6th 'Spontaneous written statement" that Knox gave police as a "gift" (as she referred to it). Mignini reiterates Knox's earlier testimony, that she was pressured by police into making the false accusations about Patrick Lumumba. He also again reminded the court that Knox had spoke of the "suggestions" made by police during the interrogation. "Then you wrote a memorandum in which you confirm everything," Mignini says. "And you weren't under pressure right then. Why didn't you just say: 'I falsely accused someone?' Can you explain this to me?" Knox agrees to explain it, but before she can, Della

Verdova makes an objection, making sure to do it calmly (but almost seems to mock Judge Massei). "Can I make an objection, very, very calmly and without animosity?" Seemingly grateful for the calm, Judge Massei shows his gratitude. "Thank you, thank you, thank you, thank you, thank you." This time Della Verdova had a good reason for objecting; over the fact that Mignini claimed that Knox wrote the memorandum "confirming" everything.

Judge Massei took note of the objection and took over questioning again briefly. "As the pubblico ministero notes, Massei explained to Knox. "You wrote the memorandum spontaneously. We heard that you yourself asked for paper to be able to write it." Knox agrees. "And writing with this liberty," Massei continues, "you even referred to it as a gift, these elements which had already emerged; you reasserted them, and this involvement of Patrick Lumumba…in these different circumstances, you weren't in the room any more, there wasn't any pressure, why didn't the truth somehow get stabilized?" Knox proceeds to give another one of her very strange answers to this question. She says, "Yes, yes. In fact, what happened is that I had literally been led to believe that somehow, I had forgotten something real, and so with this idea that I must have forgotten, I was practically convinced myself that I really had forgotten…" Knox continues with this puzzling explanation until she is interrupted by Judge Massei, who seems just as puzzled by her answer. He asks her if she remembers what she wrote in the memorandum, but he is interrupted by Mignini.

"I want to contest this point, Mignini asserts. "Two points in the memorandum. If I'm not mistaken, you weren't a witness right then. You had been the object of an arrest warrant. You had been arrested. You know the difference between a suspect and a witness. You weren't a witness. Not any longer. So in the memorandum…" Before he can finish he is interrupted by Della Verdova, who asks if Knox knows the difference between a witness and a suspect. This angers Mignini greatly, and he goes off on a tangent! "Can I continue? Sorry, avvocato (Lawyer), but I'm asking questions! Can I continue? He's continually…" Judge Massei tries again to stop and argument and apologizes for Della Verdova, and asks Mignini to continue. However, Mignini is in a rage. "This is impossible!" he shouts. "Please, pubblico ministero, go ahead, go ahead," Massei says. "I am interrogating. I am interrogating. Now I'm distracted." Mignini finally composes himself and continues.

Mignini had reason to be upset, because he was onto something. This was a pivotal point in Knox's testimony, because Mignini was now going to point out some of Knox's contradictions that would be very tough for her to talk her way out of. Knox claimed in earlier testimony that she "made these declarations [to police about Patrick] so that I could leave." Yet Mignini further explains his problems with her statements:

Giuliano Mignini: But instead, you were arrested. And you wrote the memorandum after you had been arrested. And you wrote two sentences: I'll read them. *'I stand by my statements that I made last night about events that could have taken place in my home with Patrick.'* Do you know what the word "confirm" means in Italian? 'In the flashbacks that I'm having, I see Patrick as the murderer.' There wasn't any policeman with you when you wrote that. No one! You wrote that in complete liberty. Do you know how to explain to me why? And this is even more decisive than what you said some hours earlier. Can you explain this?

Now it was Knox's time to respond to the most crucial of questions in the most crucial of moments. Yet, it was as if she still did not understand the weight of her answer, and she just couldn't pull out the rabbit.

Amanda Knox: I couldn't even explain to myself why I had these images in my head, because I didn't know if they were memories or not. And I want to say that if I made these declarations, that they asked me to sign and everything, I did it, but I wanted in the memorandum to explain my doubt, this fact that I wasn't sure about it, because no one ever wanted to listen when I said listen, I don't know.

Knox proved here that even after she was arrested for her declarations and had time to write down and re-think her thoughts, she still wrote down a very damning confession. The fact that she wrote down that she was unclear what was real and what was not from what she said makes it hard to believe; particularly considering that the murder occurred only four days before. Knox continually painted herself into a corner, and even when given the liberty to write freely, with no pressure, she faltered to what was ultimately going to be perceived as her guilty conscience.

Moreover, Knox claimed that she gave the written statement to police as a "gift." This was the same officers who she claimed "struck her twice in the back of the head," then she gave them a gift. Even Judge Massei could not refrain from making a comment on the lack of understanding of her explanation. "Effectively the memorandum was correcting what had been said, and these doubts arose?" Mignini then asks Knox if she suffered from lapses of memory. Again, seemingly not understanding the severity of the situation Knox inappropriately chuckles with levity and says, "I've had that problem all my life." Stunned by this admission, Mignini says, "What?" Knox then inappropriately jokes and says again, "I've had that problem all my life. I can't remember where I put my keys." Like a shark smelling blood, Mignini begins to circle.

Giuliano Mignini: So it happened to you at other times? Explain it to me. You previously mixed up things, didn't know whether you had dreamed things or they were real?

Knox catches herself here and seems to pull herself back in— realizing that she is digging a hole.

Amanda Knox: No, not that part about the imagination! I would forget for example what I ate yesterday for dinner, yes, that happened to me, but not to actually imagine things.

With his feet under him now, Mignini continued to hammer away at Knox's written inconsistencies following her arrest. Switching to Knox's written Memorandum on November 7th, Mignini quoted Knox: "I didn't lie when I said that I thought the murderer was Patrick. At that moment I was very stressed and I really did think that it was Patrick. But now I know that I can't know who the murderer is, because I remember that I didn't go home." Mignini then asks Knox a poignant question which raises a very interesting point. Since Knox had basically alluded to the fact that she knew on November 7th that she didn't know who the murderer was—basically exonerating Patrick—Mignini asks, "But didn't you feel the need to intervene to get an innocent person out of prison?" Knox responds by saying that the police had already branded her a liar and she didn't think that they would listen to her. It was a spiteful concept pointed out by Knox: seemingly saying that the police had already called her a liar so let them figure the truth out on their own. Mignini then scolded Knox, telling her that the right thing to do, regardless of whether she felt that the police would believe her or not, would have been to send him (Mignini) a letter declaring that Patrick was innocent and that she didn't tell the truth. Judge Massei blocked Knox from answering; pointing out that she had already given a response to that question.

Mr. Mignini then brings up the incident in Seattle when Knox was fined for having a party with loud music, sex, and kids throwing rocks at cars. He cited the article from the UK's *Daily Mail* that detailed the incident, the police report, and a witness who saw multiple sex acts and drug usage at the party. Knox admitted that there was beer and a lot of noise at the party, but denied witnessing any drug usage. Nothing relevant came from this testimony, other than Mignini's attempt to paint Knox, even further, as a drug-crazed, sex-crazed party girl. Mignini also brought up the incident when Knox was brought back to the cottage after the murder and had a break-down, of sorts, when she was shown the knives in the knife draw. Knox explained that she was disturbed when she was shown the knives and that the reality of what had occurred had hit her all at once at that moment.

Mignini then brought up the black lamp with a red button that was found in Meredith's room at the foot of her bed. Knox admitted that the lamp was "supposedly" hers (Knox's), but denied ever witnessing if it was missing from her room after the murder or if Meredith could have had one just like it. Mignini believed that the lamp was taken out of Knox's room and used to assist in the clean up effort by Knox and Sollecito, and subsequently left in Meredith's room accidentally in their haste. Knox told Mignini and the court that she knew that the boys who lived downstairs had said that they wanted to celebrate Halloween night somewhere or other, but she claimed she didn't know where or for how long they were going to be away. She admitted to being present when they were discussing their plans, but she said that she didn't really understand what they were saying (i.e. didn't understand the language). Mignini made several gestures and references (i.e. saying "Hm" several times) when Knox was answering, which he was seemingly alluding to the fact that he did not believe she was being honest with her answers. Mignini also asked Knox if she remembers if Sollecito received any phone calls on the evening of November 1st. He was referring to the call from Sollecito's father at 8:42p.m. Knox claimed that she didn't remember.

Mr. Mignini continued trying to point out inconsistencies and irrationalities with Knox's version of events. He asked her if she remembered on November 2nd if Sollecito tried to knock down Meredith's door. Knox said, "Yes." Mignini seemed puzzled and ask Knox how then later, when Filomena Romanelli arrived, that Knox told the group that it was normal for Meredith's door to be locked. Knox claimed that she never said that Meredith's door was always locked. She explained that she didn't think it strange that Meredith's door was locked, but she thought it strange that it was locked and she (Meredith) was not answering. However, she clarified that she did state to those present that it wasn't abnormal for Meredith to lock her door. This contradicted what others present at the time had stated in their testimonies, which was that Knox made it sound as if Meredith's door being locked was a normal occurrence and not something to be concerned about. Judge Massei also appeared puzzled by Knox's answer, and he grilled her on it for several minutes.

Judge Massei: "Yes, but 'per carita' ('for heaven's sake'), still on this circumstance. A door is locked; why should I think there is someone inside who isn't answering me? I could just calmly think that nobody is there…and if she's not home, why should I be worried? Enough to ruin the door by breaking it down? Why should I think that there is someone there who is not answering me? The simplest answer is that she left, locked the door and left. She's not answering, why call her? The door is locked, she's not there."

Amanda Knox: I know. But the fact that there were all these strange things in the house—

(Judge Massei clearly shows his frustration and lack of belief in Knox's answer.)

Judge Massei: No, excuse me. 'Per carita' ('for heaven's sake'). After this, the other party will continue the examination. I want to say: you find the main door open; you can think that she left and forgot to close it, but she locked her own door. Why should you be so worried that you try to break down her door? I think this is what the pubblico ministero is asking. There, if you could explain why you were so worried in relation to your knowledge, your motive for trying to break down the door?

Amanda Knox: Yes. I was worried that somehow she was inside and had hurt herself, because there were so many strange things in the house, and so I didn't know what to think. But at the same time, she could have been inside or not, but I wanted to be sure, because if she had hurt herself in some way, or if someone was in there, or if she went out because there was something in there, I didn't know. And the fact that the door was locked together with the broken window had me very worried, I didn't know what to think, but I was worried. So I wanted to knock the door down to see if there was something in there. I didn't know what. But at the same time it worried me. And when I said to Filomena 'It's not true that it's never locked,' I only wanted to explain the truth of the situation. Because someone was saying 'No, no, it's never locked,' and that wasn't true. I wanted to explain that.

Afternoon Session

Very shortly after, at 11:17a.m., Judge Massei called for a suspension of the proceedings (a break) to reconvene at 11:30a.m. Once the questioning resumed, Mignini went right back to work; again trying to prove Knox to be a liar. One of his first questions to Knox was, "Raffaele didn't by any chance try to break down the door to get back the lamp we talked about?" Perfectly calmly and reasonably sounding, Knox claimed that they didn't even know that the lamp was in there. "You didn't know that your lamp was in there?" Mignini asked, as if he was in utter disbelief. Knox's word-play and creative semantic response does not indicate that the lamp found in Meredith's room was even hers. "In the sense that the lamp that was supposed to be in my room, I hadn't even noticed it was missing." Knox then re-explains why she tried to knock down Meredith's door. Satisfied with the job he had done, Mignini wraps up his questioning and passes the floor to the other public prosecutor, Manuela Comodi.

Both prosecutors had prearranged which questions each would be asking Knox, in an attempt not to ask the same questions and to focus on certain aspects of the case. Manuela Comodi clearly had been waiting to ask Knox about the phone call she had made to her mother on the morning of November 2nd. Comodi asked Knox when she had called her mother for the first time on that day. Knox said that she had called her mother for the first time that day immediately after Meredith's door had been broken down and the group was sent out of the house by police; Knox testified that she sat on the ground outside and called her mother at that time.

Unlike Mr. Mignini, prosecutor Comodi went straight into attack-mode. Comodi—a more skilled interrogator than Mignini—pointed out that the actual phone records and pings indicate that Knox first called her mother that day at 12 noon, Perugia time. "Okay," Knox responded, as if indifferent to the facts. This is significant, because by Knox's explanation of when she called, it couldn't have been before 1:00p.m., (this is certain). There is a nine-hour difference in time between Perugia and Seattle, which means that if it's 12 noon in Perugia, its 3:00a.m., in Seattle. (Note: the call referred to here actually occurred at 12:47p.m., Perugia time.) Regardless, Knox claims that the first time that she called her mother was after Meredith's door had been broken down and they had been sent out of the house. This is also significant, because Knox's mother was scheduled to testify in the coming days, and even she had indicated early on to police that the first call from her daughter came in at the time the pings specify (3:47a.m., Seattle time). The following testimony is compelling and pivotal to the case and Knox's alibi:

Manuela Comodi: But at 12 nothing had happened yet. That's what your mother also said –

Amanda Knox: I told my mother –

Manuela Comodi: --during the conversation you had with her in prison, even your mother was amazed that you called her at midday, which was three or four o'clock at night, to tell her that nothing had happened.

Amanda Knox: I didn't know what had happened. I just called my mother to say that we had been sent out of the house and that I had heard something—

Manuela Comodi: But at midday nothing had happened yet in the sense that the door had not been broken down yet.

Amanda Knox: Hm. Okay. I don't remember that phone call. I remember that I called her to tell her what we had heard about a foot. Maybe I did call before, but I don't remember it.

Manuela Comodi: But if you called her before, why did you do it?

Amanda Knox: I don't remember, but if I did it, I would have called to--

Manuela Comodi: You did do it.

Amanda Knox: Okay, fine. But I don't remember. I don't remember that phone call.

At this point Jude Massei decides to intervene. Massei appears to be concerned that Knox is suggesting that maybe the phone call did not even take place, when in fact it is quite clear that it did.

Judge Massei: Excuse me. You might not remember it, but the Public Minister [Comodi] has just pointed out to you a phone call that your mother received in the small hours.

Manuela Comodi: At three o'clock in the morning.

Judge Massei: So, that must be true. That did happen. Were you in the habit of calling her at such an hour? Did you do this on other occasions? At midday in Italy, which corresponds in Seattle to a time when, it's just that we [in Italy] don't usually call each other in the middle of the night.

Amanda Knox: Yes, yes, that's true.

Judge Massei: So either you had a particular reason on that occasion, or else it was a routine. This is what the Public Minister is referring to.

Amanda Knox: Yes. Well, since I don't remember this phone call, although I do remember the one I made later, ah, but, obviously I made that phone call. So, if I made that phone call, it's because I had, or thought that I had, something I had to tell her. Maybe I thought even then that there was something strange, because at that moment, when I'd gone to Raffaele's place, I did think there was something strange, but I didn't know what to think. But I really don't remember this phone call, so I can't say for sure why. But I suppose it was because I came home and the door was open, and then--

Manuela Comodi: It's strange. You don't remember the phone call, but do you remember the conversation with your mother in prison?

Amanda Knox: I had so many. But yes.

Manuela Comodi: This conversation must have been the one of the 10th of November. Do you remember when your mother said 'But at 12, nothing had happened yet.'

Amanda Knox: I don't remember that.

Amanda continues to insist that she cannot recall making the phone call that looks to have triggered the self-incriminating 112 calls. To even a neutral observer those phone calls seem to indicate botched attempts to gather more witnesses to their having 'innocently stumbled upon the crime scene and then called the police.' The phone records show that Amanda had made one phone call to Meredith's phone (at 12:07p.m.) and then to Filomena (at 12:08p.m.). Then she made two more calls to both of Meredith's phones (at 12:11p.m. and again at 12:11p.m). Amanda testified that Meredith's Italian phone "just rang and rang," but phone records prove that it rang for only three seconds. Why? Maybe Knox knew that Meredith could not answer. All of these calls came before the arrival of the postal police. So, if Knox was not trying to strengthen her alibi or gain other witnesses to her having innocently stumbled across the crime scene; why exactly did she call her mother? Amanda's answer is, "I don't remember this phone call, so I can't say for sure why."

Mrs. Comodi skillfully bounced around, hitting Knox with different questions in an attempt to keep her off balance and uncomfortable. Knox responded well to the pressure in her demeanor, but not with her answers. Comodi also is a good listener, and she reacted sharply when Knox showed the slightest contradiction or idiosyncrasy in her story. For instance, Comodi asked Knox if she had left Sollecito's flat at around 10:30a.m., on the morning of November 2nd. Knox confirmed this, as she has stated several times. "You went to get the mop," Comodi asked. "Yes, to take a shower and change, and get the mop, yes." Picking up on this, Comodi asked, "But hadn't you taken a shower the evening before, at Raffaele's place?" Comodi was surely referring to Knox's "spontaneous written statement," on November 6th when she wrote, "In truth, I do not remember exactly what day it was, but I do remember that we had a shower and we washed ourselves for a long time. He cleaned my ears; he dried and combed my hair."

Although Knox did write that she didn't know what day it was, she took the bait from Comodi nonetheless. "Yes," Knox admitted, "but then we made love, so I wanted to take another shower." Not believing her, Comodi asked, "The next day? Not right away after, but the next day?" Knox claimed that she had fallen asleep after having sex with Sollecito, so she wanted to take a shower when she awoke, which she claimed was the next morning. Without pause (seeing as Knox had somewhat thwarted her efforts), Comodi switched the line of questioning, asking Knox where she bought the marijuana. Knox said that she never bought marijuana in Italy; rather she smoked only when her friends had some. Comodi then asked where Sollecito got the marijuana from that they smoked together on the night of Meredith's murder. Knox again replied sarcastically, "I don't know. I don't know the people who give out marijuana." With that, Comodi told the court that she had no other questions, and she relinquished the floor to Kercher family lawyer, Francesco Maresca.

Mr. Maresca wasted no time, and took the floor immediately after Comodi had announced she was done. Maresca went back to the November 2nd phone call between Amanda and her mother. Maresca asked Knox if she remembered calling her mother three times on that day. Knox claimed that she remembered calling her mother, but not how many times; because there was so much going on that day. Taking a page out of Comodi's book—and probably because he saw that it was an effective interrogation method—Maresca also began bounced around; not sticking with previous questions for long, particularly when the line of questioning wasn't going anywhere significant. He moved to the phone call with her mother, Edda, which was intercepted while she was in prison on November 10th. "Do you remember how surprised your mother was that you didn't even remember about this phone call?" Maresca asked, referring to the first call to her on November 2nd at 12 noon Perugia time. Knox admitted that her mother was a "bit surprised," but she reiterated that there was so much confusion that "specific things got mixed up."

Della Verdova appeared a bit uncomfortable with Maresca's questioning. He began standing up at the end of each question asked by Maresca, but had not said anything thus far. Maresca then pulls out the transcript of Knox's conversation with her mother in jail on November 10th and begins reading a passage.

Maresca: Your mother, surprised, says – 'You called me three times.' You say – 'Oh, I don't remember that.' She says – 'Okay, you called me once to tell me some things that had shocked you. But this happened before anything really happened in the house,' says your mother. You say – 'I know I was calling, I remember calling Filomena, but I really don't remember calling anyone else. I just don't remember this thing about having called you.' Your mother says – 'Why would that be? Stress, you think?' (Amanda replies "Yes, right," and the conversation continues, although Maresca has stopped reading).

Immediately after he stops reading, Della Verdova stands and appears as if he is going to interrupt Maresca before he is even able to ask a question. Maresca sees this and must have gotten wise, and also angry, from watching Della Verdova do this several times. Maresca says, "So, my specific question," but he stops in mid-sentence and looks at Della Verdova then back to judge Massei. "I don't want to be interrupted! Presidente, I am examining her as I was allowed." Judge Massei, not ready for another courtroom brawl of sorts, assures Maresca that there will be no interruption. Apparently Judge Massei had not gotten wise from the prior exchanges he so desperately tried to subdue. Yet, Della Verdova didn't seem to take the same stance as Judge Massei, and he stood trying to distract Maresca. However, Maresca was not waiting for Della Verdova to interrupt. Maresca was taking the fight to him.

"I didn't even ask the question yet!" Maresca shouts, "Avvocato (Lawyer) Dalla Vedova gets up punctually at every question!" Judge Massei again tries to assure Maresca that there will be no interruption and says, "Getting up doesn't matter, the important thing is that there are no interruptions." However, again, Della Verdova couldn't resist, and began flagging Judge Massei.

"Excuse me, please!" Massei says to Della Verdova.

"Can I make an objection to this?" Della Verdova asks brazenly.

Maresca is clearly fed-up with his antics. "Can I ask my question or not?" Maresca says in a very annoyed tone. Judge Massei orders that Maresca be allowed to ask the question before he makes an objection. Della Verdova again did a good job to try and distract Maresca—who tried to regroup quickly and ask his question. Maresca asked Knox if there was a specific motive why she couldn't remember making three phone calls to her mother in Seattle, waking her up in the wee-hours of the morning. Right on cue, Della Verdova says loudly, "I object to this question! Because the reference to the transcription was read out with one sentence skipped by the lawyer for the civil plaintiff." The question was not posed clearly because Della Verdova had thrown Maresca into a rage. However, Maresca read the transcript in perfect context. "Presidente," Maresca pleads, "this 'skipping' annoys me. I do not skip anything. I read out to the Court exactly the entire passage. If someone skipped, it was someone else. Yes?"

With that, a spirited argument ensued between Maresca and Della Verdova; each screaming at one and other simultaneously. Both were yelling so most was unintelligible, but the content seemed to center around one call, three calls, and so on. Judge Massei could be heard yelling several times "excuse me, please" at the two, but not making much headway. Without permission from Judge Massei, Della Verdova repeated his objection, which consisted of the fact that Maresca had left out that Knox had stated to her mother that "several things were happening at that point." All of that arguing for a meaningless quote left out? No, Della Verdova skillfully interrupted the opposition as he had been doing since Knox had taken the stand earlier that day. When the dust finally settles, Knox testifies that she remembers the call that she made to her mother 'after' the garden call, but not the one that she made at noon.

Knox then says something that befuddles the crowd, and gives insight into her truly darker and callus side. After reviewing her prison diary, psychologist, Dr. David Wilson, has always maintained that he has no doubt that Knox is guilty of the murder of Meredith Kercher. Among several other things, Dr. Wilson cites that Knox was self-obsessed, and that she never once mentioned being upset about Meredith's death. Knox would clearly display this "lack of remorse," per say (or for a more appropriate phrase, "lack-of-sensitivity"), in this interesting exchange with Maresca. "Did you suffer from the loss of this friend?" Maresca asks. "Yes, I was very, very shocked by it," Knox replies. "I couldn't even imagine such a thing." Maresca asks Knox if she thinks about Kercher often in her daily life. Knox replies, "Yes, I remember her. But in the end, I only knew her for one month, and more than anything, I am trying to think how to go forward with my own life…"

Maresca then asks Knox if she ever thought that Patrick Lumumba might be guilty of the murder. Knox claims that she never thought that before the November 5th interrogation, but at that time she said that she believed him to be guilty. Maresca pressed her on when exactly she realized for the first time that Patrick might not be the murderer. Knox stumbled a few times, not answering the question directly. Maresca kept poking away until he got an answer. Knox finally stated that the more time that passed, the more she realized that imaginations were not really memories, but just imagination. Still Knox was avoiding the question. Maresca pressed and pressed. "Weeks, days, hours, I don't know. The question is: when?" Maresca asked. Maresca grew more and more frustrated with Knox's evasive answers. He pressed more, but Knox skillfully avoided giving a direct date and time, or even a radius of time, when it hit her that Patrick may be innocent. Knox's final answer to the question was again a baffling attempt to explain herself:

Amanda Knox: I needed time to think. I don't know the precise moment where, bing! But it was this continuous evolution of asking myself: "So, what did I actually do?" If I didn't do these things with him, then he's probably innocent, but I only know the things that I actually do know, about what I myself did. About what I actually said about him, it was not true. It was a mistake. But—I don't know—I don't know anything anymore. In fact, the thing that was important for me was to know whether I myself was there or not, and when I remembered that I wasn't, that was the important thing which I wanted to say, and also the fact that what I had said about him was a mistake.

Knox again shows her insensitivity in the fact that she falsely accused a man (Patrick Lumumba) of a murder which he did not commit, ruined his life and his business, and "the thing that was important for her was to know whether she was there or not," not to worry about exonerating Patrick. In fact, she even admitted never formally apologizing to him for the false accusation. Then Maresca asks Knox what the words "imagination" and "state of confusion" mean to her. Knox again proceeds to give a very bizarre explanation that sounds like a mix between psychotic and just plain lying:

Amanda Knox: According to me, it depends on the situation. I can only talk about my own experience, which was, that I had to, forced myself -- because they told me that I had to remember something else -- to recall something else, so I forced myself so hard, that I was trying to imagine the reality that I had apparently forgotten, and I got confused as to whether the things I had imagined were really memories or just imagination; because they were fragmentary. They were just images of things I had seen in my life; for example Piazza Grimana that I saw every day; Patrick, whom I saw almost every day. These things, which were fragmented, I didn't know if they belonged to that evening, to that sequence of events, or that line of reasoning. I didn't know, and not knowing what was reality and what was my imagination, this was the state of confusion.

After continual questioning on the subject by Maresca, Knox stated that she has only experienced this phenomenon (state of confusion) on that one occasion, never prior to or after that. Maresca then switched to her first meeting with Sollecito, which was on October 25th. Maresca asked Knox when her first sexual encounter was with Sollecito. Knox replied, "On the first day," explaining on October 25th. Knox claimed that she had brought four other boys to the cottage prior to Sollecito (Juve, Spiros, Rezzon, and Daniel). Knox also admitted that she had sexual relations with Rezzon, Daniel, and then Sollecito. Maresca then asked Knox to take him step-by-step through the morning of November 2nd, after she left Sollecito's house and returned home. Nothing new here except that Knox stated that she did not use the bidet or even notice any blood there on that occasion. This is significant, because a mix of her blood and Kercher's blood was found inside the bidet. In regard to the footprint on the bathmat, Knox claimed that it didn't look like a footprint; rather, it looked like a large stain. Knox also testified that she was only in the cottage for less than a half-hour before returning to Sollecito's flat.

After returning to Sollecito's apartment, Knox said that she didn't know what time it was. Maresca asked her if she looked at her cell phone for the time. Knox stated that it wasn't important to her to know the time, adding that she rarely looked at the time—especially then, when she had no particular place to go. Back at Sollecito's, Knox said that she quickly cleaned up the floor then prepared coffee. As they ate biscuits and drank coffee, Sollecito advised her to call her roommates regarding the strange nature of what she witnessed at the cottage. Knox reiterates her previous testimony about what she and Sollecito did after returning to the cottage. Again, she leaves out the part about running to a neighbor's house, which she stated in her email to friends and family on November 4th. In the email Knox stated, "I ran outside and down to our neighbor's door. The lights were out, but I banged on the door anyway. I wanted to ask them if they had heard anything the night before, but no one was home." Knox never makes mention of this in her testimony, and sadly, she was never asked about it or pressed by lawyers. It must have been overlooked completely by the prosecution and not verified. Detectives certainly should have verified if the residents of the house were in fact home at the time that Knox claims to have knocked on the door.

Knox was questioned several times before her arrest (November 2, 3, & 4). She claims that these questionings were much "lighter," in the sense of pressure put on her by police. Maresca alluded to the fact that, upon her arrest, Knox signed her arrest document, which was translated into English so that she understood why she was being detained. Maresca asked her if she remembered or knew why she was being held.

Amanda Knox: I remember understanding that it was some bureaucratic issue. I didn't sufficiently understand the specific situation; but at the same time, I was extremely tired, exhausted, stressed, and I didn't understand anything anymore. So that fact is that everything they explained to me at that point, everything seemed the same to me, total confusion. I just didn't understand.

In her answer, Knox again tries to have the court believe that she wasn't aware why she was being held or that she didn't know that she was being arrested. Although she attempts to make the case that this was a long and hard interrogation (her father, Curt Knox, claiming that she was physically and mentally abused for 14 hours) and that she was tired and stressed, she falsely accused Patrick Lumumba at 1:45a.m.; less than two hours after the interrogation began. She was arrested shortly there after, and notified of her arrest by the arresting officers. Mr. Knox has stated this several times, including an article from UK's *Times Online* (January 11, 2009). In that same article, Mr. Knox claimed that there was no interpreter either, which Amanda herself testified that an interpreter was present.

When Knox returned to the cottage with Sollecito she claims that she thought someone might have broken-in and robbed the cottage, after seeing the broken window in Filomena's room. She had also previously stated that she had some money stashed away in a little draw. Maresca asked Knox if she checked to see if her money was still there. Knox said that she couldn't remember if she checked or not. This seemed to puzzle Maresca, who asked her if she remembers if the money was stolen or not. Again, Knox claims that she can't remember. Maresca had asked the question as if he assumed that if someone felt that they were burglarized, one of the first things that they would check is if money was missing—specifically their own money.

Although her testimony had almost concluded, Knox would leave with a statement that would horrify jurors and make front page news everywhere. Mr. Maresca switched the questioning to November 2nd, after Kercher's body was discovered, and all were brought to the police station for questioning. Maresca asked Knox, in regards to her stating to friends at the station that "Meredith died slowly," how she came to know this information. Keeping in total stride with her bizarre behavior, Knox replied,

Amanda Knox: I heard that her throat was cut, and from what I saw in CSI [Crime Scene Investigation] of these things, these things are neither quick nor pleasant. So when they said 'We hope she died quickly,' like I don't know, in some other way, I said 'But what are you saying, her throat was cut, good Lord, bleargh [mimicking the noise].' I had remained at that point, that brutality, this death that was really, bleargh [mimicking the noise], that made a horrible impression [The jury looked very surprised at her language]. That was what really struck me, that fact of having your throat cut. It seemed so gross, and I imagined that it was a very slow and terrifying death. So when they said 'We hope it was like this,' I said 'No, I think it was really yucky, disgusting [crossing her hands repeatedly in front of her chest].'

Mr. Maresca then brought Knox back to the conversation that she had with her mother from jail. Maresca asked why she told her mother that she was "very worried about the knife" found in Sollecito's flat that had Meredith's blood on the tip. Knox replied, "I didn't understand why there would be Meredith's blood on a knife that was found in Raffaele's house, because [nervous laugh] for me that was impossible." There was a long pause soon after, as Maresca shuffled through papers looking to see if he had any further questions. "I don't know if I have any more questions, Presidente," he stated. After another long pause and shuffling through some more papers, Maresca finally announced that he had no further questions.

With that, Mr. Maresca gave the floor to Sollecito's defense team, who would conclude the day's examination. Taking the floor was Sollecito's lawyer, Giulia Bongiorno, who has a sharp, snappy voice. Bongiorno began by asking Knox the extent of her relationship with Rudy Guede. Knox said that she "didn't have any relations with Guede," adding that she was introduced to him and saw him around a few times. According to Knox, they never exchanged numbers or called each other. Bongiorno then brought up a prior witness, Mr. Hekuran Kokomani. Knox let out a tiny snicker after Bongiorno mentioned his name. Bongiorno reiterated Kokomani's testimony (Trial—day 13) then asked Knox if what he claimed was true. Knox s testified that what he said was "totally false"—adding that he must have imagined this event. During Bongiorno's attempt to discredit the shaky testimony of Mr. Kokomani, she described an incident where he claimed to have sat at a bar in Perugia with Knox's American uncle, Sollecito, and Knox during the summer. Knox said that this was impossible, not only because she was in the United States at the time, but because no one from her family speaks Italian or ever came to Perugia before the murder.

Giulia Bongiorno then moved to the two days that Knox was brought back to the cottage by police (2 & 4 November). She asked Knox if she had been given shoe covers and or gloves when she entered the house. Knox explained that she was given gloves when she went into her apartment to look at the knives; yet, on the other occasion—when she went to look at the apartment downstairs where the boys lived—she was not given gloves. She did not refer to shoe covers at all, but when she was shown the knives police had testified that she was given shoe covers and gloves before entering the cottage; Knox even confirms this in earlier testimony. Bongiorno then asked Knox whether she noticed if police all had on shoe-covers, gloves, and suits all the time. Knox said that she noticed that the officers that she was standing with had shoe covers on, but she was unable to remember if they had gloves on.

Just about every question that Giulia Bongiorno asked Knox from that point on—in one form or another—were questions she had already been asked by other lawyers. Upon further questioning,

Knox informed the court that Sollecito had never met Rudy Guede, to her knowledge; although the two only lived about two-blocks from one another. Bongiorno then quoted a prior witness, Fabrizio Gioffredi (Trial—day 13) who claimed to have seen Knox, Guede, Sollecito, and Kercher coming out of the cottage one afternoon. Knox denied this, saying that it was "impossible." With that answer, Giulia Bongiorno relinquished the floor to Sollecito's other defense lawyer, Luca Maori.

Mr. Maori started by asking Knox if she had heard the conversation between Sollecito and his sister on November 2nd, after they had returned together to the cottage. Knox said that she was nearby, but wasn't listening. When Sollecito had finished with the call he told Knox that his sister had advised them to call the police. Knox then remembers that Sollecito called the carabinieri and Knox could be heard in the background. During the call Sollectio turned to Knox for clarification of the address of the cottage and the landline phone number. Knox claims that they were alone at the time of that call and that no one else had arrived at the cottage yet. However, as we have seen from prior testimonies, CCTV footage, and phone records; the timeframe of this call strongly contradicts Knox's account. The days' examination was taking its toll on Knox, and she spoke out on it, asking Judge Massei if she could take a five-minute break because she was tired. Judge Massei agreed, and allotted ten-minutes for the break.

The examination resumed at 1:20p.m., with an announcement from Judge Massei in regards to Knox's prior arrest in the United States. Massei announced that the FBI had faxed over the arrest report and it had just been transmitted to the court. Massei announced that it was available to all parties (lawyers). Questioning then resumed, this time with Patrick Lumumba's lawyer, Carlo Pacelli, taking the floor again. Pacelli announced that he only wanted to ask a few questions to get clarification. Pacelli brought up Rudy Guede, asking Knox if she had ever met him at the basketball court or purchased marijuana from him. Knox denied that either episode ever occurred. Pacelli again brought up Knox's interrogation on November 6th, asking her why she declared that she heard "thuds" in the cottage while Meredith was being killed.

Knox began speaking of her imagination again, claiming that she "was confused, and was trying to imagine things that she had supposedly forgotten." Pacelli became very frustrated with Knox's answers on the matter, and stated, "It's useless; she is going back to what she has already said about this." Pacelli and Judge Massei had a brief discussion about it, with Massei asking Pacelli to simply go over the information with Knox for clarification. Seeing that he was probably going nowhere with this line of questioning, Pacelli shouted, "No, no, I'm not going back. No, no, no." Pacelli clearly believed that Knox was lying, and he grew more irritated. "She won't answer me, Presidente. Ahh, you said that you had good relations with Patrick...Then why, in your statement of 6 November 2007 at 5:45a.m., did you say you were very frightened of Patrick?" Knox responded by saying, "Because, imagining him as being capable of murdering someone, at that moment I was scared." Pacelli again seemed puzzled and frustrated by her answer. He couldn't understand why Knox had told police that she had good relations with Patrick and then she switched her positioning and was then scared of him. Pacelli continued with this line of questioning for a few minutes, but Knox continued to provide confusing answers.

Mr. Pacelli then asked Knox how she could have known that Meredith had let out a scream if the police hadn't known at that time; a question that incites the last screaming match of the day. Ghirga then stands up and begins arguing very loudly with Pacelli.

"Calm, avvocato Ghirga! I'm doing this examination in a calm way! I want to do this calmly," Pacelli announces. Still, Ghirga continues screaming.

"Avvocato, please, please!" Judge Massei says to Ghirga.

"Basta" ("Enough"), Pacelli then says to Ghirga.

Pacelli and Judge Massei then begin arguing, after Massei orders that he avoid repeating questions. Pacelli points out to the judge that he asked the question yesterday, but Dalla Vedova interrupted and she (Knox) never answered. Massei said several times that she did answer the question, and the two argued back and forth for a few minutes about it. After getting a little heated, Pacelli apologizes to Massei and order finally returns to the court. Judge Massei asked Knox about the scream. Knox claimed that the police asked her if she heard a scream. Judge Massei spoke of the perplexity of the defense in regards to a witness who spoke of the scream. Knox replied obnoxiously, "Well, I would ask the police about that."

Although Knox's testimony had ended, the days' events had not. Andrew Seliber[79] (Knox's college friend from Seattle) would take the stand in the afternoon, in what would be known as a very anticlimactic finish to the day. As the skinny, dark-haired, and intellectual 'best friend' of Knox walked into the courtroom, Knox appeared encouraged. Called as a character witness for Knox, Seliber testified that Knox was "having the happiest time of her life" in Perugia. "She worked three jobs responsibly so she had the money to come here," Seliber added. Seliber had been a guest at the infamous party back in the states that saw Knox receive a $276 fine. Speaking of the shindig, Seliber told the court "It was a normal party," and there was "no rock throwing or anything like that." Seliber claimed that some of Knox's friends threw-in money to help her pay the fine. Outside of the courtroom, after his testimony concluded, Seliber told the media that "It was surreal," speaking of the carrying-on and shouting by lawyers.

Knox's testimony had certainly lived up to its billing, even outshining its expectations—in regards to theatrics. Still, the sides had been drawn, and neither Knox's supporters nor her critics would budge. Each side would take what she had said in her testimony and use it to feed their arguments. Knox's testimony was not reported in full detail, only snippets were provided to the public. Much of the raw details were left to the imagination and media spin. However, for those who witnessed it first hand, it would not be something that they would soon forget.

Chapter 10 - The Trial of the Century

Meredith Kercher Trial Day 27 – (June 19, 2009)

On the heals of Amanda's testimony just one week before, the court again geared-up for a new witness. This time, Amanda Knox's mother, Edda Mellas[80], would take the stand to answer the all important question regarding the 12:47p.m., phone call on 2 November 2007. As we recall from her testimony, Amanda claims that the first call she made to her mother on that day was after Kercher's body was discovered (circa 1:15p.m.). However, phone records—and Mellas herself—indicate that Amanda's first call to her mother was at 12:47p.m. Amanda testified that she doesn't remember making that first call. This is significant, because during that call Amanda hadn't indicated to her that police had already arrived. Moreover, in her November 4th email to family and friends, Amanda omits this call completely, and writes that police didn't arrive until after Sollecito phoned 112, which was at 12:54p.m. This timeline does not even come close to fitting with the various pieces of evidence acquired in regard to the time period; which is possibly why Amanda chose to exclude this call from her memory.

Also expected to testify is Raffaele's father, Dr. Francesco Sollecito[81] (from Giovinazzo near Bari), who is scheduled to testify on behalf of his son's character. Dr. Sollecito may also be facing an indictment—along with other family members—for interfering in the case. The investigation into Dr. Sollecito stems from a local Bari TV station called *Telenorba*, which broadcasted crime-scene video of Meredith Kercher back on 4 January 2008. The video is heinous, showing Kercher lying half-naked on her back on the floor, with the wounds to her throat clearly visible. The video has since been placed on YouTube, and has yet to be removed.

A few months ago, Italian newspaper, *La Nazione*, and *AGI* news-service, announced that the public prosecutor Giuliano Mignini has launched an investigation against four Sollecito family members, the TV journalist on *Telenorba,* and the director of the station are accused of the crimes of defamation, invasion of privacy, publication of documents during the investigation, and publication of gruesome acts. Raffaele's sister, Vanessa Sollecito, was also facing possible charges; reportedly being bugged while seeking a political favor for her brother. She has since been forcibly discharged from her job as Carabinieri-Lieutenant. Compounding their problems were the allegations that several Sollecito family members—including Francesco and Vanessa—had been overheard during police phone taps discussing plans to persuade Italian politicians to pull two hostile detectives from the case.

In a report in UK newspaper, *Daily Mail*, Kercher's lawyer, Francesco Maresca, spoke on the video: "This is an example of gross journalistic misconduct, which evidently violates all the rules of how to report a story…" In that same article, Anna Maria Ferretti, the director of the leading Italian TV program, *Antenna Sud*, said: "For five minutes of television, the ultimate taboo has been broken without any shame." According to a reconstruction by Mignini—provided in the *La Nazione* article—Raffaele Sollecito's father and sister (also from Bari) had legitimately obtained the video from police then illegally provided it to *Telemundo*. Charges are expected to be filed on this matter in the upcoming months.

Testifying on behalf of her daughter, Edda Mellas faced a most perplexing and polarizing situation. Spending 18-months flying back and forth from the United States to see Amanda, Mellas was attempting to counter the prosecution's portrayal of her daughter. Desperately trying to free her daughter, Mellas was faced with actually incriminating her further by telling the truth; as phone conversations just hours after the murder were going to be discussed—even though she was a defense witness. Nevertheless taking the stand, Mellas looked calm and spoke very credibly and precisely about the details on the day that Kercher's body was discovered. Speaking of Amanda and Meredith's relationship, Mellas told the court that "they got along great." Amanda kept her head down and scribbled on a note pad during much of her mother's testimony.

Mellas testified that she spoke regularly with Amanda via email. She said that she didn't know that Amanda was using drugs, and that they never talked about that. In regard to Patrick Lumumba, Mellas said that Amanda told her that he was a "nice man" who was "dedicated to his family." Patrick's lawyer, Carlo Pacelli, brought Mellas back to the conversation that she had with Amanda in jail on November 10th. Mellas claimed that Amanda spoke of Patrick during that conversation, saying that "she [Amanda] was very upset that Patrick was dragged into this horrible situation; she felt terrible." Seeing how it was Amanda who dragged Patrick into this mess, Pacelli asked, "Who dragged him into it?" Mellas said that Amanda was "interrogated all night long" and she was pressured into it by police (when in fact, not even two-hours of interrogation had passed before she incriminated Patrick). When asked if she herself went to the police or informed anyone that Patrick was innocent after that conversation with her daughter, Mellas said "No." The reasons she gave for not telling anyone was that she doesn't speak Italian, and that she didn't speak to Amanda's lawyers that often in the beginning.

In regards to the first phone call that she received from Amanda on November 2nd (12:47p.m., Perugia time), Mellas claimed that Amanda told her that she tried to call Meredith's phone several times, but there was no answer. In reality, Amanda only called Meredith twice and both calls lasted less then four-seconds. After informing her to call the police, Mellas claims that Amanda told her that "Raffaele was finishing a call with his sister and then was going to call police." This was a telling statement by Amanda; because it shows premeditation, showing that is was predetermined that they were going to call the police; and that the call to her mother and Sollecito's call to his sister were part of their newly reconstructed alibi. Moreover, phone records indicate that the call with her mother started at 12:47p.m., and lasted only a minute-and-a-half. Sollecito didn't call his sister until 12:50p.m., and that call lasted only about a minute or less. Therfore, Sollecito hadn't even started dialing his sister until after Knox's call with her mother had ended.

Needless to say, Amanda never mentioned to her mother that the police had already arrived. Mellas said that during the second call (1:24p.m.); Amanda informed her that someone had seen a foot under a blanket. During the third call (Approx. 2:00p.m.), Amanda was at the police station and told her mother that they had found a dead body in Meredith's room. However, Amanda did not know at that time, according to her mother, that it was Meredith's body. According to Mellas, Amanda told her on that third call that "all she could understand is that it was a person and there was a closet" and she was worried about Meredith because they still couldn't get a hold of her. So, Edda testifies that on the third call—while Amanda was at the police station—she was not informed by Amanda that it was Meredith's body that was discovered; meaning that Amanda was unaware whose body was found in Meredith's room at that time; or, Amanda knew that it was Meredith's body and omitted this important fact to her mother, which seems highly unlikely.

Neither the USA nor the UK were particularly interested in the testimony of Dr. Francesco Sollecito. However, in Italy, Dr. Sollecito's testimony was eagerly anticipated, because of the almost certain charges that he would be facing, as well as that his son was Italian born and bread. Speaking of his son's predicament, Dr. Sollecito said, "To me and my family it is obvious that some very big mistakes have been made and my son is innocent. He has spent nearly two years in jail for something he did not do." Dr. Sollecito also spoke of Raffaele's fascinations with knives, claiming that he carried "small knives" in his pockets. "It's a habit he has had since childhood," he told the court. "He grew up in the country and he always carried a knife. He is not violent; he would not hurt a fly. I had told him not carry a knife around." In regards to his son's relationship with Amanda, Dr. Sollecito said, "He spoke to me about her in a way that he had never done about other girls. Raffaele had a certain affection towards Amanda."

In defense of his actions of interfering in the case, Dr. Sollecito said, "Everything I did was in complete respect of the law. Once I saw the film of the scene from the first search after the murder and the subsequent one in December it was clear that mistakes had been made." Dr. Sollecito testified that he was aware that Raffaele had issues with drugs, adding that he had "received a letter from police in Giovinazzo" informing him about his son's "drug habit." Once again, speaking of the case against his son, he said, "We were always convinced as to the absolute innocence and total strangeness of the allegations against Raffaele."

Meredith Kercher Trial Day 28 – (June 20, 2009)

The Knox family would now make an all-out assault on the media now that Edda Mellas's testimony was over. Breathing a sigh of relief, Mellas was now able to sit in the courtroom to support her daughter, as she was not allowed to attend court sessions prior to her own testimony. Likewise, Dr. Francesco Sollecito would also be on hand to show support for his son. Knox and Sollecito's defense teams would also get a boost today, as an Italian coroner, Francesco Introna[82], would be called to Sollecito's defense. It would be a long day for the coroner as he would be the only witnesses to take the stand on this day. Again, due to the graphic nature of the testimony, the session would be closed to the public, including the media.

Mr. Introna was brought in to give testimony on the type of weapon used in the murder and the number of attackers involved. Introna told the court that one of the stab wounds on Kercher's neck was caused by a shorter knife than the one believed to be the murder weapon. Introna testified that the cut on Kercher's neck was made by a knife with a 3-3 1/2-inch-long blade, as opposed to the knife that the prosecution claims was the murder weapon—which is the 6 1/2-inch knife found at Sollecito's flat. Introna also testified that it would be "physically impossible" that three people could have attacked her, because Kercher's bedroom was too small. With the help of two assistants (both substitute lawyers); Introna physically demonstrated how he believed that Kercher was assaulted from behind.

Mr. Introna demonstrates that the lone killer grabs Meredith from behind—as she was already naked from the waist down—and lifts her t-shirt. He then covers her mouth and nose with his left hand and cuts her bra with a knife in his right hand. He then pushes her down to the floor, where she rests on all fours, in an effort to rape her, according to Introna. However, not explaining what turned this possible rape into a killing before the rape even occurred, Mr. Introna explains that the killer snapped; putting the blade first on her face. He then grabbed her jaw and plunged the knife in completely—once, then once more. He then cuts her throat, which was stopped by its impact with the jawbone. Meredith rolls over on her back and gasps for air. The killer straddles her with his knees. According to Introna, Meredith bled to death in 10 minutes, suffocating on her own blood.

Mr. Introna's reconstruction of the crime only had one major flaw, plus a questionable time of death calculation and a questionable room size calculation. The big flaw in Introna's diagnosis is that if the knife was stopped by the jawbone, then why was there no damage reported to the jawbone in the original autopsy? This is not something that even a novice coroner would miss. The remainder of the questions surrounding his analysis could be explained; however, Introna does not offer an explanation. For instance, what caused the murderer to go from the possibility of rape to a killing? Some speculate that the scream might have scared the killer, but Introna never explains this. Also, why did his reconstruction start with Meredith's pants already off? How did this occur? As for the time of death being 10 minutes, according to Introna; someone's calculations is way off (as originally it was determined that Kercher died an agonizing 2 hours after she was first stabbed)!

Another questionable call from Introna was his determination that there was only one killer. From his reenactment and room-size calculations, he theorized that there was only one killer involved in the murder and one knife used. However, under cross-examined by prosecutors, Introna admitted that he had never been to the cottage nor did he use forensic data to work out the size of the bedroom. Furthermore, Mr. Maresca informed the media after the session that when the court went to inspect the crime scene in April they determined that six or seven people could fit into the room.

That being said, Introna's analysis of the cuts on Kercher's hands was very plausible. Meredith had cuts on her hands which, during a knife attack, normally indicate defense wounds. However, Introna explains that these wounds came when the killer pushed her to the floor; explaining that Meredith received the cuts from glass that was on the floor. The cuts on Kercher's hands were about the size of the tip of a ball-point-pen. Normal defense-wounds coming from a knife attack are usually much more severe. In this instance,

Introna's analysis of these wounds seems to be spot-on. The broken glass appears to have come from a drinking glass in Kercher's room that was broken during the struggle.

Meredith Kercher Trial Day 29 – (June 23, 2009)

With the summer break fast approaching, it was decided that they would cram a few trial days within the next week. Knox and Sollecito's defense were in full swing, with two witnesses testifying today on their behalves. First up was Pasqualino Coletta[83], the man whose car had broken down near the cottage on the night Kercher was murdered. Coletta testified that he had been stuck in front of the cottage between 10:30p.m., and 11:00p.m. During that time, Coletta told the court that his "attention was not caught by anything in particular." Coletta also said that he did not hear anyone scream in the half hour that he was near the cottage.

How significant is this testimony? Well, the defense appeared to be trying to show that the crime occurred before 10:30p.m., seemingly, with this testimony and the assertion a day before by coroner Francesco Introna who testified that it took Meredith only ten-minutes to die after first being stabbed. In contrast, both Nara Capezzali and Maria Dramis claimed in earlier testimony to have heard a bone-chilling scream at approximately 11:30p.m., that night. Timelines were not adding up for the defense, and this was a huge problem for them. In contrast, the prosecution had built a solid case, and their timelines were supported on several fronts. Pasqualino's wife, Mrs. Coletta[84], would also testify, confirming her husband's story. She was present with him when the car had broken down in front of the cottage.

Next to testify was one of the boys who lived on the first floor of the cottage, Marzana Marco[85]. He testified that he noticed no friction between Knox and Kercher. Marco also explained the two times that he witnessed Rudy Guede at the cottage, with nothing new added. The final testimony of the day came from Raffaele Sollecito's landlady[86]. She testified to the character of Sollecito for the most part, painting him as a good tenant who never gave her any problems or any complaints from neighbors. She did, however, help Sollecito's credibility in a way, by explaining that his sink had broken in the past. She clarified that Sollecito had called the plumber himself and had the sink fixed. Now, this can be seen in two ways. First, it confirms that there was a previous problem with the sink, essentially validating his claims that it could have broken again on the night of the murder. However, the other side of this is that he didn't feel the need to call the plumber after the hydraulic issue after the night of the murder; rather they (Knox and Sollecito) decided to fix it themselves. This does not eliminate the question of whether the sink had even broken at all that night, and was just another part of their alibi.

Meredith Kercher Trial Day 30 – (June 26, 2009)

With Solleciot's father and Knox's mother in attendance for the third hearing in a row, both defense teams would have the most promising day in court since the trail began almost six-months earlier. On this day Sollecito's lawyers would call two witnesses—who happen to be lawyers—that would tell of a recent burglary that had an eerie similarity to Kercher's murder, in terms of circumstances. That recent burglary also may have involved Rudy Guede, who had already been convicted of Kercher's murder at this point. Also testifying during this relatively short session would be Sollecito's ex-cleaning lady. The defense's aim would be to show that Rudy Guede acted alone (lone-wolf-theory), and had committed at least one known crime in a similar fashion—minus murder.

First to take the stand was Paolo Brocchi[87], a lawyer whose office is not far from the cottage. Brocchi described to the court that back on 14 October 2007, an intruder broke the window of his law studio by throwing a rock threw it. The intruder then entered through the broken window and stole a laptop computer and a cell phone. Police later determined that the thief (or thieves) had disabled the alarm system, used a rock to break through the double glass, and then scaled a 12ft. high terrace and entered through the window. About two weeks later Rudy Guede—armed with a knife—was arrested for breaking into a school in Milan. During that arrest, police found the stolen goods in Guede's possession.

Police called Brocchi on October 27th and informed him that they had retrieved his stolen laptop and cell phone to his surprise, as he was not even aware that those items had been missing. Police informed Brocchi that the items had been recovered from a thief who had been arrested in Milan, but they did not tell him the burglar's name. However, two days later, Brocchi said that a young black man—who he later identified as Rudy Guede—appeared at the steps of his office, wearing gym shorts, a tank top, and holding a basketball. He testified that Guede spoke "perfect Italian with a Perugia accent," and told Brocchi that he had bought and paid for Bocchi's stolen items at the Milan train station. Brocchi informed the court that he had later recognized that Guede was the man who had visited him after seeing his photo in a newspaper reporting his arrest.

Alberto Palazzoli[87], a lawyer who shared an office with Brocchi, confirmed his story. The testimony provided by the two lawyers certainly had an impact on the court. Sollecito's defense was able to provide convincing evidence that Guede may have been involved in a similar incident only weeks before the murder—even establishing a possible M.O. Although nothing was stolen from the cottage, one can speculate that Guede broke in, saw Kercher alone, tried to rape her, and things got out of hand. The result: murder. However, with all of the other evidence (against Knox and Sollecito), the defense was going to need much more than this common link to exonerate their clients.

The final witness of the day was Marina Chiriboga[89] from Ecuador. The very attractive Latina had worked as Sollecito's cleaning lady until September 2007, at which time she went on maternity leave. Marina told the court that just before she went on maternity leave she had asked Sollecito to purchase some bleach for her to use to clean his apartment. Sollecito did so, purchasing two-bottles of *Ace bleach*. When she stopped working for Sollecito in September, one and a half bottles of bleach were still left in his flat. After the murder, police had recovered both bottles of bleach from Sollecito's flat in relatively the same place that Marina claims to have seen them last: one still sealed and the other one half-full. Marina also worked at the same supermarket (*Conad Store*) that owner, Marco Quintavalle, testified that he had seen Knox on the morning of November 2nd, when Knox claimed that she was still asleep. Marina testified that she was working on the morning after the murder. When asked if she had seen Knox come into the store that morning she simply answered, "No." When pressed by Judge Massei—who asked her if she was sure that she didn't see Knox or if she was sure that she was present at all times that morning—Marina said she was sure, she was present at all times, and that she didn't see Knox.

Meredith Kercher Trial Day 31 – (June 27, 2009)

Three witnesses would take the stand on this day, but the best testimony of the day for both defense teams came from a person not present in the courtroom. Entered into the recent evidence log was a statement made to Perugia police 1 January 2008, from Perugia bar owner, Christian Tramontano[90]. In his statement to police, Christian said that he and his girlfriend were awakened by noises in their apartment at around 6a.m., on September 1st or 2nd, 2007. He looked down from his bed loft and saw a young black male who was drunk going through his things. Christian told police that he then chased the man towards the front door, which was locked. Like a rat in a corner, the man fought back, using a chair to keep Christian at a distance; then the intruder pulled out a switchblade knife and threatened him. The thief then escaped with 5 euro bills and three credit cards.

After Kercher's murder, Christian remembers seeing Rudy Guede's picture in the paper and thinking that he looked like the thief that he had come-across in his place. However, Christian was not sure if it was Guede or not who he had encountered at his place that night. The credit cards were never recovered or used in any place where Guede had been, according to police: in his report, Judge Micheli wrote-off this evidence against Guede for these reasons. This may seem like promising evidence but, again, it is more speculative than it is valuable informative. Keep in mind that, according to the *National Institute of Justice*, eyewitness-misidentification-testimony was a factor in 75 percent of post-conviction DNA exoneration cases in the United States; making it the leading cause of wrongful convictions—and these numbers are from those who claimed that they were sure that they identified the correct person.

The assault on Guede continued Saturday, as the owner of a nursery school in Milan, Maria Del Prato[91], took the stand. Del Prato testified that she had stopped by the school on October 27th, even though the school was closed that day. She said that when she entered her office she saw Rudy Guede there. "I asked him who he was," she told the court, "and he replied perfectly calmly, even though I had caught him red-handed." Guede had responded by saying that he was "a kid from Perugia" who had arrived the night before and had nowhere to sleep. Seeing that a locker had been opened and some change was missing, Del Prato did not believe his story. When police arrived they found a large knife with a 16-inch blade in Guede's backpack that had been taken from the school kitchen. Guede was arrested and fingerprinted by Milan police and charged with theft, receiving stolen goods, and detention and transportation of a weapon. It was those fingerprints that later identified Guede to the scene of Kercher's murder or he may have never been caught. We see here that Guede can be quite creative with his lies, but a few things probably had been perplexing the jury after this story. We do not see a violent person from this account. In fact, Guede does not even try to run; instead he calmly waits for police arrive.

One of Knox's good friends from Perugia, Spyros Gatsios[92], was next on the stand. Spyros, a Greek student studying in Perugia, worked at a local internet café where Knox had frequented. He said that he and Knox had met in October 2007, as Knox would often be at the café that he supervised to chat with her love back home (DJ); she would use the computers in the café to do so. Spyros testified that he and Knox went out a number of times; the last being on Halloween night 2007. After hitting a couple of night spots together, Knox asked Spyros to escort her to the *Fontana Maggiore*—the fountain in the heart of old Perugia—where she was meeting Sollecito, whom she had just started dating. Spyros said that Knox had expressed to him her discontent and confusion over the fact that she had just started dating Sollecito, but still felt an emotional attachment to DJ, who was in China at the time. Knox and DJ had agreed to keep their relationship open prior to being separated by different countries. The last communication that Spyros had with Knox was when she had sent him a text message the day after Miss Kercher's body was discovered reading, "I'm so tired."

Knox's best-friend from Seattle, Madison Paxton[93], also testified today as a character witness. As Paxton took the stand she and Knox made eye contact. Knox then took a deep breath, a gesture signaling for Paxton to relax. Knox held-onto her necklace, a signal that Paxton received as a 'thank you' & 'solidarity' between the two; as Knox and Paxton both wore identical necklaces; both made by Knox. Paxton told the court that Knox is the complete opposite of how she is portrayed in the tabloids, as a sexual deviant and manipulative person. "Amanda is one of the few people I actually trust with my life," Paxton said. "I will never stop sticking up for her. I know she's innocent." Paxton, a great friend, worked two jobs in order to save money to make the trip to testify on behalf of her best friend.

Meredith Kercher Trial Day 32 – (July 3, 2009)

Over the weekend excerpts of Knox's diary were released, in an effort—no doubt—to offset some of the good things that were being said about her by recent witnesses in court. In the excerpts released, Knox boasts of all the fan mail that she has received. "I've received blatant love letters, a marriage proposal and others wanting to get to know 'the girl with the angel face.'" In another passage Knox writes of her experience as if she has been lucky to go through it; sounding as if she will be home soon and wants to remember this time. "I'm writing this because I want to remember," she says. "I want to remember because this is an experience not many people will ever have. I am not saying I am glad everything that has happened has happened. If it were up to me, my friend would never have been killed." In other passages Knox appears narcissistic, boasting about a prison guard who is obsessed with her and about her looks. "Apparently someone out there saw me on TV and thought I was 'hot,' so they set up a Web site where people comment on how pretty I am," Knox writes. "If I were ugly, would they be writing me wishing me encouragement? I don't think so."

Several witnesses were called by the defense on this day, but none bigger than the first person called to the stand, Francesco Pasquali[94]. A retired Non-commissioned officer (NCO) and a ballistic expert formerly with the Carabinieri, Pasquali took the stand with video, ready to show a re-enactment of how he believed that Filomena's window was the entry point of the murderer. Filomena's second-floor window is located approximately 13ft. off the ground. For his re-enactment, Pasquali constructed a window of the same size and with the same type of glass. Standing at a distance, which he estimated where the rock was thrown from, Pasquali threw a rock (of the same weight), from the exact angle of the garden in front of the window—with the thrower standing outside the fence and throwing the rock with one hand. Two video cameras—one inside and one outside—recorded the event, as he provided three different scenarios of how the rock could have been thrown from the outside to break the window. From his analysis of the trajectory of the rock and the projection of the glass shards, Pasquali testified that he could "exclude that the glass could have been broken from the inside."

Pasquali also shows how easy it is to scale the wall and climb into Filomena's window. His scenario shows that the intruder would have broken the window with a rock and then climbed up the wall, using the first floor window—which is gated—as a ladder to get to Filomena's window. He did prove that it doesn't take an amazing climber to pull off this feat. Yet, if the shutters were partially closed, the intruder would have had to climb first, open them, climb back down, go to the garden and throw the rock, then climb back up. This side of the cottage is also very well lit by the light of the car-park across the street. It is very likely that the intruder would have been seen in this scenario. Regardless, Pasquali did answer the question: "Could this have been done?" Regardless, it does not prove that Guede broke into the cottage. Since it was seen as a staged break-in by the professionals first on the scene; it is just as likely, if not more, to assume that Knox or Sollecito threw the rock from the outside after throwing Filomena's clothes around on the floor. Pasquali may have only confirmed how Knox and Sollecito staged the break-in.

Although Pasquali admitted that he was not a physicist, nor an engineer—or that he's never worked on a rock throwing re-enactment before—he did a relatively convincing job. However, his re-enactment was not without its faults. The prosecution maintains that the shutters were partially closed on the morning after the murder. Filomena testified, "I almost closed the shutters when I left" (and police testified that they "found the shutters almost closed"). "It does not take a technician," Pasquali told the court. "If the shutters were ajar then the rock couldn't fit through." According to Pasquali, the trajectory in which the rock was thrown would have made the glass "explode" on the inside, spreading glass fragments everywhere—on the inside and the outside of the windowsill. Nevertheless, if this scenario were correct, glass fragments would have also fallen outside the house as well; yet nothing was found there. The theory also does not explain how there could have been glass on top of the clothes. Also, there would have been glass on the window's ledge, and the climbing intruder would have likely cut his or her hands climbing with the force necessary to pul one's self up and into the room.

The next witness to testify was Paolo Fazi[95], the director of a local bank in Perugia. Fazi told the court that 20 Euros ($28) had been withdrawn from Kercher's bank account on November 2nd, using her ATM debit card. Fazi also said that the person withdrawing the money had used Kercher's pin-code for the ATM withdrawal. He did say, however, that the actual date of the ATM withdrawal would only be known for sure by the British bank which held Kercher's account. Someone from that bank is expected to testify in the upcoming days to clarify the exact date that the transaction had taken place.

Raffaele Ariro[96], a prison guard who gave Knox a pen and paper on November 7th, testified next. His testimony was relatively short and had no real bearing on the case. He claims when Knox had finished writing she gave him the paper, which he then gave to Mignini. Pietro Camplongo[97], a student at the University of Perugia, told the court that he had witnessed Rudy Guede dancing alone at a local disco in the early morning hours after Kercher's murder. Camplongo said that people were keeping their distance from him, because he smelled "as if he hadn't washed." The final witness of the day was Riccardo Luciani[98], one of the boys who lived on the first floor of the cottage. He was in Bologna during the murder.

Meredith Kercher Trial Day 33 – (July 4, 2009)

Previously scheduled to testify on this day were two defense DNA experts Carlo Torre and Sarah Gino. However, their testimonies had been rescheduled for the following week. Instead, the court will hear from five of Sollecito's friends (four from his hometown of Giovinazzo, Italy, and the other a friend from Perugia). Raffaele Sollecito was born in Giovinazzo on the under populated south-eastern coast, just north of Bari. Although it was the 4th of July, there would be no fireworks in court on this day. Just the opposite actually; this day would provide no startling evidence.

However, Sollecito would be happy to see some of his old friends testify on behalf of his character and non-violent nature.

They described Sollecito as a quiet, calm, and a helpful boy who used reason to combat the arrogance of others. He is a sensitive boy, they said, who did have sexual relations with a woman before Knox. He was kind to woman and caring in his relations with others. "The television described him as a womanizer; in fact he was shy and introverted," said Saverio Pinetti Mofetta[99], who has known Sollecito for 10 years. "He [Sollecito] was excited about his new relationship with Knox," said Sollecito's college friend, Angelo Cirillo[100]. "Raf is a big romantic," said Mariano De Martino[101], who was a classmate of Sollecito's since elementary school. When asked about the knives, they admitted that Sollecito carried two small pocket knives. Speaking of the knife, De Martino said that Sollecito carried a knife with him "as an ornament to match with clothes." Speaking of Sollecito's first sexual experience, Corrado De Candia[102] said that "it must have been back in 2004 or 2005."

Perhaps the most courageous act came from his longtime friend, Gabril Traverso[103], who spoke of the incident when Sollecito was arrested for having two-grams of hash. "In fact, the hash was mine," Traverso asserted; and he claimed that Sollecito took the hit for him. After Sollecito was arrested, a photograph of Sollecito dressed as a mummy, wrapped in toilet paper, and wielding a meat clever had appeared in virtually every newspaper. Cirillo testified that he was the one who took that picture, claiming that it was a joke and that it was his idea to rap him in the toilet paper. Outside the courtroom Sollecito's father expressed his love for his son, saying "Finally the courts have come to know the real Raffaele...quite different from that described by newspapers and television."

Meredith Kercher Trial Day 34 – (July 6, 2009)

Amanda Knox, who would celebrate her 22nd birthday in three days (July 9), entered the courtroom on Monday looking for an early birthday present. This session would be the first Monday assembly of the trial. No cameras or reporters allowed in the courtroom for most of the day as an Italian medical examiner hired by Amanda Knox would provide grisly testimony about how Kercher was likely killed. Just two days after the uneventful July 4th

proceeding, the fireworks would be set off, as one of Italy's foremost forensics experts, Dr. Carlo Torre[104], took the stand. Judge Massei was noticeably ill, but would try to make it through the day. He would need to seek out a doctor immediately after the day's events, as he was suffering through the early stages of pneumonia.

Before Dr. Torre took the stand, Judge Massei ordered everyone out of the courtroom, except for the legal teams and the parents of the defendants. Aside from Knox's mother, Knox's sister, Deanna [20], and her best friend, Madison Paxton, were on hand and allowed to stay in the courtroom. However, the judge ordered that Knox's other sister, Ashley [14], leave the courtroom, because she is a minor. Armed with a Styrofoam head, Torre took the stand and demonstrated that the cuts on Meredith's throat could not have been made by the 12-inch blade found in Sollecito's flat. Torre believed that the blade used to make all three cuts on Kercher's throat was about 3-inches long. Dr. Torre showed close-up images of the actual wounds on Kercher's neck and demonstrated that the larger wound was made by a sawing action from a smaller blade. As Torre displayed these images, Amanda kept her head down and doodled on her notepad. Dr. Torre's version of the murder is that the killer—facing Meredith—grabbed her by the jaw with his left hand and stabbed her repeatedly with his right.

"The smaller wound is absolutely incompatible with the knife in question," Torre testified. "For the larger wound, I cannot rule it out, but it could have been made by a number of different knives." This was an important caveat by Dr. Torre. When asked by Mignini if two knives could have been used, being the great showman that he is Torre replied, "It would be the first time in history that a murder was committed with two knives." Dr. Torre contradicted the Italian coroner, Francesco Introna's version, as well as the prosecution's version of how the murder occurred. Torre said it was "more logical to think" that she was killed from the front, and that "it seems difficult that it was from behind," but he did not totally discount the idea. Dr. Torre also had a chance to examine the luminol footprints that the prosecution says are Knox's barefeet. Torre contested this theory, testifying that Knox's second toe is longer than her big toe, and that characteristic is not apparent in the luminol-enhanced prints. He also criticized the prosecution for not taking comparison prints from the rest of the roommates, including Kercher. "There is not a single element that leads one to think more than one person could have committed the crime," Dr. Torre asserted to the court.

Dr. Torre's assistant, Sarah Gino[105] (who is a private coroner), took the stand next to dispute the lab results provided by Dr. Stefanoni. Gino's critique of Stefanoni's centered on the DNA found at the tip of the blade that Stefanoni claimed was Meredith's. Dr. Stefanoni used the Low Copy Number (LCN) DNA method to obtain her results. This DNA profiling technique, developed by the *Forensic Science Service* (a government owned company in the UK), had come under scrutiny in the United Kingdom and was suspended between 21 December 2007 and 14 January 2008 while the *Crown Prosecution Service* (a non-ministerial department of the Government of the United Kingdom responsible for public prosecutions of people charged with criminal offences in England and Wales) conducted a review into its use. LCN is a form of generic low template DNA analysis in which scientists can copy and obtain a genetic profile from just a small amount of biological material; as small as a millionth the size of a grain of salt (typically using 5 to 20 cells). After a thorough review, by the *Crown Prosecution Service*, they reinstated the technique on 14 January 2008.

In their 'Review of the Science of Low Template DNA Analysis,' conducted at the University of Strathclyde, they concluded that:

> "From our detailed review we find that the science supporting the delivery of Low Template DNA (LTDNA) analysis is sound and that the three companies (the Forensic Science Service Ltd, LGC Forensics and Orchid Cellmark Ltd) providing this service to the Criminal Justice System have validated their processes in accord with accepted scientific principles using both 28 and 34 PCR cycles for extracts containing less than 200 picograms (pg) of DNA. At these levels, stochastic and inhibition effects have an impact upon the DNA profiles produced and all those involved in this process have established guidelines for profile interpretation. Work on interpretation is continuing and it is for the Forensic Science Regulator to monitor this and to

bring about some standardization in interpretation amongst all providers."

Gino testified that because the sample amplified was less than 100 fluorescence units (RFU) that, "we are allowed to assume that it resulted from a contamination from the machine." Gino explained that, "The electrophoretic run should have been done on the substrate as well." The substrate is the gel on which the electronic field is applied. What Gino means is that in case of a stronger than recommended electric field, if pieces of DNA from a previous test are present the machine may read them, as she is claiming occurred in this case. As Gino further explained, unfortunately, because the test cannot be repeated (and no pictures from stereomicroscope have been taken), the results cannot be validated; or even if there was biological matter to begin with. "It is likely just noise from the reagents used in the test," she asserted, "something that a control run on the reagents would have proven." After three hours on the stand, Gino produced some pretty convincing testimony. For the defense it was a good day in court, and Knox did receive her early birthday present.

Two days later Amanda Knox celebrated her twenty-second birthday behind bars. In attendance was her mother-Edda, sister-Deanna, 20, half-sister-Ashley, 14, best friend-Madison Paxton and her aunt from Germany, Dorothy Craft Najir. Amanda surprised her family by baking a chocolate cake with icing and serving it with pear juice. Although wrapped gifts were not allowed, her family brought her shirts, music CDs, books, and a ton of birthday cards from friends and family back home. Even Raffaele Sollecito sent her a birthday present; Sollecito sent Knox a CD by Italian singer Elisa titled "Lotus," and he included a note that read, "A keepsake from a friend for what we are going through together." Court was expected to resume on July 10th, but Judge Massei was diagnosed with full-blown Pneumonia. President of the Tribunal, Aldo Criscuolo, took Judge Massei's place on Friday, but just too formally announce that the trial is suspended until July 17th.

Meredith Kercher Trial Day 35 – (July 17, 2009)

The defense had picked-up momentum in the previous weeks with some substantial expert testimonies. Earlier in the trial it looked almost hopeless for them. However, as the trial has gone on, a formidable battle was brewing, and things were starting to look better for the couple. Only one expert witness would be called today, and the testimony would again contradict what other experts have testified. But first to the stand was Knox's aunt, Dorothy Craft Najir[106], from Hamburg, Germany. Najir, first-cousin to Edda Mellas, testified that she was in close contact with Amanda everyday (telephonically) following the murder. She claimed that they spoke at least six-times after the murder. "I told her to come see me in Germany so she could calm down," Najir told the court. She claimed that Knox had declined.

"She said she wanted to help the police and answer their questions." Knox herself had testified that police had informed her that she couldn't leave Perugia. Najir spoke of Knox's state of mind after the murder, saying that she was terrified that "someone going around killing girls." Najir's account of Knox's demeanor following the murder directly contradicts several witnesses, who have claimed that Knox seemed indifferent and even callous. Najir also told the court that Knox wanted to stay in Perugia to meet Meredith's father; to console him and tell him what she knew. Judge Massei jumped in on the questioning of Najir, asking her about the morning after the murder. "When she got out of the shower, Amanda noticed something was strange," Najir replied. "Only after she got out of the shower?" Massei asked, as if the story just didn't make sense to him.

Next to the stand was Bruno Pellero[107], a mobile telephone expert from Liguria (coastal region of north-western Italy) called by Sollecito's defense team. Pellero looks like a grown-up Harry Potter, with a drab voice, which had the effect that acted almost like a sleeping pill for those present in the courtroom. Still, Pellero acknowledged that he "often gives classes" to the same experts from the Scientific Police (who had testified earlier in the trial). Pellero testified that Sollecito was at his house on the morning of November 2nd because his cell phone was turned on at 6:02a.m., in that location and remained there until 9:30a.m. As compelling as this testimony seemed, though, even Pellero acknowledged that he could not say any of this with 100 percent certainty.

Finally, the defense called toxicologist, Dr. Maurizio Taglialatela[108], to the stand. When asked to describe the affects of the drug, Taglialatela said, "Marijuana can have psychotropic effects for up to six hours from the initial consumption and it can affect the memory in particular, especially short term memory. The user will remember clearly what happened before they took the drug and after but the period they were under the influence of it will be very vague. Marijuana affects your reaction time and it can make you dream more, it leaves you relaxed but unlike other drugs, such as cocaine, it does not make you aggressive." Under cross examination, however, Dr. Taglialatela did say that a violent reaction was possible if marijuana was mixed with alcohol.

Meredith Kercher Trial Day 36 – (July 18, 2009)

On the final day before the summer break, the defense would call one expert witness that would spend all day refuting the DNA evidence from what he called a "sloppy investigation." Legal doctor specializing in genetics and professor at the Università Politecnica delle Marche in Italy, Professor Adriano Tagliabracci[109], took the stand. Dr. Tagliabracci spent all day contesting damning DNA evidence found against the two accused, particularly Meredith's bra clasp, which was said to have traces of Sollecito's DNA on it. The hotly contested bra clasp—which wasn't found until more than a month after the murder—had a high chance of contamination, according to the good doctor. "The clasp goes from one scientist to another, and we don't see gloves being changed. We then see it being put on the floor and picked up again. These procedures are all wrong," Tagliabracci told the court. "By not changing gloves and by touching other objects, cross-contamination of DNA is highly possible," he testified.

The debate over the DNA results ragged on in a big way, fueled by the fact that there is no law that obligates a lab to follow certain protocols; only recommendations of what standards work best. Dr. Tagliabracci stressed that the DNA found on the bra clasp was not enough for a reliable test.

In attendance was Dr. Stefanoni who, through prosecutor Comodi, expressed that the quantity found (1.4 nanogram or 1400 picograms) was sufficient enough to receive a satisfying result. In theory, the amount needed to obtain a DNA profile is only one cell; although in practice, the required amount (using the PCR Process) is about 1 nanogram; which contains approximately 160 cells. So, Dr. Stefanoni is correct when she states that there was a sufficient amount of Sollecito's DNA on the bra clasp to achieve reliable results. Moreover, it was much more reliable than the tests run on the knife, for sure. Any novice forensic specialist would know that there was plenty of DNA on the bra for a reliable test; therefore it is safe to assume that Dr. Tagliabracci knew this as well.

Dr. Tagliabracci's testimony seemed more confusing than anything, even mixing up some basic scientific methodologies at times. When Judge Massei took over questioning at one point, Dr. Tagliabracci actually declared to the court that Sollecito's DNA on the bra clasp cannot be ruled out, but Rudy Guede's can. But it was Kercher's lawyer Francesco Maresca who somehow got Dr. Tagliabracci to admit that there was no contamination, which oddly contradicted his original theory.

Sollecito has claimed that he has only been in the cottage a couple of times and that he has never been in Meredith's bedroom. However, the defense made an attempt to capitalize on the one mistake that Dr. Stefanoni made; she provided the results of the tests but not the data that led to these results. When Della Vedova had finished his questioning of the witness, Bongiorno jumped up and requested an immediate suspension of the trial until all missing data (quantities, registries, rough copies, charts, etc.) were produced by Dr. Stefanoni. Judge Massei accepted the request. And so the trial had reached a pivotal point. They would break for the summer and not return until September 14th. What now loomed over the break was the question: would some of the crucial physical evidence against the two suspects be held inadmissible when the trial resumed? It was a long-shot for the defense, but a point worthy of camping on the doorstep for.

Summer Break…

Chapter 11 - The Trial of the Century

Meredith Kercher Trial Day 37 – (September, 14 2009)

After a long, hot summer in Capanne prison, Amanda Knox and Raffaele Sollecito returned to the courtroom on Monday where their trial had resumed. Almost two-months after Judge Giancarlo Massei called for summer break; the players once again took their places, in what was shaping up to be the longest trial in history. Knox was escorted into the courtroom wearing white trousers, a yellow shirt, and a throwback red-hooded Beatles sweatshirt promoting one of the most famous shows in rock-n-roll history (Beatles concert at Shea Stadium, New York City, 23 August 1966). Sollecito entered the courtroom more modestly, looking clean-cut, wearing glasses and a white button-down collared shirt, with blue stripes.

The order of the day was not to call witnesses, but to discuss the defense's previous request: for the judge to rule on whether to declare the DNA evidence against the two accused null and void. During the summer break, both defense teams were provided with more than three-hundred pages from Dr. Stefanoni regarding the tests conducted. They passed those pages to their experts and they got word back from them that the data was unsatisfactory and did not justify the results. The defense filed a motion with Judge Massei, asking for a cancellation of the trial based on Judge Micheli's diktat of a trial that was primarily based on the DNA evidence. The motion took the two judges into a private deliberation. Surely most people braced themselves, thinking that they may return and call-off the whole trial. However, when they returned Judge Massei refused the request, declaring that "the tests had been carried-out correctly and the defendants' rights had not been violated." With that business out of the way, and no witnesses scheduled, the trial was adjourned until Friday, when further forensic consultants will be called by the defense.

Meredith Kercher Trial Day 38 – (September, 18 2009)

On Friday the trial resumed and was back to weekend sessions. Sollecito's defense continued their assault on the physical evidence, calling Dr. Francesco Vinci[110] to the stand. Dr. Vinci—a coroner and forensic specialist—had been hired by Sollecito's father in the beginning of this case. He is the one who originally discovered that the shoe print found in Meredith's room—which was believed to be Sollecito's print—was in fact Rudy Guede's. The print was the only piece of physical evidence at the time that put Sollecito at the murder scene. According to Vinci, the print was made by a sneaker compatible to one which was retrieved from Rudy Guede. Dr. Vinci simply counted the circles on the bottom of the shoe and concluded that there were too many to be Sollecito's, a contention that the prosecution later agreed upon. Now, Dr. Vinci was back; this time to challenge the prosecution's evidence that the barefoot-bloody footprint on the blue bathmat and a luminol-enhanced print found in the hallway of the cottage were both attributed to Sollecito.

Armed with a laptop computer, Dr. Vinci facilitated a detailed PowerPoint presentation to the court. Dr. Vinci's presentation incorporated Crimescope images that changed colors, which highlighted the details of the prints. He also used slides featuring photographs, grids, and different measurements. Dr. Vinci was given access to the bathmat at forensic headquarters in Rome, so he did have a chance to study it in person. His analysis focused on discrepancies in the print left on the mat and the print that Sollecito provided to police. During a podiatrist visit back in 2006, Sollecito's right foot was diagnosed with a particular footprint characteristic which has the hallux (big toe) lying on a different axis than on a normal foot. Dr. Vinci also noted that, on that same foot, Sollecito's second toe is a hammer toe, so it does not touch the floor or leave an imprint. From this he concluded that Sollecito could not have made the bloody footprint on the bathmat.

Not surprisingly, Dr. Vinci attributed the footprint to Rudy Guede. "I am not saying that this print certainly belongs to Guede," said Vinci, "but it is attributable to Guede; it is compatible." The fact that there is a debate over two very different size feet—Guede's being much larger than Sollecito's—is fairly disconcerting to the process. Moreover, Dr. Vinci failed to make the connection between how Guede could have left a right sneaker print in Meredith's room and a barefoot right print on the bathmat. Certainly a shoe could have come off during the bludgeoning, a defense lawyer pointed out; but figuring the attributes of the foot left on the bathmat and Guede's print is a stretch, particularly for a doctor. Recalling Dr. Lorenzo Rinaldi's testimony (back on trial day – 19), he said that Sollecito's big toe was much wider than either Knox's or Guede's, as was the ball of his foot and the arch. As Rinaldi told the court, "it can absolutely be concluded that the print is compatible with that of Sollecito and not compatible with that of Guede. It gives us a probable identity of Raffaele Sollecito."

Dr. Vinci believed that the extension at the top of the big toe (on the bathmat print) was not an extension, but the second toe of Rudy Guede's; which is much longer than Sollecito's second toe. He also believed that the region of Rudy's foot just below the big toe was compatible with that of the bathmat print. Dr. Vinci also superimposed Guede's print on top of the bathmat print in an attempt to show the compatibility. However, he did not do the same with Sollecito's print. Mignini pointed this out to him, which Dr. Vinci replied that he did not feel the need to make that comparison.

As for the luminol print in the hallway, that prosecutors say is compatible with Sollecito, Dr. Vinci offered a simple explanation. He stated that "the only thing we can say for sure is that it is a human footprint, but it can't be attributed to anyone." He offered an explanation that his measurement of the print was shorter than Sollecito's print, and because of this he ruled out Sollecito. Yet, measurements of pictures favor a slightly shorter measurement. Dr. Vinci attributes all of the luminol prints, simply, to those of old prints left by the occupants. However, he didn't explain why anyone would have been walking around with blood, chlorophyll, fruit juice, detergent, horseradish, or bleach on their feet, or one of the other luminol-sensitive substances on their feet.

As for the two shoe prints on the pillow found underneath Meredith's body, Dr. Vinci claims that both were made by the same shoe. Examining the pillowcase personally, Dr. Vinci calculated that both prints (which prosecutors believe that one is a partial print of the bottom of Guede's right sneaker—a Nike Outbreak2—and the other the heel of a smaller shoe, probably a woman's size 37, which they attributed to Knox) are of a similar pattern of that found in Meredith's room (which has been attributed to Guede).

Dr. Vinci also had a chance to examine blood traces left on Kercher's mattress sheet when he participated in one of the crime scene investigations by forensic experts at the murder scene. According to Vinci, two of these traces were left by the same bloodied knife (with a 3 1/2-inch-long blade that had been placed on the bed); which again contrasts with prosecutors' allegations that the 6 1/2-inch knife found at Sollecito's flat matched Kercher's wounds and may have been the lone murder weapon. The knife that prosecutors allege is the murder weapon is expected to be shown in court for the first time during the next session.

Meredith Kercher Trial Day 39 – (September, 19 2009)

The day had finally arrived when everyone would get a firsthand look at the Marietti knife that was found in Sollecito's flat that the prosecution claims was the murder weapon (marked "Exhibit 36"). Earlier in the trial Dr. Stefanoni testified that the knife possessed Knox's DNA in a groove on the black handle of the knife and Kercher's DNA on the tip. Also scheduled to testify were three expert witnesses called by the judges. The court would finally be privy to expert witnesses that were purely independent, per say; a refreshing change from the perceived partisan expert witnesses, on both sides thus far. Initially the judges had asked the witnesses to focus on the time of death, whether there were signs of sexual assault on the victim, and the characteristics of the possible murder weapon. Their testimony's today were expected to focus on those elements.

The time for the knife viewing was the first order of business; there would be no more waiting. Everyone in the courtroom stood in anticipation, as two court officials (both wearing gloves and masks) entered the room. One of the assistance was carrying a small-white cardboard box (marked "Evidence – handle with care"). Holding the box as if some kind of ancient relic was inside, it was carried to and placed on a viewing table. Suddenly, the box was opened and everyone in the crowd began elbowing others to get the first look at the knife of doom. The other assistant carefully cut open the cellophane bag with a pair of scissors and removed the knife, while Judge Massei instructed the jurors to strap-on surgical masks and step forward to take a look. The jurors all crowded around to get a look at the 6 ½ inch stainless steel blade as judge Massei reminded them, "Please touch only with your eyes." Knox, wearing blue jeans and the same red sweatshirt with the Beatles design that she had worn the previous day, seemed impassive as the knife was being viewed. Sollecito, wearing a white jacket and rimless glasses, bit his fingernails during the viewing and throughout much of the testimony on the knife.

When people were done gawking at the star of the show, the first of the judge's witnesses, Giancarlo Umani Ronchi[111], was called to the stand. A professor and forensic specialist, Ronchi told the court that there was an escalation in the injuries to Meredith Kercher; evolving from a "modest size until they ended with more important wounds that determined her death." Ronchi testified that there were traces of alcohol in Kercher's blood, and that there were signs and traces that she may have been sexually assaulted, "but there just isn't irrefutable certainty in any of it." Ronchi was originally critical of the initial examination of the body. "We were asked to determine time of death," Ronchi explained, "but they had already made outrageous mistakes: first, the failure to analyze the corpse by the coroner who arrived first at the scene." Ronchi was speaking of Dr. Luca Lalli's failure to examine the body until the following day. Dr. Lalli had first arrived at the cottage on November 2nd at 2:00p.m., but had to wait for the forensic team to finish their initial examinations before examining the corpse. He did not get to do so until 1:00p.m., the following day.

Ronchi also stated that the gastric content in Meredith's stomach was about 200 cubic centimeters; not the 500 cubic centimetres indicated by Dr. Lalli's report. Professor Ronchi made a backhanded comment about Dr. Lalli's examination, saying that "the examination performed by the person who carried out the autopsy [Dr. Lalli] does not appear to have been conducted according to the prescribed techniques of forensic pathology..." Professor Ronchi specified that gastric digestion is very much debatable insofar as time necessary for gastric emptying: he stated that it can take three, four, five hours for the stomach to empty; although it could also take much, much longer.

The second witness, Professor Mariano Cingolani[112], also testified to the presence of alcohol in Meredith's system. This can change the calculations of the time of death, which is based partly on digestion, and alcohol affects the rate of digestion. Kercher's blood alcohol levels were tested both in Perugia and Macerata and came out differently, even though the two samples were supposedly taken from Kercher's corpse at the same time. "The amount of alcohol in the system determines how much it affects digestion," said Cingolani. "But because the amounts differ, it was either a lab error or an unexplainable anomaly." Cingolani concluded that Meredith was not in a condition of alcoholic intoxication.

Professor Cingolani testified that he thought Meredith had died within a few minutes of the fatal wound to her throat, which he attributed to a combination of strangulation, suffocation, and loss of blood. "It was maybe no more than seven to ten minutes, and she possibly screamed out," he told the court.

Judging from when the scream was heard by witnesses, at around 11:30p.m., the ten-minute time of death, and the purported alcohol in Kercher's system, this would significantly change the dynamics of the crime. We know that Kercher arrived home at around 9:00p.m. We've also heard witnesses claim to have been with her just prior to that testify that they weren't drinking alcohol that evening. This would mean that at sometime between 9:00p.m., and 11:30p.m., Kercher was drinking alcohol. Mr. Ronchi had originally admitted, back in 2008, that Kercher was extremely drunk at the time of her death, adding that he was not certain of this. From the testimony of the first two witnesses today, we see that there may have been a noteworthy amount of time between Kercher having fun and enjoying a few drinks and her being violently murdered. Was she drinking alone when Rudy Guede allegedly climbed through a window and murdered her, or was she drinking with supposed friends (Knox, Sollecito, and at some point Guede) when things suddenly got out of hand? These questions resurfaced and were certainly amplified by this testimony, which had to have the jury thinking something similar.

However, Mr. Cingolani testified that it was impossible to confirm Kercher's alcohol toxicity levels because test results from Perugia were so different than results he obtained later in his laboratory in Macerata. The first round of tests, done by the coroner in Perugia, showed a low alcohol level of .04, consistent with about one glass of wine, one shot of whiskey, or one 12oz bottle of beer. Cingolani's results weeks later showed a much higher alcohol level .27, which would be consistent with about eight beers. This major inconsistency led Cingolani to believe the blood samples had been either contaminated, poorly conserved, or even inadvertently swapped. This major discrepancy makes establishing her exact time of death laborious, because varying alcohol levels severely affect digestion.

At one point, holding the knife in his hands, Mr. Cingolani raised doubts about it being the murder weapon. He testified that it did not match one of the two knife wounds on the right hand side of Kercher's neck; saying that the three cuts on the Kercher's neck—which range from a depth of less than an inch for the smallest cut to the 3 inches of the deepest gash—would have been bigger if that knife was used, given the wound's depth. "A blade of that dimension going in 4 centimeters would have made a wider wound," Cingolani said. "Many other knives in general are probably more compatible with a lesion of that type." However, he also cautioned that "no firm conclusion could be drawn without knowing the position of Kercher's neck during the attack or the elasticity of her tissues." According to Cingolani, whose team examined photos and videos of the procedure, Kercher died of combined loss of blood and suffocation. He said that the bruises on her neck suggest she might have been strangled and may have choked on her own blood.

A third judge's expert, Anna Aprile[113], testified that while it could be determined that Kercher's body showed evidence of sexual activity close to the time of death, it could not be directly determined whether she was raped or not; as she noted: two-thirds of rape cases show no visible physical injury upon gynecological examination. Aprile said, "The fact that she was found in a pool of blood, with multiple wounds and bruises, suggests violence during intercourse."

Meredith Kercher Trial Day 40 – (September, 25 2009)

The Court of Assizes in Perugia was back in session on Friday morning with two more defense witnesses. Professor Carlo Caltagirone[114], a neurologist who had spent a few hours with Knox the previous winter, explained to the court that stress can affect the memory. "All aspects of memory can be modified by stress and certain circumstances can produce false recollections in perfectly normal people who are completely in good faith," Caltagirone testified. His testimony enraged the prosecution and all civil parties. They wanted to know why the stress of the situation had affected Knox so differently than the rest of the parties involved. Caltagirone could not speak directly to Knox's state of mind during the days following the murder, but he did speak of other cases that he had studied.

"When people are threatened, and accused of not remembering things, they become confused and cannot distinguish what they remember; it is as if they cannot manage their thoughts," he said. Caltagirone's psychological evaluation of Knox explained that she was a typical girl of her age with a flexible mind and that she was in very good general and cognitive condition. The prosecution sarcastically pressed Caltagirone about his evaluation, asking him if the cartwheels and stretches that Knox did at the police station indicated a relaxed frame of mind. Caltagirone said that "the cartwheels were certainly incongruous"; yet, he said that it "reflected great stress," which helped her try and relax. Caltagirone also emphasized that false memories produced by a great deal of stress "is a documented phenomenon." He further explained that it can be scientifically reproducible. Patrick Lumumba told reporters after the session that Knox lied intentionally to throw-off the investigation, period.

The last witness of the day was well-know Italian coroner, Walter Patumi[115]. It has been apparent that this trial, particularly the knife evidence, was as much about the debate over the legitimacy— or lack thereof—of low copy number LCN-DNA than anything else. Another witness, Patumi, would throw in his opinion on the matter, testifying that Kercher's DNA on the knife is too low to be attributed to her with any reasonable certainty. His analysis was based primarily on the sequencer that Dr. Stefanoni used to get her results. Patumi gave the court an example of how the sequencer can be contaminated. He explained—in a separate incident, with a similar machine—that after repeated attempts to clean it for about six months the machine kept reading sheep's blood instead of the human blood that they were testing for on various different samples. Patumi brought in the instruction manual for the sequencer and showed it to the judges. In it, he referred to a particular section which read, "Don't go below 50rfu." However, according to Sarah Gino's testimony on day 34, anything under 100rfu can be considered contamination. The manual is correct, not Gino.

Patumi also contended that the knife was not compatible with Kercher's wounds. Patumi had also been a witness in a different Italian murder trial—also presided over by Judge Massei. Patumi brought pictures of the wounds made in that murder and tried to demonstrate his theory about the type of blade used. He explained that the wounds on the victim in that case were made by a cutters tool and were cuts of 5, 10, and 20 centimeters. He theorized that with a small blade one can make a large cut; drawing the similarity that Kercher's wounds suggest a smaller blade. In particular, Patumi pointed out the deepest would on Kercher's neck (8cm wide & 4cm deep) was absolutely not compatible with the knife held as the murder weapon, which has a blade of 17.5cm.

Meredith Kercher Trial Day 41 – (September, 26 2009)

As the trial neared its dramatic conclusion, the last two scheduled defense witnesses took the stand today in what would be a climactic ending to the trial of the century. One returning expert witness—who would again dispute DNA evidence—and one computer expert would round out the defenses' case. Knox entered the courtroom with Sollecito only a couple of steps behind, as the two were escorted to their seats. The atmosphere was loose, as everyone sensed that a verdict was getting close and that the testimony that would shape the outcome was behind them. However, there was speculation that the defense was likely to request the appointment of an independent expert to evaluate conflicting DNA and other evidence, which would extend the trial and thus the verdict. This would be decided on October 9th, as court is scheduled to meet on that date to hear possible requests for further evidence to be presented or witnesses to be heard again. At this point, closing arguments are scheduled for late October.

Police experts had preciously testified that there was no human interaction on Sollecito's computer after 9:10p.m., on 1 November 2007, when Sollecito finished watching the movie "Amelie," until the following morning at 5:42a.m. However, computer expert, Antonio D'Ambrosio[116], contradicted police experts, testifying that the hard drive on Sollecito's laptop showed that his computer connected with a provider for four seconds at two-minutes before 1:00a.m., on November 2nd. Mr. D'Ambrosio confirmed that he found no other sign of human interaction with the computer after that until 5:42a.m., when an application on the computer crashed. Then, in a strange twist of fate, D'Ambrosio testified that someone had used Sollecito's home computer twice on the night that both Knox and Sollecito were being questioned by police (November 5th), and were subsequently arrested. D'Ambrosio told the court that the computer was used to read ANSA's reports and other news websites detailing Kercher's murder. He added that this computer usage had caused some data to be lost, data that might prove Sollecito's alibi for the night of the murder.

This means that according to D'Ambrosio someone was at Sollecito's apartment on the night that both he and Knox were arrested, while they were already at the police station. The defense made a huge mistake here trying to use this evidence to help prove Sollecito's innocence, when in fact it could more likely be used as further evidence against him. Sollecito would never return to his apartment, as he was arrested and jailed that night (early morning). Why was someone tampering with his laptop computer? Had Sollecito—the Italian engineering graduate—gotten one of his friends or even classmates to tamper with potential incriminating evidence against him? Or, did Sollecito himself tamper with the computer before arriving at the police station, anticipating that the police were getting close and an arrest was near?

Outside the courtroom, Luca Maori, Sollecito's lawyer, did not say who he thought was on the computer. Instead, Maori said told reporters, "Whoever it was cancelled valuable data that showed Raffaele was on the computer the night of the murder." Somehow he had spun this 'incident' in Sollecito's favor; when it was more likely that it was a premeditated attempt to erase valuable and incriminating information. Surprisingly, the prosecution did not pick-up on this huge misstep by the defense.

Sarah Gino[117], the geneticist who had testified only a few sessions ago, was the last witness scheduled for the defense. She told the court that in her opinion "the levels of DNA found on the knife were too low to be considered as evidence." Ms. Gino also suggested that the evidence should be treated as "flawed," because of the strong possibility that it might have been the result of an inadvertent contamination in the police lab. "In a lab where hundreds of samples are tested the risk of contamination exists and should be taken into consideration," Gino said. Then, in a sarcastic rebuttal to Alberto Intini's (the Director of Italy's National Forensic Police who testified on day 17) comment, "DNA doesn't fly," Gino replied, "DNA doesn't have wings but it can fly." It should be noted that her response, although witty, is inaccurate. Ms. Gino also ridiculed the prosecution for providing amplified DNA samples with the dates missing. "These dates are important," Gino testified, "because they would tell us what samples were tested together on the same day, which might indicate if some of them could have been contaminated."

Dr. Patrizia Stefanoni, the Chief of the Italian Scientific Police Unit in Rome, contended Sarah Gino's assertions of contamination by explaining that "...in performing the various analyses on the biological traces in question, there was no anomaly found which could have caused such a contamination," and she gave evidence of the presence of a whole series of checks [controls], precautions and procedures, intended so as to eliminate this risk. Moreover, Dr. Stefanoni declared that she had been working as a biologist for seven years, had always used the same methodology, and had never heard that any problem of contamination of exhibits had occurred.

Meredith Kercher Trial Day 42 – (October 9, 2009)

Having provided several expert witnesses that contradicted just about all of the physical evidence put forth by the prosecution, both defense teams were upbeat and confident as they entered the courtroom. It would be the day that Judge Giancarlo Massei would rule on whether to appoint an independent expert to review the prosecutions DNA evidence. The defense was hopeful that this review would lead to the elimination of the DNA evidence all together; which was a shot-in-the-dark at best; yet, the defense truly felt confident that these events would take place. Even if Knox and Sollecito's lawyers knew it was a long-shot, they did not let it show. Knox, Sollecito, and their family members, however, did not only believe that this was a possibility, they were expecting only this outcome. Curt Knox echoed these very sentiments at the end of the previous session, expressing to reporters outside the courtroom that he couldn't see how the judge could not order an independent review.

The day started with Knox's layers asking the court—just as expected—for an independent review of the evidence. By the evidence, Knox's lawyer Carlo Della Verdova explained that he wanted an independent review of the following:

- DNA on the knife,
- DNA on the bra clasp
- Sexual violence
- Time of death
- Compatibility of the knife
- Dynamic of the attack
- Physics of the scream
- Footprints
- Luminol
- Pillowcase
- Computers
- Phone records

In essence, both defense teams were asking for a new trial with independent experts—a long-shot indeed. After a two hour deliberation—which included all defense lawyers, both judges, and both prosecutors (supported by both Francesco Maresca and Carlo Pacelli)—it was dejavu all over again: the request was denied. Judge Massei explained to the court that if the jury still had doubts about the evidence by the time that both sides had concluded their closing arguments, that they could ask for a review by independent experts.

Overwhelmed and surprised by the decision, Knox appeared visibly upset. Upon hearing the judge's refusal, Knox put her head back and closed her eyes in astonishment. Meanwhile, looking even more distraught, Sollecito put his head down on the table and wept; while his lawyer, Luca Maori, patted his client on the back to comfort him. With that Judge Massei adjourned the trial until November 20th, at which time the closing arguments will begin. The court told reporters after the session they expected a verdict by December 5th. With the trial suspended until November, the prosecution, defense teams, and civil lawyers would begin to prepare their closing arguments. The prosecution was scheduled to go first, to which Mignini told reporters outside the courtroom, "I will surprise you all."

Meredith Kercher Trial Day 43 – (November 20, 2009)

Amanda Knox and Raffaele Sollecito entered the courtroom for what was surely going to be a very draining emotional day for them. Scheduled to give his closing arguments was the public prosecutor Giuliano Mignini. The two suspects would have to settle in and tough it out, as Mignini's summation would last for over seven-hours. During his closing speech, Mignini confidently and lucidly described how Knox, Sollecito, and Guede brutally murdered Mereidth Kercher; he explained the motive and means behind it, from his perspective. Judge Massei started by making it very clear that neither defense team was allowed to interrupt or object during closing arguments. It would be the most compelling day in court as Mignini would remorselessly, ruthlessly, and unapologetically provide every detail that led up to the brutality of this crime.

Mr. Mignini began by explaining the strained relationship between Knox and Kercher. "Amanda had the chance to retaliate against a girl who was serious and quiet," Mignini said. "She had nursed her hatred for Meredith and that was the time when it could explode. The time had come to take revenge on that smug girl." Mignini gave a detailed reconstruction of the crime that began with Knox, Sollecito, and Guede arriving at the cottage together. He stressed that they had arrived together most likely to settle some drug issues with Guede—who was known in Perugia for dealing drugs. He claimed that Sollecito and Guede were smitten with the young American and that they would both do anything to please her. Mignini explained that Sollecito was "dependent on Knox," and that she "dominated" their relationship. Mignini asserted that this could be seen in TV footage from the time of the murder in the way Sollecito was "following behind her, often kissing and cuddling her."

As the three arrived at the cottage Mignini said, "Meredith and Amanda began to argue over money; Meredith was also upset that Amanda had brought another man [Guede] back to the house." According to Mignini things quickly got out of hand as Kercher was not going to back down to the bullying. "They argued about this ugly habit of hers and the three who had arrived were also under the influence of drugs and alcohol." Mignini occasionally raised his voice which added quite an effect to his speech. The more serious the circumstances, as he described them, the louder and more poignant his vocal inflections became. At some point during the argument, Mignini alleged that Knox hit Kercher's head against a wall then tried to strangle her, as Sollecito held her and Guede sexually assaulted her.

"They realized that Meredith would not give up fighting and at that point the match had to be brought to an end," he said. Mignini alleged that the men pinned Kercher down by her arms while Knox threatened her with the knife, prodding at her throat and saying, "Ah, you were pretending to be such a little saint, now we are going to show you." Mignini then said that Knox used the 6 1/2-inch Marietti knife (16.5-centimeter blade) to cut Kercher's throat, causing the deepest wound, while Sollecito used another knife to threaten her. "It is easy to imagine Amanda, with her sexual confidence, insulting the more reserved Meredith," he told the jury. "Amanda was in charge. She plunged the knife into the side of her neck with the intention of killing her friend."

Knox appeared disheveled and drained as she sat listening to Mignini accuse her of being a cold-hearted assassin. Knox looked straight ahead as tears flowed down her cheeks. Luciano Ghirga held her hand and hugged her in an effort to comfort her. During a brief break, she broke down crying as she left the courtroom. Yet, the break was shorted lived, and Mignini was right back to his all-out assault on the two suspects. He described Kercher as a woman full of life and potential, "the young woman we too often forget." He quoted the testimony of Kercher's father John when he described his daughter as a woman who would have fought back endlessly against an attack. The courtroom was silent as he recalled the words of Kercher's father: "Meredith would have fought with all her life."

"Meredith was far too serious a girl for her," Mignini claimed. "Amanda didn't like her; she didn't like her friends because they were critical of her hygiene and habits," he added. Mignini quoted Kercher's British friends, who testified to the strained relationship between Knox and Kercher, as well as their surprise and irritation with Knox's behavior after the murder. Mignini described the murder as "an unstoppable crescendo of frenzied violence," which began with Knox and Sollecito trying to take off Kercher's clothes and threatening her. He said that the fatal blow occurred around 11:30p.m., when her horrible scream was heard by two neighbors. He went into great detail; at one time describing the sound of dry leaves crunching underfoot as the murderers ran from the crime scene.

Mr. Mignini was most animated when he discussed what he termed as a "staged burglary" after the murder. "The key to the mystery is in that room," he said: adding that it would be nearly impossible to climb that window and enter without hurting oneself and leaving blood traces on the shattered glass. He also argued that window was the most exposed window; clearly visible from the nearby road and illuminated as well, making it an unlikely choice for a burglar. "All of this was done to channel suspicions on a stranger, and divert them from those who had the apartment keys," he said. Mignini also pointed out how fragments of glass had been found on top of clothes scattered on the bedroom floor and that the wardrobe had been ransacked after the window was broken.

Giuliano Mignini: It would have been manna from heaven for them if blood or other genetic evidence had been found on the broken glass or window frame, but nothing was found. This hypothetical thief then did something quite remarkable—he didn't take anything of value. No jewelry was missing; computers were left at the scene as well as designer bangs and clothes. A 'very strange break-in' was, in fact, how the first police officer who arrived at the house described it—they could not believe that nothing of value was taken.

Mr. Mignini also got animated when discussing the events that took place when Knox returned to the home the next morning, just before Kercher's body was discovered. Knox had testified that she noticed blood in the bathroom, but proceeded to take a shower anyway. Acting sarcastically puzzled, Mignini looked at the jury and asked them rhetorical questions. "Is this normal?" he asked while waving his papers. "Why would anyone do that?" Mignini also defended the investigation, explaining that the criticism came from journalists, detectives, bloggers, and lawyers from Italy and abroad who were seeking fame. He added that police and prosecutors handled the case professionally and that it was time to bring the saga to a close. Mignini also defended some of the seemingly less-credible prosecution witnesses, such as Mr. Kokomani (whom Mignini said was "commendable under pressure"), and homeless man, Mr. Curatolo (whom Mignini termed "educated" and "extremely credible").

Although it appeared to be over, Mignini was scheduled to finish-up the following day. It was then that Mignini was going to reveal his surprise to the court. Also, the prosecution was expected to formally make their sentencing requests to the eight-member jury, which most would bet would be a life sentence request for both suspects. Kercher family lawyer, Francesco Maresca, told reporters outside the courtroom that he was "very satisfied" with Mignini's argument, adding that the crimes should bring a life sentence.

Meredith Kercher Trial Day 44 – (November 21, 2009)

Wearing her Beatles hoodie for the second time during the trial and with her hair held up by a clip; Amanda Knox entered the courtroom looking battered from the events of the prior session. The day was expecting both prosecutors to say their final words, as well as their requests to the judge to sentence the suspects to life in prison. Furthermore, prosecutor Giuliano Mignini's surprise was also looming (which would be a complete video reconstruction of the crime).

Continuing where he left off the day before, Mignini told the court that he had "gotten to know Amanda Knox fairly well" during the interrogations. Continuing, Mignini said, "and I have observed her at length in court." He quoted an evaluation of Knox by a well-known criminologist—to which he did not name (very likely criminal psychologist Dr. David Wilson)—and he read the evaluation aloud in court.

According to the evaluation, "Knox has a tendency to develop a dislike for people who do not agree with her, and her feelings are anesthetized." Mignini described Knox as a "narcissist; someone prone to aggressive anger, manipulative, theatrical and lacking in empathy." Mignini said that he was struck by how much the profile of the criminologist matched his own impressions of Knox. Raffaele Sollecito's profile also fit, Mignini said; describing him as someone who depends on others for approval—a "dependent personality." Mignini added that he also "found Sollecito to be cold." Knox and Sollecito remained expressionless as Mignini continued his assault.

However, when Mignini had finished, Knox took a deep breath and stood up to make a brief spontaneous statement to the court. "Meredith was my friend, and I did not hate her. The idea that I wanted revenge on a person who was always kind to me is absurd. I never had any acquaintance or relationship with Rudy Guede. The things that were said in the past two days are pure fantasy. It is not the truth and not the reality of the situation."

Next it was prosecutor Manuela Comodi's turn to give her final statement to the court. "The DNA was not contaminated," Comodi asserted. She declared that the proof which has emerged from the investigations is "irrefutable and overwhelming." Comodi stressed that not one right of the defendants had been harmed. "The only right offended was that of the scientific police and the postal police to see their work recognized," she stated. "In every biological analysis the risk of deterioration and contamination is inherent," Comodi said. "Patrizia Stefanoni, the biologist of the scientific police has, however, put in action all the due procedures to avoid these phenomena and nobody can affirm the contrary. Dr. Stefanoni expolained that deterioration is caused by an attack on the evidence sample by fungi or bacteria, but such an event has no effect on the reliability of the result. According to Stefanoni, deterioration impacts samples in the sense of causing "a loss of information;" thus, it is not the same as unreliable data."

Comodi spent her time discussing the evidence against the two, mostly criticizing the defense's expert witnesses. "At the scene of the crime there is a footprint made in blood on the bathmat and Knox and Sollecito's footprints made in blood on the floor"— Comodi said—"and these were supposedly made at some different time because they stepped in bleach or rust or fruit juice? It's up to you to decide."

Nearing the end of the day, Mignini revealed his surprise. Using Google maps of the town of Perugia, and avatar figures resembling Knox, Sollecito, Guede, and Kercher superimposed on actual photos or digital re-creations of the scene of the crime; he showed a twenty-minute video of what prosecutors believe was the dynamic of the murder; retracing events from the hours before the murder through to its aftermath. Autopsy photos were also included to illustrate how the injuries found on Kercher's body were produced by the actions of the alleged killers. Below is the timeline of the re-enactment as read in court by prosecutor Mignini.

15:48 - Meredith texts to her English friends that she will be slightly late for her dinner meeting with them. 16:00 - Meredith leaves the house in Via della Pergola to go to the home of her friends. A few minutes later Raffaele and Amanda leave the cottage in Via della Pergola to go Sollecito's place. 18:00 - Amanda Knox leaves Raffaele Sollecito's house. This is indicated by cell phone records. 18:27 - Raffaele Sollecito interacts with his laptop to watch the film "Amelie" alone at home. 20:18 - Amanda Knox in Via Ulisse Rocchi receives a text message (sms) from Patrick Lumumba telling her not to come to work that night. 20.30 - Amanda Knox goes back to Via Garibaldi to the apartment of Raffaele Sollecito. 20:38 - Amanda sends a text message (sms) in reply to Patrick Lumumba. 20:46 - Sollecito turns off his mobile phone. He is still at home in Via Garibaldi.

20:45 – Meredith's meal of pizza with her English friends' ends. She starts off in the direction of Via della Pergola with a girlfriend who will leave her halfway to go to her own home. 21:00 - Meredith is at home, she eats a mushroom, she lies down on her bed, and she reads some university lecture notes. 21:10 - From this point on there is no more human interaction with Raffaele Sollecito's computer. 21:45 - Amanda and Raffaele leave his apartment and go to the Piazza Grimana. Less than 100 meters away from the house in Via della Pergola, the two talk and watch the house and decide what to do. They show a suspicious attitude which is reported in court by the witness Curatolo 23:20 - Amanda opens the door of Via della Pergola. 23.20 - Amanda, Raffaele and Rudy enter the house in Via della Pergola, where Meredith is already present in her room [On the court video there is no simulation of the meeting between Amanda and Rudy, because the reconstruction is based on testimony, the autopsy evidence and medical findings.]

23:21 - Amanda and Raffaele go into Meredith's bedroom, while Rudy goes into the bathroom. 23:25 - A scuffle begins between Amanda, helped by Raffaele, and Meredith. The English girl is taken by the neck then banged against a cupboard. Rudy Guede enters and joins in. 23:30 - 23:45 Depiction in the timeline and computer simulation of a horrific struggle with Meredith 23:50 - Amanda and Raffaele take Meredith's mobile phones and they leave the apartment. Guede goes into the bathroom to get several towels to staunch the blood then puts a cushion under Meredith's head. 00.10 - Meredith's mobile phones are thrown into a garden in Via Sperandio. 00.15 - From this moment, there are no certainties on the times for the rearrangement of the crime scene carried out by Amanda and Raffaele Sollecito.

At the end of the session, both prosecutors (Comodi and Mignini) requested a life sentence for Amanda Knox and Raffaele Sollecito. "This was a murder accompanied by sexual violence which was done for petty reasons against a girl 21 years old who was soon due to return to London for the birthday of her mother; but Meredith would never go home to embrace her loved ones," Mignini said. "Her mother, father, sister, Stephanie, and two brothers, who now have no choice but to go to the cemetery to be near her remains; she was literally eliminated."

He closed the session by reading a Latin phrase about justice from ancient Roman jurist, Eneo Domizio Ulpiano: "*Iustitia est constans et perpetua voluntas ius suum cuique tribuendi. Iuris praecepta sunt haec: honeste vivere alterum non laedere, suum cuique tribuere*" ("Justice is the constant and perpetual will to render to every man his due. Live honestly, don't hurt others and to each his own").

"You must give them what they deserve," Mignini pronounced, "ergastolo" ("life in prison").

Chapter 12 - The Verdict

Meredith Kercher Trial Day 45 – (November 27, 2009)

Italy's trial of the century was nearing a dramatic conclusion; but first the world would have to wait a bit longer, as all litigators would have a chance to add their closing arguments for their clients. Possibly causing further delay was the fact that Sollecito's lead lawyer, Giulia Bongiorno, had been diagnosed with appendicitis just three days earlier. All civil lawyers were expected to plead their cases in court today, asking for monetary compensation for various reasons.

The first to provide closing arguments for the day was Letizia Magnini, a lawyer for civil-plaintiff, Aldalia Tattanelli-Morrone (owner of the cottage where the murder was committed). The cottage had been seized by police for nearly 16-months before it was released back to its owner; the cottage had been confiscated by police and released back to Morrone back in April 2009. Since the release, Morrone had changed the locks on the doors and cleaned it thoroughly, as blood remained on the walls until its release. Letizia told the court that her client was looking for compensation from either the state or the defendants if found guilty. "In rent alone my client has lost more than €20,000," Letizia said, "and then on top of that there is the cost of the cleaning and the repair work. So that is why we are civil plaintiffs to try and get some of this expenditure back." All in all, Letizia formally requested $57,000 for lost rent and the cost of renovating the house that was dubbed by many "the house of horrors" in the aftermath of the crime.

Patrick Lumumba's lawyer, Carlo Pacelli, was up next. Pacelli attacked Knox, describing her as "satanical and diabolical" for blaming Lumumba for a crime that she (Knox) knew he did not commit. "Knox is a talented and calculating liar who had deliberately gone out of her way to frame Patrick," Pacelli asserted. He noted that "Just a few words said by the nefarious and astute Amanda Knox to police, 'I confusedly remember that he killed her,' have destroyed Patrick Lumumba as a man, father, and husband." Pacelli told the court that a separate hearing would be needed to figure out the total monetary damages that he and his client are requesting for slander. He noted that the reason for the uncertainly at this point is because Patrick is still suffering the consequences of being named by Knox, and is undergoing psychiatric treatment.

Lumumba had only been awarded $12,000 in compensation for unjust detention, although he had requested nearly ten-times that amount. He was also forced to close-down his club, *Le Chic*, after Knox's accusations. Pacelli ended his address in dramatic fashion, posing to the court a question that can be viewed as the most poignant of the trial—while providing his own answer. "By naming him [Lumumba], she hoodwinked the officer in charge of the murder investigation. *Who is the real Amanda Knox*? Is it the one we see before us here, simple water and soap [Italian phrase meaning *wholesome*], the angelic St Maria Goretti [A teenager made a saint by the Catholic Church after she was murdered by an attempted rapist]? Or is she really a she-devil (a diabolical person focused on sex, drugs, and alcohol; living life to the extreme and borderline?)— this is the Amanda Knox of November 1st 2007 [the night Meredith was murdered]."

The day saved the best for last, as the highly anticipated closing arguments from Kercher family lawyer, Francesco Maresca, got underway. Maresca told the court that the case against Knox and Sollecito was "crystal clear," and sufficient enough for the judges and the jury to find them guilty. "We often hear from families of victims that they do not want revenge," Maresca said, "just justice and justice means punishment." However, Maresca formally requested $36 million in damages from Knox, Guede, and Sollecito ($12 million each). He noted that "These damages requested are symbolic to the injuries suffered by the whole of the Kercher family, her parents, her two brothers, and her sister." Maresca explained that the Kercher family had showed the world "the elegance of silence," and he slammed the Knox and Sollecito families for their furious media campaigns "putting an abyss between them [Kercher family] and the Knox and Sollecito clans," he said. "Meredith no longer has a life and perhaps the only thing left in this case is repentance," Maresca told the court. "Personally, I hope she did not die for 300 euros [about $450 that was missing from the crime scene], for no real reason, as the prosecutors indicated." In closing Maresca stated, "The Bible says that the judge is a minister of God, and inflicts a just punishment on those who do evil; those who cause suffering must be made to suffer by having their freedom taken away."

Meredith Kercher Trial Day 46 – (November 28, 2009)

With the prosecution and civil lawyers out of the way, it would be up to Sollecito and Knox's defense teams to close out Italy's trial of the century. Previously scheduled to speak first was Sollecito's lead litigator, Giulia Bongiorno. However, since she had been diagnosed with appendicitis, the court made a special ruling (back on November 24th) that she could begin her summation on Monday. Taking her place on this day was Sollecito's other lawyer, Luca Maori.

Trumping that information, the real news of the day came at the end of Friday's (November 27th) session when Knox's parents, Curt Knox & Edda Mellas, were informed that they had been brought up on defamation of character charges for giving an interview in a newspaper recounting Amanda's statement that the police struck her head, deprived her of food and water, and refused to provide her with an English translator. The defamation accusation was filed by the officer in charge of the Perugia Murder Squad, Inspector Monica Napoleoni and five of her colleagues involved in the case. In Italy defamation is punishable with a minimum fine of 500 Euros and a jail sentence of between six months and three years. The suit was based on an interview that Curt and Edda gave to a British newspaper eighteen months before (*Sunday Times*, published on 15 June 2008). That case—along with a similar charge against Amanda Knox—would likely take place sometime in the fall of 2010.

With the buzz about the new defamation suit against Knox's parents, Luca Maori took the floor for his final attempt to defend his client. "Defending an innocent person is always more difficult than defending a guilty one" Maori told the court. "Raffaele has been described as the worst of young men; he has been insulted and wounded in his dearest affections. Raffaele is the second victim in this event. He is twenty-three years old and he has spent two of these years in prison. They have wanted to tailor him a suit of clothes which does not belong to him; he has been described as a fellow addicted to drugs, porno films, and the search for strong emotions. His past has been morbidly delved into and that of his family, as has the premature death of his mother."

Mr. Maori played an audio conversation via Skype to the court that took place between Rudy Guede and a friend while Rudy was in Germany. Unknown to Rudy at the time, his friend was speaking to him from an office in Perugia police headquarters.

Friend: Ciao Rudy, how are you?

Rudy Hermann Guede: Not too well.

Friend: Where are you?

RHG: I'm in Dusseldorf and I have no money.

Friend: Where are you staying?

RHG: I'm living in a barge on the Rhine and sleeping on trains, without paying for a ticket. It's tough, I can't do this any more.

Friend: Would you like me to send some money?

RHG: Well, that would be useful.

Friend: OK, look, I'll send you 50 Euros through Western Union, then you can pick it up.

RHG: Thanks, but it's already late in the evening.

Friend: They're talking about you here [in Perugia].

RHG: I know what happened in Perugia, but they're making a mistake. I am not 'The Baron.' I'm called Byron after Byron Scott, the famous basketball player.

Friend: But they are saying other things.

RHG: Listen, you know I knew those girls, I knew them both, Meredith and Amanda, but nothing more, you know that. I've been to their house twice, the last time a few days before all this business, but I didn't do anything. I have nothing to do with this business. I wasn't there that evening. If they have found my fingerprints it means I must have left them there before.

Friend: But your photo is everywhere.

RHG: I've seen it, the police were wrong to put my photo around like that. I'm not how they describe me. I have nothing to do with that night.

Friend: But if you have nothing to do with it why don't you come back? I'll help you to find a good lawyer who can clear things up.

RHG: I'm afraid. But I don't want to stay in Germany, I'm black and if the police catch me I don't know what they might do to me. I prefer Italian jails.

During his six-hour summation, Mr. Maori placed the responsibility for the crime solely on Rudy Guede, and spent a majority of the six-hours refuting the evidence presented against Sollecito. "There is one fact that must not be forgotten in this trial, and that is that there is already a guilty person: Rudy Hermann Guede condemned to thirty years for the crime," Maori stated. "The DNA is his; as are the fingerprints, and the footprints." Maori defended Sollecito's character, calling him "quiet, shy, and romantic." He also reiterated that the DNA on the bra is probably due to contamination, and that the footprint (that the prosecution attributes to Sollecito) belongs to Guede. Maori also brought to light some new evidence that his forensic experts had discovered. He said that his experts believed that the biological substance visible on the pillow found underneath Kercher's body, contained semen. According to Maori, the substance was never tested by the forensic police. "Why were the two spots visible on the pillow found under the victim not tested?" Maori asked. "The crime against Kercher was sexual," Maori added, "but no one tested those stains."

Meredith Kercher Trial Day 47 – (November 30, 2009)

Monday had been reserved for Sollecito's lead attorney, Giulia Bongiorno, after a bad case of appendicitis forced Judge Massei to reschedule her closing arguments until today. However, Bongiorno was ready, and she came out swinging for her client. Bongiorno went right to attack on the forensic evidence, calling it "contaminated and flawed." Bongiorno claimed that Sollecito "raised the alarm and waited for the investigators on the doorstep of the house of the crime." She then asked the court, "Now would a killer do that?" She stated that Sollecito barely knew Kercher and didn't know Guede at all—adding that the prosecution failed to establish any link between Sollecito and Guede. "In this trial there are many doubts, but one certainty, that the two did not know each other at the time of the crime," she proclaimed. In regard to Meredith's bra clasp, which the prosecution says had Sollecito's DNA on it; Bongiorno claimed that it was due to contamination, citing 46 days between the murder and the time that it was collected.

Bongiorno surprised the court, however, spending most of her time defending Amanda Knox. Her plan was clear: it would be hard for the jury to convict Sollecito if Knox was found not guilty. "Throughout this trial I have heard Amanda described as someone who nursed a hatred, someone who was a man-eater, and someone who was a diabolical witch. But Amanda is a little girl with child-like eyes, full of energy who is given to imprudence and spontaneity. She is not Amanda the Ripper; she is a fragile and weak girl who had only been in Italy a short while and did not know the language or the law." Then she made another one of her memorable comments similar to the "Little lovebirds" comment that she made earlier in the trial. "Amanda, just like Amelie, has a lot of energy; she is naive and candid like the French film character," Bongiorno said. "The approach of Amanda toward life is exactly the same of Amelie, spontaneous, immediate, and imprudent." Bongiorno then sarcastically asked the court, "Are we to believe that selective cleaning was carried out by Raffaele and Amanda? They said 'oh there are my fingerprints, there are my footprints, there's my DNA' and then cleaned it all up; leaving only Rudy's handprint and DNA at the scene." Closing out Sollecito's defense, Bongiorno stated, "The train of absolute proof has not left the prosecution's station, because there are no tracks for it to travel on. Open your souls and examine each piece of evidence."

Meredith Kercher Trial Day 48 – (December 1, 2009)

After a long, arduous trial it was finally time for Knox's defense team to give their closing arguments. Today would be reserved for the naturally argumentative Carlo Dalla Vedova, who had put up quite a fight throughout the trial—often frustrating Mignini and Judge Massei. "The truth comes out in a trial and we have been patiently waiting for this moment, especially Amanda Knox, who has been sitting in jail with patience and determination, waiting to get her life back," Dalla Vedova told the court. "Amanda Knox never should have been arrested. And everything that has happened since then has been part of an attempt to maintain an accusation that, bit by bit, has disintegrated." Dalla Vedova cited Edgardo Giobbi, the former director of the violent crimes division of the central operations unit in Rome, as the first to suspect Knox. "Immediately after the crime, they focused attention on her," said Dalla Vedova. "They started recording her conversations. They were quick to say 'case closed,' but it was a mistake the police made in the beginning, then they couldn't let it go." Dalla Vedova claimed that it was more than 53 hours of police questioning that made Knox blame Patrick Lumumba for the crime as well as falsely implicating herself. "She can hardly speak Italian," he said, and she was "confused and terrorized."

Although Dalla Vedova did not make mention of any physical abuse suffered by Knox at the hands of police, he did acknowledge that she was questioned without an attorney present. Dalla Vedova accused the prosecution of changing the motive at the last minute and not supporting it with evidence. "It is no longer the result of a sex party gone wrong," he said. "Now it is Amanda who organized the crime out of vengeance." He played up his perplexity over this 'so called' hatred that Knox had for Kercher. Citing Kercher's British friends—who testified that Kercher had criticized Knox for her cleaning habits, for her guitar playing, and because she brought random boys home—Dalla Vedova said, "And yet it is from this hate that everything else is meant to follow; according to the prosecutor, it is all Amanda; Amanda against another girl? You have to explain the hate to me. Where is it?" he asked. "This cannot be used as evidence." Dalla Vedova described Knox as a "clean-faced young girl" who he knows well.

"Amanda stayed in Perugia, she did not run away; she did not go to Germany when her aunt told her to come. On the morning of the 5th, the day she was interrogated, she went to school. She wanted to be in Perugia," claimed Della Vedova. According to him, the police were in a rush to solve the crime. "It was a mistake from the beginning," he said. "They called her an assassin based on the fact she did a cartwheel," Dalla Vedova sarcastically pointed out. Dalla Vedova disputed the evidence against Knox that was proposed by the prosecution, reiterating points testified to by expert defense witnesses. In closing, Dalla Vedova said, "She is soap and water (wholesome)," a phrase used by Carlo Pacelli in his summation. "I've known her for years," he said. "Remember that life in prison is the most severe punishment in our country, there is nothing worse; that what the prosecutor has asked for Amanda. But Doubt remains in this trial today, and a young girl is waiting to be judged. There is a lack of clarity with all the evidence in this trial, and as jurors you have a very difficult job. But if you have even a minimal doubt, you must acquit this girl."

Meredith Kercher Trial Day 49 – (December 2, 2009)

The last day of summations had finally arrived. Today would be the last day of court before the verdict. Anticipation and anxiety was growing day by day, and today it was one day away from its peak. The best was saved for last, as Knox's lead attorney, Luciano Ghirga, would give an emotional closing argument that would bring tears to his eyes. Ghirga's emotional four-hour plea to acquit his client started with an attack on the prosecutions' evidence against her. He also heavily criticized the way that the investigation was handled, claiming that prosecutors leaked investigative documents that were to be kept secret. Ghirga focused some time on the interrogation of Knox and her allegations that police hit her. "This is a privation of the right to defense of a person who was at that moment effectively a suspect, and," he said as his voice rose to a shout, "we will not accept it! It is a very serious omission that we cannot bear—something we did not know how to explain to her and her parents!"

Ghirga showed remorse for Kercher, but also asked the jury for similar mercy for Knox. "We suffer for what happened to Meredith, but also for the future of Amanda." Ghirga turned to Knox's parents, who have been ever present in the court room, and said tearfully, "Amanda's parents ask you for her acquittal. There is no Knox clan, just two desperate parents." Ghirga apologized to the court for his emotional outpouring, and he was forced to take a long pause as tears ran down his face. Ghirga stood at Knox's side with his head down trying to fight back the tears, as Carlo Dalla Vedova comforted him by putting his left hand on Ghirga's right arm. As he composed himself and continued; Ghirga said in closing, "The prosecutor is right about one thing: you should not forget the victim, Meredith," he said. "And there is one thing the prosecution should have done for Meredith and that is an investigation done well from the beginning, with rigor. Amanda asks you for her life. Give Amanda her life back, by acquitting her." Addressing the jury, Ghirga ended by saying, "You the jury will have to decide whether what Amanda said that night [the night of her arrest], her implosion, was the collapse of her alibi or evidence of utmost stress."

As the court took a short recess, Knox was escorted out of the courtroom. She turned back and smiled at her mother, father, and three sisters—whose eyes were welling-up with tears—as she exited. Upon commencement of the session, prosecutor Mignini ended the case with a rebuttal statement. Mignini called Knox a "coiled spring that was unleashed" during the night of her arrest. "Meredith accused Amanda of a series of things," Mignini said, "that Meredith must have considered unbearable—she brought boys home; she had a vibrator and condoms; she didn't flush the toilet." Mignini told the court that Sollecito helped Knox because he was always following her, and that Guede was also trying to please her as well. "The three of them were full of drugs and alcohol," he said, "and things degenerate quickly in those conditions." Recalling the night of Knox's confession to police Mignini said, "Her confession of having a vision of being at the murder scene was not coerced and it was not improper that a lawyer wasn't present." Defending his own actions on that night Mignini said, "I asked Amanda if she wanted to make a spontaneous statement, and she said yes. In that situation the presence of a lawyer is not necessary." With all sides resting at this time, the judge ordered that the jury would begin deliberations on Friday, December 4th.

Meredith Kercher Trial Day 50 – (December 4, 2009) – The Verdict

Eleven grueling months after the trial had begun; the day of the verdict had finally arrived. News media from all over the world gathered inside and outside the courthouse to get the dramatic decision. Unlike the United States, a guilty verdict and sentencing in Italy can be handed down on the same day. The Kercher family, the Knox family, and the Sollecito family—who were all present in the courtroom—all braced themselves for what was sure to be an emotional day, no matter what way the decision went. TV Stations in America, Italy, and the UK reported the story, providing non-stop analysis throughout the day as they awaited the final decision.

Meredith's parents, John and Arline Kercher, had arrived in Perugia earlier that evening, accompanied by their surviving children—Stephanie, John, and Lyle. Hoards of photographers and television cameras surrounded them as they made their way into a nearby hotel. Reporters asked them what they expected from the verdict, but received no response from the grief-stricken family. The Knox family, however, continued their vocal campaign, saying that the jury has the lives of two twenty-year old children in their hands.

Amanda Knox entered the courtroom wearing a lime jacket over a yellow shirt, with white pants and her hair pulled back in a single braid. All eyes focused on the six independent jurors as they entered the courtroom wearing red, white, and green sashes—the colors of Italy's flag. The American media continued to slam the Italian justice system and the way that they handled the case. The overall sentiments of the American media was that there was not enough evidence against the two suspects, and that jurors were not sequestered in the same fashion as in the United States, a method seen by the American media as antiquated and unfair.

As the final day of trial began, Amanda Knox was scheduled to give a final statement to the court. Raffaele Sollecito, on the other hand, continued to maintain his right to silence. As Knox stood to address the court for the last time, she appeared much more sullen and serious; realizing the weight of the situation. As she began to speak her voice trembled, and a hush fell over the Italian courtroom. Speaking fluent Italian, Knox tried one last time to convince the court that she was not the killer.

Amanda Knox: *I would like to take this moment because it is my right to speak in this case. I have thought a lot over the past days on what to say. Very often people have asked me how I manage to stay calm. I am not calm. In these days I wrote on a piece of paper that I was scared to lose myself for deeds that weren't of my doing. I am scared of having the mask of an assassin glued to my face. The decision to keep me in prison for the past 2 years has made me sad, delusional and frustrated. Many say to me 'I would have already ripped my hair out or wrecked my prison cell,' but I don't let my moral go down. In these cases I try and stay calm and look for the positive side and this is one of those cases. The moment in which a decision has to be taken you must understand. I feel vulnerable in front of you, but I am sure of what happened and for this I would like to thank you for having followed, listened to me. My family and my friends have been the ones who have supported me and help me go forward day by day; making me able to bear all this and I thank them. But I would also like to thank the prosecutor because sincerely I know they are doing their job even if they don't understand. They don't understand because they are trying to bring justice to a fact. But I thank you because it's up to you now.*

At 10:40a.m., the two judges (Giancarlo Massei & Beatrice Cristiani) and the six jurors withdrew into the council chambers to begin their deliberations. In the deliberation room, which is just beside the courtroom, there were eight comfortable armchairs, shelves full of the files from the trial, a computer, printer, coffee machine, and water dispenser. Judge Massei sat at the head of the table and Judge Cristiani sat just to his right. The judges would first summarize the entire trial, then questions, and then an extensive deliberation period in which they discussed the evidence. This process was expected to take several hours, and a verdict could come the next day, even. As the judges and jury deliberated; so to did the Italian, American, and UK TV stations. All other news was virtually passed-over, as the coverage continued almost without pause on CNN and FOX News here in the United States.

After several hours of coverage the media was informed at about 3:00p.m., Eastern Standard Time that the jury would announce a verdict by 6:00p.m., Eastern Standard Time. At midnight Perugia time (6:00p.m. New York time), after deliberating for 14 hours, the jury had finally reached a verdict. The man in the black gown (Judge Massei) walked into the courtroom like the grim-reaper with a piece of paper in his hand that had the fate of Knox and Sollecito written on it. Judge Massei walked up to the podium—with judge Cristiani standing to his right and the remaining six jurors reaching their places. Judge Massei bent his head down and began to read the paper without expression, words that would make history.

"La Corte d'Assise di Perugia, in the name of the Italian People...in regard to Knox Amanda and Sollecito Raffaele...the articles 533, 535...declares Knox, Amanda and Sollecito, Raffaele guilty of the crimes they are accused of..." The Knox family immediately broke into tears as the gut-wrenching verdict was announced, sobbing loudly. Amanda Knox began to sob and sniffle as her fate was being announced. Judge Massei continued reading, convicting both Knox and Sollecito on all counts except theft. This meant that the jury had probably theorized that Rudy Guede had left with the money and credit cards, while Knox and Sollecito disposed of the two cell phones that belonged to Kercher. Knox was given a sentence of 26-years; Sollecito was given 25-years. In regard to the civil suit, both were ordered to pay a total of 5 million euros ($7.4 million USD) to the Kercher family. In addition, Knox was ordered to pay 40,000 Euros ($60,000 USD) to Patrick Lumumba for falsely accusing him of being the killer. Judge Massei concluded the trial with his final words, "L'udienza è sopra" ("The hearing is over").

As the judges and jury step aside, the guards come forward to take Knox and Sollecito away. Knox continues sobbing as her lawyer, Carlo Dalla Vedova, holds her tightly for a moment then delivers her to the guards. Sollecito, on the other hand, showed little emotion—sitting stiffly while staring into space. No cameras flashed in the courtroom this time, however, as the deafening sounds of shock and horror filled the air. As Sollecito and Knox were led from the court, Sollecito's stepmother appeared to be hyperventilating, as she cried-out his name twice, "Raffaele, Raffaele!" His father sat silently, with his head in his hands—composed, but visibly distraught. As Knox passed the door she looked up and saw the Kercher family standing there. She gave them a desperate look, but they just looked at her with stone faces. Prosecutor Mignini appeared to be enjoying the moment, even taking some pleasure in the reactions of the relatives.

Outside the courthouse, flocks of media swarmed like flies trying to get shots of the two recently convicted youngsters. Knox and Sollecito were escorted by guards into the night, and placed into two separate black vans. Camera flashes lit-up the night's sky as Knox and Sollecito were slowly driven away. Some reporters even chased behind the vehicles, snapping pictures into the back of the van's tinted windows with bars on them, in an attempt to capture the look on Knox's face.

Knox's father, Curt, walked the four blocks from the courtroom to Perugia's Brufani Hotel—where they were staying—staring into space and holding the hands of his other two daughters, who were sobbing profusely. Back at the hotel, the Knox family held a press conference where they reacted to the verdict. "While we always knew this was a possibility, we find it difficult to accept this verdict when we know that she is innocent, and that the prosecution has failed to explain why there is no evidence of Amanda in the room where Meredith was so horribly and tragically murdered."

The American news media continued their coverage of the event, as shock and dismay was the overall pervasive theme. U.S. Senator, Maria Cantwell, of Knox's home state of Washington, said she was "saddened by the verdict." The Democratic senator said she had "serious questions about the Italian justice system and whether anti-Americanism tainted this trial." Cantwell also publically vowed to call for a review of the trial through Secretary of State Hillary Clinton and the Italian embassy in Washington. Meanwhile, the complete written ruling of the judges and six jurors, as prescribed by Italian law, is expected to be released within 90-days.

Chapter 13 - Forensic Analysis of the Evidence

Footprint Analysis (Lone Wolf Theory)

The phrase 'Lone Wolf' has been a popular phrase throughout history. This phrase refers to one individual who favors to go without the company or assistance of others. The phrase 'Lone Wolf Theory' has long been synonymous with crime. Police use this phrase in order to explain a disputed case which they believe only one person was involved in the crime. Such case examples are the *D.C. sniper* and the *holocaust museum shooting*. In the case of this theory the burden is usually on those who are attempting to disprove it rather than the other way around. The lone wolf theory in essence is somewhat of an oxymoron, because wolves hunt in packs. Nonetheless, the phrase is intertwined in police jargon and widely accepted. The phrase has been introduced to a large number of the population through the murder of Meredith Kercher and has come to be known as one of the cases top 'buzz words.' The convictions of both Amanda Knox and Raffaele Sollecito were based heavily on disproving this theory. There were certain pieces of physical evidence that helped the prosecution do this; one being the footprint evidence.

One of the oldest papers in Italy, *La Nazione*, released pictures (on 14 May 2008) of three of the prints revealed by luminol. Additional photos were then released by an Italian news website owned by Mediaset *(TGCOM)*. These pictures showed six barefoot-prints pressed in blood, not in Meredith's room, but in other areas of the cottage. Five of these prints were only visible after police used the chemical *luminol* and viewed them under fluorescent lighting.

Luminol (3-aminophthalic hydrazide) is a chemical that reacts with the microscopic particles of iron found in hemoglobin, causing an organic peroxide reaction. If blood is present, its oxidized state is expressed by a chemoluminescent burst, i.e. the sample glows with a bluish color in the dark. Luminol evidence can be very convincing. If blood stains appear while using luminol, but are not visible to the naked eye, it is proof positive that a clean-up was initiated. Luminol is superb at detecting minute traces of blood that are not visible to the naked eye. Luminol is so effective that it can detect bloodstains that have been diluted up to 300,000 times. The only noteworthy limitation of luminol is that it also reacts to other substances such as copper ions, horseradish, and bleach. So in order to positively identify the substances as blood evidence, samples need to be sent to the laboratory for testing (where the *Kastle-Meyer test* and other tests can be performed by forensic biologists).

In the case of Meredith Kercher the lone wolf theory states that there was only one killer, and only the killer had access to Meredith's bedroom before the body was discovered by the group the following afternoon. In order to disprove this theory we must come up with conclusive evidence that puts at least one of the prints as belonging to Raffaele Sollecito. If one or more of the prints were Amanda's then one can still make an argument that it was her house, leaving room for doubt or speculation as to how that print got there. This would open-up another line of questioning which requires further evaluation. However, if we can simply prove that one or more of the prints belonged to Sollecito, then we would have pretty conclusive evidence that there was more than one wolf. Keep in mind that the murder, by all expert accounts, took place in Meredith's room (i.e. Meredith never left the room once blood was shed). The importance of this is that any other blood evidence found outside her room could only have been brought out of the room by the killer(s). However, if we somehow find that one of the bloody footprints match the victim, then this would mean that the crime had at some point taken place in another location of the cottage before Meredith was locked in her room and left to die. This would indicate a massive clean-up had taken place. Nonetheless, let's not digress, but instead cross that bridge when and if we come to it.

Living in such a digital age has given an advantage not only to the hardened forensic experts, but also to the armature armchair detectives. By using the right techniques and measurements, just about anyone can come up with relatively accurate calculations. Moreover, professional forensic specialists who don't have access to evidence can now weigh-in using technological advancements to study the evidence. As long as one has the right programs and know-how to use them, it becomes a matter of creativity, basic math, and experience. It's axiomatic that different factors—one being camera optics—will impede an exact measurement. The real test is comparing our results with what the experts have tallied. Nevertheless, the key aspect to each measurement is the ruler(s) laid down by the forensic team and the dimensions of the floor tiles. This is the exact reason that forensic experts use such tactics. These rulers can give us an exact estimate of the size of the objects shown. Moreover, they can be used to give us an accurate measure of the surrounding area; thus, helping get a precise measurement of the object(s) in question.

We start with the foot sizes of the four in question. Using the shoe size conversion table, we can list the appropriate sizes as defined by the different regions. Keep in mind, for obvious practical purposes; we will be focusing on centimeters for our analysis.

Shoe Size Conversion Table

Smallest to largest	Euro size	US/Canada	Centimeters
Amanda Knox	37	6.5W	23.8cm
Meredith Kercher	38.5	8W	24.8cm
Raffaele Sollecito	42	8.5M	26cm
Rudy Guede	46	12M	28.4cm (Approx.)

There was one sneaker print found in Meredith's room that has been identified as Rudy Guede's (Evidence maker "C"). Since Rudy has admitted being at the scene and in the room at the time, we won't need to concern ourselves with it. We can safely assume that is Rudy's print based on its size and distinctness anyhow. Our focus must be on the prints that were wiped clean to the naked eye as well as the bloody footprint left on the bathmat.

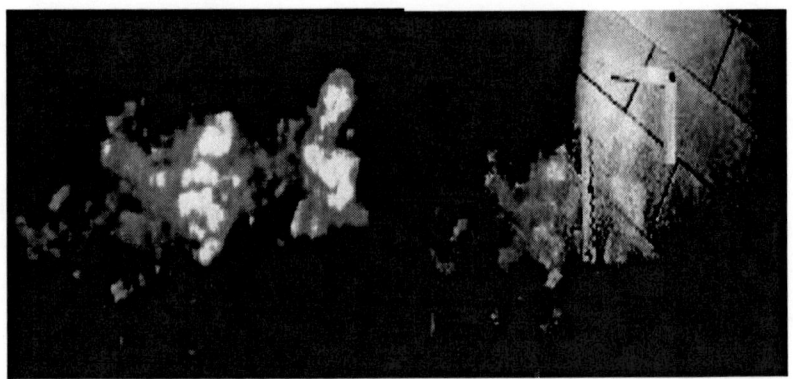

Print A – (Print on the left) - FIG 1   Same photo, different lighting - FIG 2

Print A

At first glance it's hard to tell, but if you look close enough you can see that both pictures are of the same two footprints, just under different lighting. Keep in mind that we are only examining "Footprint A" (Footprint on the left in both pictures) at this time. Looking at FIG 1 we can tell that this print did not come from a 'rolling heal,' which signifies the motion of the foot at the time the print was made. The rounded heal of the print as well as the arch and the sides all denote a stationary foot at the time the impression was made. Also, we notice that the smaller toes do not appear, which could indicate that they were not as blood-soaked as the rest of the foot. Most importantly, we see the distinct impression of the big toe, which corresponds with a motionless print. FIG 2 is the picture we must use for our measurements, since the floor tiles are visible; making accurate measurements possible. The surrounding area is four-tile-lengths wide; and the corridor, where these footprints were found, is 1.45 meters wide (approx. 5ft). The amount of blood found in this area could be a result of a less than thorough cleaning in this particular vicinity. Now, we must superimpose the left footprint in FIG 1 over the corresponding print in FIG 2. Next, we sharpen the ruler and draw lines—highlighting the floor tiles.

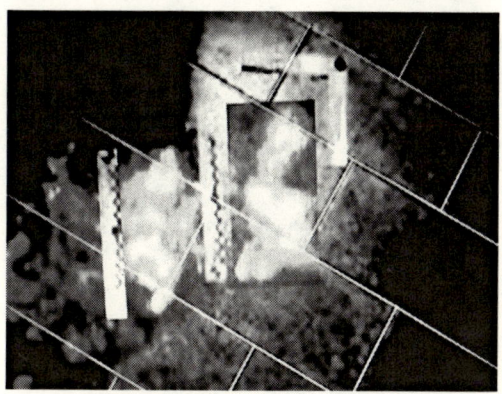

Superimposed prints - FIG 3

The next step is to figure out the dimensions of the tiles, doing this in three steps. We know that all the tiles in the north wing of the cottage are the same size. To get an accurate measurement we simply need to go into the victim's room and use the ruler at marker "C." By copying and duplicating the ruler in Meredith's room then extending it proportionately, we can create an accurate measuring stick. Using our new ruler we then measure one of the tiles. When we do so, we get a measurement of 16cm. in width. Our second test is then to use the ruler in FIG 3 to measure the width of the floor tiles near the luminol prints. Doing so, we again come up with 16cm. As a third point of reference, we go into the bathroom and use marker "6" (bloody footprint on the bathmat) in the same way to get the calculations of the floor tile in that room. Again we come up with 16cm. Now that we have taken the preliminary steps and know that we are getting accurate measurements, it is time to measure the first print. For optimal results, we should use the ruler at evidence marker "C" and just recalibrate it so that it measures the width of the floor tile at 16cm.

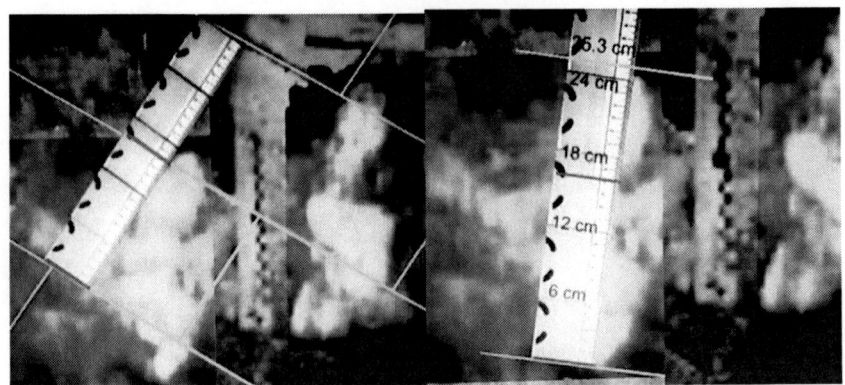

Evidence marker "C" - FIG 4　　　*Measurement of "Footprint A" (25.3cm.) - FIG 5*

By using this method we can determine the length of "Footprint A" to be 25.3cm. (Note: measurements through photography favor a slightly larger measurements rather than smaller). From this we can clearly rule out this print belonging to Rudy Guede, as his foot size is approximately 28.4cm. The next person we can easily rule out is Amanda; her foot size is too small (23.8cm.) to have made this impression. At this point we can rule out—to a very high degree of certainty—that either of these prints were made by Amanda or Rudy. This one piece of evidence alone completely changes anything that we knew or assumed about this case before it. From this—at this stage of experimentation (if we believe all expert accounts to be accurate)—we must conclude that either this print was made by Raffaele, Meredith, or someone else.

Meredith's footprint could be a contender for this print (24.8cm.), although her print is a bit smaller. Whereas, Raffaele's size (26cm.) is slightly larger than the measurement he is the most likely contestant for this print. Centimeters can be deceiving to us here in the United States. For instance, Meredith and Raffaele's foot sizes both seem to be close in size when comparing them in centimeters. However, Raffaele's foot size is two-sizes bigger than Meredith's by United States calculations. So we must adjust our prejudices. From these calculations we can make a very strong argument that "Footprint A" belongs to Raffaele Sollecito. In fact, this is just what the prosecution asserted! Keep in mind that it was not this evidence alone that convicted them. Continuing with the above steps for the remainder of the prints and tallying the results, we get two prints belonging to Sollecito; thus disproving the lone-wolf theory in this case.

[4]*Footprints as per the Prosecution:*

- Sollecito – Bare footprint highlighted by luminol (found in the hallway)
- Sollecito – Bare footprint in blood (found on the bathmat in the bathroom by Kercher's room)
- Knox - Bare footprint found with luminol (Located in the hallway outside Kercher's door)
- Knox – Bare footprint found with luminol (In Knox's room)
- Knox – Bloody shoe print, size approx. 37-Euro size (found on pillow underneath Kercher's body)
- Guede – Bloody shoeprint (Found on pillow underneath Kercher)
- Guede – Bloody shoeprint in Kercher's room (Found on floor near body)

Phone Call Confusion

It's clear from analyzing the trial that the results of the expert witnesses (defense vs. prosecution) were vastly different. The question is—who is correct? Picture yourself as a juror trying to decipher the believability and credibility of witness testimony. To do so, we must try and make a determination based on thorough analysis and scrutiny of each testimony. In doing so, we must look at the reasonability of their assertions and the contradictions within each testimony. The case brought-on by each defense team has several holes and contradictions; whereas the prosecution did a more thorough job piecing the puzzle together. Each prosecution witnesses complimented and corroborated the next, which provided a complete picture of the events. As for defense testimony; some of them contradicted themselves while some contradicted the testimony of other defense witnesses. Moreover, most of the theories posed by the

---

[4] To view a detailed analysis on each footprint, view:
http://truejustice.org/ee/documents/perugia/Kermit06LuminolEvidence.pps by Kermit.

defense can be disproven, whereas the prosecution holds a solid lead in this area. Let's take a look at one small, but very significant, example of this.

This section is a complete reconstruction of the anatomy of events that occurred on Friday, 2 November 2007, between the hours of 12 noon and 1:30p.m. As we know, Meredith's body was discovered by police in the early afternoon hours on this day (within the above indicated timeframe). There were eight people present when the door to Meredith's room was broken-into:

1. Amanda Knox (Suspect)
2. Raffaele Sollecito (Suspect)
3. Filomena Romanelli (Knox's roommate)
4. Marco Zaroli (Filomena's boyfriend)
5. Paola Grande (Filomena's friend)
6. Luca Altieri (Paola's boyfriend)
7. Michele Battistelli (Postal Officer)
8. Fabio Marzi (Postal Officer)

This section is based on:

- Knox's 4 November email to friends and family
- Sollecito's prison diary
- Cell phone records from police
- Testimonies of Filomena Romanelli, Paola Grande, Luca Altieri, and Edda Mellas,
- Judge Micheli's report

Sequence of cell phone calls starting at 12 noon:

A. 12:07 – Knox calls Meredith's English phone *(call lasted 3 seconds)*
B. 12:08 – Knox calls Filomena
C. 12:11 – Knox calls Meredith's Italian phone *(call lasted 4 seconds)*
D. 12:12 – Filomena calls Knox (no answer)
E. 12:20 – Filomena calls Knox (no answer)
F. 12:20 – Sollecito added more credit to his phone

G. 12:34 – Filomena calls Knox (*she finally gets through*)

H. 12:40 – Sollecito receives a call from his father

I.   12:47 – Knox calls her mother for the first time *(call lasted a minute and a half)*

J.   12:50 – Sollecito calls his sister

K. 12:51 – Sollecito calls 112 (equivalent to 911 in USA) – connection failed

L.   12:54 – Sollecito calls 112 (call successful)

M. 1:00 – Meredith's Italian phone is activated by postal police

N. 1:24 – Knox calls her mother for the second time

Intro: Amanda Knox testified that she spent the night of Meredith's murder (November 1st) at Raffaele Sollecito's apartment. She then said that she woke-up and left his place at around 10:30a.m., the next morning. She immediately returned to the apartment, noticed the door was left wide-open, blood on the bathroom near her and Meredith's rooms and feces in the toilet near Laura's room. She proceeded to take a shower, retrieve a mop (to clean the leaky facet that allegedly had broken at Sollecito's flat the previous night), and returned to Sollecito's place. Once there, she quickly cleaned up the messy facet water that had spilled on the floor, made coffee, and discussed the strange circumstances of her apartment with Sollecito over some muffins. Deciding that they would return to her apartment together, Sollecito advised her to contact her roommates to see if everything was ok.

Commentary: Disregarding whether these previous events were fact or fiction, reconstructing the time period between 12 noon and 1:30p.m., is quite simple using all of the information that we have available.

Sequence: We begin with Knox's phone call to Meredith's Italian registered phone, which only lasted three-seconds. A minute later, at 12:08p.m., Knox called her roommate, Filomena Romanelli, from the cottage.

Commentary: Knox testified that this call to Filomena was made from Sollecito's flat (She also wrote in her November 4th email that she was at Sollecito's place when she made the call). However, in

265

his letter to his father, Sollecito claimed that this call was made from the cottage, and that he was with Knox at the time of the call and that he is the one who advised her to make the call. Furthermore, Filomena testified that during that conversation, Knox told her that she was at the cottage alone and said she was going to phone Raffaele. Filomena asks Knox to call Meredith then call her back. Why didn't Knox tell Filomena that she had already called Meredith? Moreover, Knox testified that she had returned to Sollecito's flat at about 11:30a.m. Why didn't she tell Filomena that she was already with Sollecito?

Sequence: Knox then calls Meredith's English registered phone, but hangs up after only four seconds.

Commentary: Why did Knox tell Filomena that she was at the cottage, but tell the court that she was at Sollecito's flat during that call? The answer is simple, because the postal police arrived unexpectedly, which made Knox have to change her story. Knox couldn't have been at the cottage at 12:08p.m., alone, return to Sollecito's, do all that she claimed to have done there then return to the cottage in time for the postal police to arrive (at 12:25p.m.). She had to change her story to fit her new timeline. Knox was clearly establishing her alibi when she called Meredith's phone twice. These calls lasted under five-seconds, yet she testified and wrote in the email that when she called Meredith's phone it "just kept ringing, no answer." Why didn't Knox leave a message or text message Meredith as she did several times on Halloween night? Knox sent Meredith several text messages that night, even though Meredith hadn't responded. Before returning to Sollecito's, why didn't Knox call him to inform him what was going on? Simply put, because they were together the whole time. They had pretty much spent every minute of their free time together since the day they had met. Even at the police station on November 5th they wanted to stay together, but the police had to separate them. So, Knox's original plan was to say that she was at the cottage, which is why she said that to Filomena on the phone. However, after postal police surprised them, she needed to switch up her alibi, starting with where she was during that call.

Sequence: Filomena calls Knox back at 12:12p.m., and 12:20p.m., but Knox does not answer either call.

Commentary: In Knox's email, she wrote that "Filomena seemed real worried" so she told Filomena that she would call Meredith and call her right back; Filomena testified that she asked Knox to call Meredith and call her right back. The purpose for Knox's original call to Filomena was to have her rush over to the cottage so that they could walk in together and discover the body. This is why Knox didn't answer either of these two calls from her. Knox wanted Filomena to discover the broken window, the locked door, etc.

Sequence: Two Postal Police officers (Michele Battistelli & Fabio Marzi) arrive, to the surprise of Knox and Sollecito at 12:25p.m.

Commentary: As the officers arrive, they witness Knox holding a mop and bucket. This is significant, because it speaks about the nature of Knox and Sollecito's plan. Knox was waiting for Filomena to arrive. She wanted to make it look like she had not even entered the cottage since coming back with Sollecito. It would have looked as though they had almost arrived simultaneously, or she could have told Filomena that they waited for her so that they could all go in together. The arrival of the two officers threw a huge monkey-wrench into their plan. Now they would have to scramble to reconfigure their alibis and this would contribute heavily to the huge mistakes made thereafter by the inexperienced criminals.

Sequence: At 12:34p.m., Filomena calls Knox again, this time she answers. At 12:40p.m., Sollecito receives a call from his father.

Commentary: Of course Knox answers this call. Now she is frantic, because police had arrived before Filomena. In an effort to get Filomena into frenzy and rush over, Knox tells her that her window had been broken and her room ransacked. "Come home immediately!" Knox commands. Filomena tells Knox to call the police and says she is on her way. Knox doesn't make mention that the postal police had already arrived. What Knox did not anticipate, however, was that Filomena would call Marco and Luca, asking them to head over to the cottage before her, because they were in closer proximity. Knox and Sollecito were giving the officers a tour of the cottage when the call from Sollecito's dad pulled him away. Knox continued showing police around when Marco and Luca arrived. Knox tells them it's normal for Meredith to lock her door.

Sequence: Knox slips away into her room with Sollecito soon after and at 12:47p.m., she calls her mother for the first time. (Note: because of Daylight Savings Times changes, the actual difference on 2 November 2007, would have been just eight hours. So the time would have been 4:47a.m., in Seattle, WA.) Edda described the content of that call speaking to ABC's 20/20 a few weeks later:

> *[Amanda] goes, "I'm back at my house, and I want you… first I want you to know I'm okay." And I said, "Okay, what's goin on?" And she said, "Well, I was at Raffaele's last night…and I've come home now and I think somebody's been in my house…" And she told me, "We can't find Meredith. We can't get a hold of Meredith. And her room is locked." And I said, "Hang up and call the police."*

At 12:50p.m., Sollecito calls his sister, Vanessa, who is a lieutenant in the carabinieri. Raffaele briefly explains the problem at the cottage and she gives him the same advice that Knox's mother had given her: to hang up and call the police. At 12:51p.m., Sollecito makes his first call to 112 (equivalent to 911 in USA), but the connection fails. At 12:54p.m., Sollecito calls 112 back, this time he informs them of the problem, and they advise that they are sending over a car to take a look at the house. These four calls made by Knox and Sollecito take a total of eight-minutes.

Commentary: Knox and Sollecito made these four calls while Marco and Luca spoke to the officers, essentially distracted them. Not during any one of these four calls did either Knox or Sollecito mention that the police had already arrived. These calls were simply made to further establish their newly reconfigured alibis. Being young, naive, and in a time-crunch; the couple did not realize that there moves and the moves of others would be easily traceable. For instance, they didn't realize that the CCTV footage from the car-park across the street had captured the postal police's vehicle (black Fiat Punto) pulling-up in front of the cottage at 12:25p.m.; nor did they realize the fact that officer Battistelli radioed back to headquarters (HQ) at 12:30p.m., to inform them that they had arrived at the cottage. Knox tells the officers and Luca that it is normal for Meredith to lock her door, even when she takes a shower. Knox is trying to stall for time, delaying the discovery of the body until the carabinieri and Filomena to arrive.

According to the testimony of her mother, Edda Mellas, Amanda told her that she tried to call Meredith's phone several times, but there was no answer. In reality, Amanda only called Meredith twice and both calls lasted less then four-seconds. This lie, from Amanda to her mother, was part of their (Knox and Sollecito's) originally constructed alibi. After informing her to call the police, Mellas testified that Amanda told her that "Raffaele was finishing a call with his sister and then was going to call police." However, phone records indicate that the call with her mother started at 12:47p.m., and lasted only a minute-and-a-half. Sollecito didn't call his sister until 12:50p.m., and that call lasted only about a minute or less. So we can deduce from this that their newly constructed alibi was formed between the times that Sollecito had gotten off of the phone with his father and before she had called her mother. Within that time, they had quickly prearranged who they were going to call and in what sequence the calls would be made. This would help establish their new alibis.

Sequence: Just before 1:00p.m., Filomena and Paola arrive at the cottage. At 1:00p.m., Battistelli calls HQ and has Meredith's Italian phone activated, this happens almost instantaneously. Meredith's Italian phone was registered to Filomena. She had lent it to Meredith so that she could make calls while in Italy without incurring international charges on her English phone. During Battistelli's conversation with HQ, he mentions Filomena's presence, and the information she's given them about the phone registered in her name. Paola witnesses Knox and Sollecito emerging from Knox's room.

Commentary: From this we can determine the exact time that Paola and Filomena arrived at the cottage (Just before 1:00p.m.). We can also determine, with great accuracy, that the postal police had been there for a while. First, radioed back to HQ at 12:30p.m.; and second, they toured the cottage with Knox and Sollecito, looking for signs of a burglary. After Knox and Sollecito had slipped away to Knox's room, Marco and Luca got briefed and also toured the cottage briefly. They had arrived about fifteen-minutes or so before Filomena and Paola, according to the testimony of all who were present (at approx. 12:47p.m.). Finally, when Marco and Luca arrive, the postal police are already there, and have already inspected Filomena's room. When Luca informs Filomena what Knox said about it being normal for Meredith to lock her door, she becomes worried and animated. "Meredith only locks her door when she leaves the house!" Filomena exclaims. This prompts a discussion which leads to a decision to break-down Meredith's door.

Sequence: At approximately 1:10 – 1:15p.m., a decision is made to break-through Meredith's door. As Knox and Sollecito retreat into the kitchen, Luca Altieri kicks the door in. Meredith's body is discovered lying under a duvet with one of her feet sticking out. Police order everyone out of the house and into the garden. Officer Battistelli radios headquarters and describes the scene. At 1:24p.m., Knox calls her mother for the second time, this time from the garden and explains to her that police have arrived and have found a foot in Meredith's room (but she does not tell her mother that it is Meredith). The Carabinieri arrived soon after.

Commentary: According to her testimony, this call that Knox made to her mother from the garden is the first call that she claims to have made to her mother on that day. As we clearly see from phone records, this is not the case. Knox testified that she did not remember making the first call to her mother. Even her mother was puzzled by this. According to her email, Knox does not mention the 12:47p.m., call to her mother, and she writes that the decision was made to call the police after Sollecito tried to break down Meredith's door (before anyone else had arrived). Also in this fictitious email, Knox claims to have run outside and down to our neighbors house where she banged on the door, but no one answered. She makes no mention of this in her two-days of testimony or at any other time. According to that same email, Knox states that she called Filomena back and told her to come back to the cottage. However, phone records indicate that the only call that Knox made to Filomena was at 12:08p.m., (which was the first and only call to her).

Just eight-days after Kercher's body was discovered, Knox's mother visits her in jail. The conversation was intercepted by police. During the conversation, they begin to discuss the pre-dawn call (12:47p.m.), and Edda seems surprised that Amanda has forgotten this conversation, or that she makes no mention of it in her email just two days after the body was found.

Edda (surprised): But you called me three times.

Amanda: Oh, I don't remember that.

Edda: Okay, you called me first to tell me about some things that had shocked you. But this happened before anything really happened in the house.

Amanda: I know I was making calls. I remember calling Filomena, but I really don't remember calling anyone else. I just don't remember having called you.

Edda: Why would that be? Stress, you think?

Amanda: Maybe because so many things were happening at once.

Edda: Okay, right.

Conclusion: Some might ask why this phone call is important. Well, because the postal police had already arrived, and Amanda makes no mention of this to her mother. Moreover, Edda advises Amanda to call the police, and Amanda makes no reference of that whatsoever in her decision to call them. She even acts as if the call didn't actually happen because she didn't remember it. In other words, Amanda's version of events in this hour-and-a-half conflicts with the testimony of all other witnesses, with the phone records, with police records, with the CCTV footage from the car park, and even with the testimony of her own mother. With all that has been mentioned hitherto, it is easy to see why Judge Micheli determined in his report that the cell phone records clearly do not support the couple's story.

Also puzzling is the fact that Amanda's own mother's testimony contradicts her story. Edda Mellas testified that after informing Amanda to call the police, Mellas claims that Amanda told her that "Raffaele was finishing a call with his sister and then was going to call police." This was a telling statement by Amanda; because it shows premeditation, showing that is was predetermined that they were going to call the police; and that the call to her mother and Sollecito's call to his sister were part of their newly reconstructed alibi.

Email Fiction

Many of Knox's supporters believe that her November 4th email sent to family and friends represents what actually happened. They have emphasized that this email represents the truth before she was "abused and coerced into a confession by police." However, for Knox's email to be true (based on the fact that she states that police arrived after Sollecito's call to his sister at 12:50p.m.), then about a half-hours-worth of events would had to have been squeezed into about five-minutes. Even then, there would still be mistakes and contradictions with it.

10 clear contradictions which make Knox's email fiction, not fact:

1. Knox makes no mention of her first phone call to her mother at 12:47p.m., nor does she claim to even remember it
2. Knox claimed to have called Filomena after calling the police; phone records oppose this
3. Postal police had already arrived (she claims they arrived after Sollecito had called 112, which was at 12:54p.m.)
4. Knox claims that she "ran outside and down to a neighbor's house and banged on the door" (she never makes mention of this in her testimony or in any other version)
5. Marco & Luca arrive at approx 12:47p.m., and postal police have been there for a while already
6. Postal police call HQ at 1:00p.m., and inform them that Filomena is already there
7. Knox claims that "Filomena arrived with her boyfriend Marco and two other friends of hers" and they "all checked

out the house together" (As we see here, this was her original plan, but just to have Filomena check out the house with her and Sollecito)

8. Knox claimed that she called Meredith's Italian phone, "and it just kept ringing, no answer" (Phone records indicate that both of her calls to Meredith lasted less that four seconds)

9. Knox claims to have called Filomena for the first time from Sollecito's flat (Sollecito and Filomena both said that Knox made the call from the cottage)

10. Knox claims that she called Filomena before calling Meredith (Phone records indicate it was the other way around)

It is also significant to point out that Edda Mellas testified that during the second call (at 1:24p.m.); Amanda informed her that someone had seen a foot under a blanket. During the third call, Amanda was at the police station and told her mother that they had found a dead body in Meredith's room. However, Amanda did not know at that time, according to her mother's testimony, that it was Meredith's body. According to Mellas, Amanda told her on that last call that she was worried about Meredith because they still couldn't get a hold of her and had found a body in her room.

More Major Contradictions & Cover-ups

Perhaps the biggest contradiction in Knox's email, not identified above, is when she states that when she first noticed that Meredith's door was locked, she went into a "panic." It was then that she went out on the terrace to see if she could get a look into Meredith's room, but didn't report seeing anything. She then claims it was at that point that Sollecito tried to break down Meredith's door. It was this event that prompted them to call police, she writes in the email. However, in absolute contrast to this, when Postal Police arrived the panic expressed in the email over the locked door *did not exist*. In her phone conversations with Filomena (at 12:34p.m.), Knox *did not mention the locked door*. Moreover, Postal Officer Battistelli testified that it was *Filomena* who first raised concerns over Meredith's door being locked. In fact, Knox *reassured* Marco Zaroli, Luca Altieri, and both officers that Meredith was in the habit of locking the bedroom door, even just to go to the shower. Knox completely downplayed the locked door, and it wasn't until Filomena arrived (at about 1:00p.m.) and expressed panic about Meredith's door being locked that it was decided to break it down.

Amanda Knox has stated on numerous occasions—including in her testimony—that she ate dinner with Sollecito at his apartment between 10:00p.m., and 11:00p.m., on the night of the murder. However, this can easily be disproven. Raffaele's father, Dr. Francesco Sollecito, stated that he spoke to his son on the phone at 8:42p.m., on that night. This is corroborated by phone records. During that phone conversation, Raffaele told his father that he was at his flat with Knox. Mr. Sollecito also testified that his son told him "that while he was washing dishes he realized he had a water spill." By Knox's own admission, she claimed that this water spill occurred after dinner while Sollecito was washing dishes, Sollecito said the same. This places the time of dinner at sometime prior to the phone call with his father. This attempt by Knox—to determine that dinner was between 10 and 11 was one that would appear to provide an alibi, putting her at Sollecito's flat during the time of the murder. Knox had already turned off her cell phone by the time that this call had taken place, and Raffaele turned his phone off immediately after the call had ended. An examination of Sollecito's computer indicated that there had been no activity on it between 9:10p.m., and 5:32a.m.; although Sollecito claimed to have been surfing the internet for the better part of the night. Witness Antonio Curatolo testified that he saw Knox and Sollecito at Piazza Grimana just after 9:30p.m., that night.

Sollecito activated his computer at 5:32a.m., for a period of one-half hour. Sollecito then turned on his cellular phone at precisely 6:02 a.m., at which point he received the text message that his father had sent him the prior evening (at 11:14p.m.). Dr. Sollecito testified that he sent his son a text message instead of calling him because he was made aware that he was with Knox and didn't want to interrupt them with a phone call. Knox claims to have woken up in Sollecito's arms, but makes no mention of the call that Raffaele received from his father at 9:30a.m., that morning. Dr. Sollecito testified that he placed the call to his son because he knew that Raffaele and Amanda had plans for a trip to Gubbio that morning and he had called to see if they had left yet; he understood by how his son answered the phone, he testified, that he was still in bed. Amanda has spoken of a long, deep sleep that lasted until 10:00-10:30a.m.

Simply put, Amanda did not mention this call because she was not aware of it. She had already left the apartment and had no knowledge of the call. Instead, Knox went to *Margherita Conad* convenience store located on Corso Garibaldi at 7:45a.m., that morning; as indicated by store owner, Marco Quintavalle. Laura Mezzetti testified that Knox was a morning person, and the call from Raffaele's father at 9:30a.m., is significant because it indicates his knowledge of his son's sleeping habits. Yet, Dr. Sollecito testified that his son said that he was still in bed. All of these inconsistencies appear to indicate that something different must have happened to alter the normally planned events.

As we know, Sollecito made a call to 112 at 12:54p.m., to report that the cottage had experienced a break-in; with a window being broken and Filomena's room in disarray. Officer Daniele Ceppitelli answered the call and noted that Sollecito proclaimed, "No, there has been no theft." Officer Ceppitelli asked him a second time, "What have they taken?" Sollecito responded, "They have not taken anything." How could Sollecito know that money, jewelry, or other valuables that Filomena could have kept in any box in her own room had not been taken? Simply put, he knew that nothing was taken because he took part in the staging of the break-in. He knew that there was no burglary and the Freudian slip on the 112 call confirms this. There could have very well been valuables that only the owner knew about and verified. Yet, Sollecito makes the bold and quick assumption that nothing in the house had been stolen. One of the Postal Police officers first on the scene, Fabio Marzi, testified that when they arrived, Sollecito and Knox told them that "they were awaiting the arrival of the Carabinieri because there had been a burglary inside the house."

Amanda called Meredith's Italian registered phone at 12:07p.m., then called Filomena at 12:08p.m. Aside from making no mention of the call to Meredith's phone prior to the current call to Filomena, the bigger significance lies somewhat covert: the fact that Knox only called Meredith's English registered phone and not the Italian registered phone immediately after, poses a considerable point. Knox already knew that both phones were together and the reason for the first call to Meredith was to be sure that no one had found the phones yet. Only once Knox had the reassurance that the phones had not been found yet, could she then raise the alarm. If she had a genuine interest in contacting Meredith—and she wasn't involved or aware of the murder—her first call to Meredith's English phone would have been followed directly by contacting Meredith's Italian phone. It should be noted that no evidence confirms that the two remained at Sollecito's flat from 9:10 p.m., on November 1st until 10:00a.m., on November 2nd.

DNA Clarification

Much of the defenses' case centered on their declarations that the DNA evidence found to be their clients' was contaminated. It must be noted and understood that they never disputed that the DNA evidence was not correctly identified (i.e. they never disputed that it was not Raffaele or Amanda's DNA found). The defense acknowledges that the DNA was correctly identified as Raffaele and Amanda's; but they argue that the reason for this is that their DNA profiles found on these evidentiary items was due to "circumstances of contamination." There are three main questions to consider in this case in regard to contamination before making a decision whether or not the DNA should be held as valid against the defendants: the first is how can DNA evidence be contaminated? The second is what DNA testing methods were used on what items? And from that, what is the possibility, and or probability, of contamination? Let's take a look.

DNA contamination can occur in three ways: *mishandling, cross-contamination,* and *machine contamination. Mishandling* of DNA is the most common error made in DNA handling and can occur in several ways. If a forensic specialist sneezes or coughs over the evidence or touches his/her mouth, nose, or other part of the face and then touches the area that may contain the DNA to be tested, this could cause a host of problems.

Cross-contamination can occur when microscopic traces of unrelated evidence and forensic scientists accidentally mixing their own DNA with the collected sample. This type of cross-contamination is classified as mishandling. This can certainly destroy valuable DNA information that may help solve the crime. The more covert and sinister type of cross-contamination, and the one that Knox and Sollecito's defense teams are claiming is when DNA is transferred from one item to another. For instance, a forensic specialist collects a sample then, without changing their gloves, they collect a separate sample; thereby leaving traces of the first sample on the second. So, Knox and Sollecito's camps are claiming that some of the DNA found in the cottage—particularly the bra clasp; which was recovered 18 days after the murder that had Sollecito's DNA on it—were a result of this type of cross-contamination. They claim that poor forensic work led to a transfer of DNA from one item to another.

Another way that contamination can occur is from the *machine* itself. When DNA machine is not cleaned properly and previous samples from previous tests are left on the machine and mix with current samples. The only DNA evidence that the defense claimed was contaminated in this way was the alleged murder weapon. The—8.5cm long and 2cm wide—Marietti knife that was found in Sollecito's flat which the prosecutions claims was the murder weapon showed DNA of Knox on the handle and Kercher's blood on the tip of the blade. This was the only piece of DNA evidence that the defense disputed outright, claiming that because of the minute traces of DNA found on the knife, that it was the machine that caused the contamination. In doing so, the defense claimed that previous tests run on the machine, without it being cleaned properly, had caused this.

There are five major ways of limiting the influence of contamination:

1. It is extremely important to run negative controls and background controls through the entire procedure.
2. Once contamination has been detected, it is important to discard all current reagents and clean relevant equipment and work surfaces.
3. Thermal cyclers (where PCR is carried out) need to be cleaned.
4. It is critically important to store samples in proper containers and keep known samples well-segregated from other evidence, particularly evidentiary samples that have small amounts of DNA.

5. The laboratory should be extremely careful not to overstate the scientific value of the evidence.

To avoid mishandling, the following precautions should be made:

- Wear gloves, and change them after each sample collected.
- Use disposable instruments or clean them thoroughly before and after handling each sample.
- Avoid touching the area where you believe DNA may exist.
- Avoid talking, sneezing, and coughing over evidence.
- Avoid touching your face, nose, and mouth when collecting and packaging evidence.
- Air-dry evidence thoroughly before packaging.
- Put evidence into new paper bags or envelopes, not into plastic bags.

Dr. Torre's assistant, Sarah Gino (who is a private coroner), took the stand to dispute the lab results provided by Dr. Stefanoni. Gino's critique of Stefanoni's centered on the DNA found at the tip of the blade that Stefanoni claimed was Meredith's. Dr. Stefanoni used the Low Copy Number (LCN) DNA method to obtain her results. This DNA profiling technique, developed by the *Forensic Science Service* (a government owned company in the UK), had come under scrutiny in the United Kingdom and its use was suspended between 21 December 2007, and 14 January 2008, while the *Crown Prosecution Service* (a non-ministerial department of the Government of the United Kingdom responsible for public prosecutions of people charged with criminal offences in England and Wales) conducted a review into its use. LCN is a form of generic Low Template DNA analysis in which scientists can copy and obtain a genetic profile from just a small amount of biological material; as small as a millionth the size of a grain of salt (typically using 5 to 20 cells). After a thorough review, by the Crown Prosecution Service, they reinstated the technique on January 14, 2008.

In their 'Review of the Science of Low Template DNA Analysis,' conducted at the University of Strathclyde, they concluded that: "From our detailed review we find that the science supporting the delivery of Low Template DNA (LTDNA) analysis is sound and that the companies providing this service to the Criminal Justice System have validated their processes in accord with accepted scientific principles…"

Gino testified that because the sample amplified was less than 100 fluorescence units (RFU), that "we are allowed to assume that it resulted from a contamination from the machine." However, the manual on the machine stated less than 50 fluorescence units was not reliable. Gino explained—in regard to exhibit 36 (the knife), that, "The electrophoretic run should have been done on the substrate as well." The substrate is the gel on which the electronic field is applied. What Gino means is that in case of a stronger than recommended electric field, if pieces of DNA from a previous test are present the machine may read them, as she is claiming occurred in this case.

With specific reference to the knife (Exhibit 36), Dr. Stefanoni stated that this was an Exhibit that was analyzed during the course of 50 samples attributed to the victim, some of which came before and some of which came after the analysis of the knife. She further emphasized that each sample was separately analyzed, and that it was absolutely impossible to mix one sample with another. She excluded the possibility that, in the machine used for the analysis of the various samples, any secondary deposits might have formed from which it would have been possible to transfer DNA onto other specimens. With respect to this, she stated that the machine is equipped with a security system which prevents such an occurrence. As Gino further explained, unfortunately, because the test cannot be repeated (and no pictures from stereomicroscope have been taken), the results cannot be validated; or even if there was biological matter to begin with. "It is likely just noise from the reagents used in the test," she asserted, "something that a control run on the reagents would have proven."

The debate over the DNA results ragged on in a big way, fueled by the fact that there is no law that obligates a lab to follow certain protocols; only recommendations of what standards work best. Dr. Tagliabracci stressed that the DNA found on the bra clasp was not enough for a reliable test. Dr. Stefanoni expressed that the quantity found (1.4 nanogram or 1400 picograms) was sufficient. In theory, the amount needed to obtain a DNA profile is only one cell. Although in practice, the required amount (using the PCR Process) is about 1 nanogram; which contains approximately 160 cells. So, Dr. Stefanoni is correct when she states that there was a sufficient amount of Sollecito's DNA on the bra clasp to achieve reliable results.

DNA Fingerprinting (a.k.a. DNA Profiling or DNA analysis) is a sub-category of Biotechnology that has several uses among scientists as well as other fields. A broad definition of Biotechnology is, "any use or alteration of organisms, cells, or biological molecules to achieve specific practical goals."

Deoxyribonucleic acid (DNA) is located in the nucleus of every cell that has a nucleus. Its appearance is similar to a twisted ladder or staircase, which is referred to as a double-helix. DNA is an extremely long polymer made from four nucleotides: Adenine (A), Guanine (G), Cytosine (C), and Thymine (T). It is the sequence of A, G, T, and C that codes information for each gene.

In 1986 Kary B. Mullis developed the Polymerase Chain Reaction process (PCR), that produces Short Tandem Repeats (STR) which are relatively small fragments of DNA (Audersirk, Audersirk, & Byers, 2007). This means that very small amounts of DNA, found at a crime scene for instance, can be multiplied by the PCR process.

There are two main reasons why the PCR process was such a huge breakthrough. The previous system took nearly four-five weeks for results to return from the lab, but PCR could return results within twenty-four hours. Another reason was that the previous process required almost perfect samples of DNA, and there has to be a large amount to test successfully; meanwhile, the PCR process requires a relatively small amount of DNA and is successful with almost every sample.

Once in the lab, the DNA sample needs to be amplified. To do this, the DNA double-helix needs to be separated first. Heating a solution of the DNA to a temperature of 90C separates the two strands. After the strands unwind and cool, they are put into a DNA Amplifier and an enzyme called polymerase makes two new DNA strands; which are exact duplicates of the original. It takes approximately 4 minutes per cycle; each cycle doubling the amount of DNA. This process can be repeated every 4 minutes, which comes to 30 cycles every 2 hours. This means that in 2 hours, the small sample has been amplified 2^{30} or 1 billion times.

In 1999, British and American law enforcement agencies agreed to use a set of 10 to 13 STR that vary greatly among individuals. A perfect match of 10 STR's in a suspects DNA and DNA found at a crime scene means that there is less than one chance in a trillion that the two DNA samples did not come from the same person. In this can be realized the power and significance of this system.

The defense maintains that the bra clasp was contaminated by a transfer of DNA by means of mishandling. Regarding the possibility of transferring exfoliated cells that may be found on a hand or a glove, Dr Stefanoni explained that in the abstract, anything could be transferred, but it remained to be seen in practice. So, with specific reference to exfoliated cells, she stressed that it would be necessary to press down with force or scratch over a surface where these would have to be present (for example, the back of a person). She emphasized that when referring to exfoliated cells, she does not mean skin cells "that come off naturally from the skin because they are dead cells." She further explained that "it's not even possible to extract DNA from those cells, because the nucleus is practically dead."

In regard to the mixed DNA of Knox and Kercher found in five spots in the cottage: Dr. Stefanoni identified three blood spots (in the bathroom next to Kercher's room) that were mixed with the genetic profiles of Knox and Kercher: (1) On the drain of the bidet; (2) on the Q-tip box located at the ledge of the sink; (3) and on the edge of the sink. (4) Dr. Stefanoni also indicated that a luminol-enhanced bare footprint in the hallway outside Kercher's room contained Knox and Kercher's DNA. (5) The most interesting of these mixed DNA spots was the luminol-enhanced spot revealed in Filomena Romanelli's room that also contained Knox and Kercher's DNA. Dr. Stefanoni was unable to determine definitively whether these last two spots were blood or not, because luminol reacts with other substances.

Of these five spots, the fifth spot is very significant, as it was located in Filomena's room, which was at the opposite end of the cottage from Meredith's room. It's hard to cry "contamination" for this piece of evidence. It's hard, if not impossible, to assume that a forensic specialist retrieved Knox and Kercher's DNA separately, combined the two, and then negligibly trotted down to Filomena's room without changing gloves and dumped this mixed spot—or that this spot was left there at another time. Moreover, by Knox's own admission she had not gone into Filomena's room during her first visit to the cottage (when she showered). No explanation was given by either defense team of how potential contamination may have occurred for this piece of evidence.

The mixed genetic profile in the bidet is significant for various reasons; one being that Knox testified that she did not use the bidet when she returned from Sollecito's the morning after the murder to take a shower. So, how could mix have occurred? Dr. Stefanoni also emphasized that both in the bidet and in the sink, "the traces were not separate, but presented themselves as physically united, without any break in continuity, and thus each one appeared to constitute a *unicum* (unique specimen)." Stefanoni could not say whether the blood was mixed with other blood, saliva, or simply exfoliated cells.

It is also important to note that a blood sample was taken from the front part of the faucet of the sink, which yielded the genetic profile of Amanda Knox. Knox, herself, dated that blood spot to that time when she stated that she "had recently gotten ear piercings that had gotten a bit infected, and she thought the blood in the sink might have been from her own ear." Without speculating further here, this lone blood spot speaks volumes about the mixed traces as well.

The footprint sample taken from the hallway—in front of the wall that separates Kercher's room from Knox's room—yielded a mixed genetic profile of both Knox and Kercher. Although luminol also detects substances other than blood, Dr. Stefanoni pointed out that the presence of DNA also meant that biological material from Knox's foot and from Kercher was present, but could not definitively say blood was present. However, it is safe to assume that Knox was bleeding around that time, as her blood was found on the front part of the faucet of the sink.

Many of Knox's supporters claim that the Marietti knife (a.k.a. the double DNA knife)—found in the cutlery drawer in Sollecito's kitchen and marked "Exhibit 36" with a 6 ½ inch stainless steel blade that the prosecution alleged as murder weapon—was randomly picked out of Sollecito's drawer and showed Meredith's DNA on the tip of the blade and Knox's DNA on the handle because it was contaminated by forensic specialists in the lab. However, they have no answer to Sollecito's response to this news.

When confronted by police about the knife early-on in the investigation, Sollecito cooly explained that Meredith's DNA should be on the blade of the knife because he accidentally pricked her with it while he was cooking a fish diner at his place. "The fact that Meredith's DNA is on my kitchen knife is because once, when we were all cooking together, I accidentally pricked her hand," he said. It was later proven that Meredith had never even been to Sollecito's place. In fact, she had only seen him once or twice very briefly: remember Knox and Sollecito had only met a week before the murder. Furthermore, the girls who lived in the flat testified that they had never seen the knife at the cottage. Sollecito has not spoken about that statement since and has yet to retract it; he did exercise his *right to silence* during the original trial.

Several doctors testified that the knife matched the most significant wound on Kercher's neck—the deepest and fatal wound. During an independent review of the forensic evidence in 2008, Dr. Renato Biondo, the head of the DNA unit of the scientific police, reviewed Dr. Stefanoni's investigation and the forensic findings. During his testimony he confirmed that all the forensic findings were accurate and reliable. Dr. Biondo and Dr. Stefanoni (Shown in pic above) are among the top forensic experts in all of Italy. The Kercher family hired their own DNA expert, Professor Francesca Torricelli (Director of a genetic facility at Careggi University Hospital). She also agreed with Dr. Stefanoni that Meredith's DNA was on the blade of the double DNA knife. Moreover, by the admission of Sollecito himself; Meredith's DNA was on the blade, as he recalled pricking her with it while preparing a meal at his apartment—not only was he not surprised, he confirmed it to be true.

Is Lumumba Really in the Clear?

Patrick Lumumba was cleared by police of having any involvement in the murder, and he was awarded money for Knox falsely accusing him of murdering Meredith. However, does Patrick know more than he's leading-on? Patrick was released by police because there was no evidence linking him to the murder, other than Knox's bogus accusation. Yet, it was later determined that Patrick's cell phone was in the vicinity of the cottage on the night of the murder, at 8:38p.m. The question is, did he in fact visit the basketball court at Piazza Grimana at that time and did he meet up with Amanda, as she stated in her confession? No one is inferring that he is guilty, he has been cleared of any involvement, and rightfully so; however, he may know a bit more than he is leading on—about Knox's whereabouts.

Lumumba told police that he opened Le Chic at about 5:30p.m., – 6p.m., on the night of the murder, but other witnesses told police that they had passed by around 7:00 p.m., and it was closed. While in custody, Lumumba had informed police to contact Swiss university professor, Romano Mero, to corroborate his alibi. Mero was visiting Perugia at the time and Lumumba claimed that Mero had been present at the bar that evening. In a phone conversation with police, Mero told them that he was at the pub for two hours, from 8:00p.m., to 10:00p.m. But police still didn't believe either of them, because they had evidence that Patrick Lumumba's cell phone was recoded in the vicinity of the cottage at 8:38 p.m.

When Zurich born Romano Mero finally arrived in Perugia and met with police in person he changed his story, telling them that he left his hotel to eat a pizza at 8.30p.m., on the evening of November 1st, and he was at *Le Chic* by 9:00p.m., where Patrick was behind the bar. Lumumba also said that his Senegalese friend, Usi, arrived at the bar at 8:00p.m., but professor Mero says he remembers Usi arriving about 10:00p.m. Usi himself told police that he arrived at about 10:40p.m. Bar records indicate that the first receipt wasn't issued until 10:29p.m., (note: in Italian bars payment is usually made before consumption of food or drink, but in pubs or bars regular-customers are sometimes presented with the check when they are leaving).

Records indicate that Lumumba sent Knox a text message at 8:18p.m., which he deleted shortly after. The contents of the message are not known as Knox deleted the message as well. Knox replied at 8:35p.m., "Certo. Ci vediamo piu` tardi. Buona serata!" ("Certainly. See you later. Good evening!"). Knox turned her phone off immediately after sending this message to Patrick. Knox testified that the message from Patrick was in Italian and stated that "there wasn't anyone at *Le Chic*" so she didn't have to go into work that evening. Patrick put it similar to police, saying that the message said that there were not many customers at the bar and she was not to bother to come in to work that evening.

It is also important to note that upon his arrest, Patrick has repeatedly denied being physically or verbally abused by police in interviews with Italian newspapers and on Italian television programs. He blamed the wrong report in *The Daily Mail*—in which he was quoted saying he was abused by police—on mistranslation and misinterpretation of his words.

Time of Death

The experts heard by the court on this matter were, The Coroner, Dr. Lalli, Professor Mauro Bacci (appointed by prosecution), Professors Giancarlo Umani Ronchi and Mario Cingolani (appointed by the court), Professor Gianaristide Norelli (appointed by civil party), Professor Carlo Torre, Professor Francesco Introna, and Professor Vinci (all appointed by the defense).

There have always been some discrepancies with the exact time of death (TOD) of Meredith Kercher. Perugia Police Pathologist, Dr. Luca Lalli, was the first to examine the body. His first post-mortem examination took place at 12:50 a.m., on 3 November 2007. Dr. Lalli first tried to determine the TOD by using the *Henssge's nomogram* (my calculations below are based on a standard *TOD nomograph*). Dr. Lalli calculated that the ambient temperature (surrounding temperature) was 13 degrees and Kercher's rectal temperature was 20 degrees. Dr. Lalli was unable to get Kercher's exact weight, so he estimated—based on her height and size—that she weighed 55 kilograms (or 121 lbs).

The key variable to this type of calculation is the *corrective factor* (CF), which takes into account the special conditions in each situation. The way that the CF is calculated is dependent upon whether the body was found naked or clothed (if clothed, how much clothing?), whether the body was found in water (still water or flowing water?), whether the body was found in an air conditioned room, etc. To give a frame of reference, there is a standard table to facilitate the calculation of the CF. For instance, if the body is found naked and the air is still (the CF is 1.0). If the body is found covered with more than four thin layers of clothing (or covering) and the air is moving or still (the CF is 1.4). If the body is covered by a thick bedspread and clothing combined, with the air being still or moving (the CF is 2.4). Dr. Lalli determined that because the body was covered by a heavy duvet—which is considered a thermally protected microclimate—that the corrective factor was 1.7 (which is considered very high, but likely an accurate determination).

"T" stands for temperature (°C), "t" stands for time, and "e" stands for the mathematical constant.

Formula: $(T_{rectum} - T_{ambient}) / (37.2 - T_{ambient}) = 1.25e^{(Bt)} - 0.25e^{(5Bt)}$

Where: $B = -1.2815 (kg^{-0.625}) + 0.0284$.

Determined at 12:50am on 3 November 2007:

- Ambient temperature 13 degrees
- Rectal temperature 22 degrees
- Victim's Weight 55kg
- Corrective factor 1.7
- Initial body temperature 37.2 degrees
- Estimated time of death: 26h 0min (95% tolerance: *21h 30min* to *30h 30min*); rounded to 30min.

Using these numbers for the calculation—along with the initial body temperature of 37.2 degrees, which is considered standard— indicates that the most probable time of death was 10:50p.m., with the "range of times of death" lying between 8:20p.m., and 3:50a.m. Axiomatically other factors need to be considered, such as stomach contents (digestive process), hypostatic stains, and the state of rigor mortis. This is exactly what Dr. Lalli needed to consider in order to come-up with a more accurate scientific determination of the TOD. Moreover, Dr. Lalli acknowledged that if Kercher's exact weight was 1 or two 2 kilograms either-way, that this would affect the outcome of the nomographic calculations.

Both Dr. Lalli and Italian coroner, Francesco Introna, observed that neither the hypostatic stains nor the state of rigor mortis could offer useful indications for determining the time of death. When considering the digestive process, Professor Introna testified that "the stomach contents represent a concrete problem...because there are so very many variables, above all at moments of stress...the analysis of the stomach contents implies technical knowledge, is physiologically quite difficult, and the results are always open to some doubt..." In order to get an accurate estimate of the TOD by studying the digestive process it is necessary to know the values of certain initial parameters: the time when the last meal began; whether the stomach had any pathological problems which might slow down the digestive processes; whether the stomach was quite full or had already begun to empty itself. Meredith had no prior pathological stomach problems, according to Dr. Lalli and Professor Introna.

Recalling the testimony's of Meredith's British friends, Meredith had begun eating a homemade pizza with various toppings (cheese, mozzarella, eggplant, and perhaps also onions) and then ate apple crumble with ice cream at around 6:00-6:30p.m. According to them, this meal ended at about 8:30p.m. Upon examination, Meredith was recorded as having 500cc of stomach contents; experts stated that under macroscopic examination, the stomach contents revealed a piece of apple and floury fragments which might have been from the crumble or from the pizza. The emptying of the stomach under standard conditions starts around three-and-a-half hours after the start of a meal—"emptying" indicates the stomach emptying its contents (into the duodenum or the first section of the small intestine).

Dr. Lalli, noted that the duodenum was still empty "because the stomach had not even begun to empty itself," so the time of death must lie between 9:30p.m., (three-hours after 6:30p.m.) and 10:30p.m. (four-hours after 6:30p.m.). Professor Introna indicated that the beginning of the attack must have been a moment of tremendous stress for Kercher and may have arrested the digestive process. From this he concluded that the initial attack took place sometime between 9:30p.m., and 10:30p.m. Dr. Lalli theorized that it took Meredith some time to die, based on these calculations.

In order to create the most accurate reconstruction of the crime we must first indicate the TOD and the beginning of the altercation. To do so, we must consider the information considered hitherto along with witness accounts. We know that Meredith was alive and well at 8:45p.m. The impending altercation had not yet begun, as Meredith was still on her way to the cottage. We know this by the testimony of Sophie Purton and footage from the CCTV camera in the car-park across the street from the cottage which captured video of Meredith walking home at that time. Rudy Guede has maintained that he witnessed Meredith was fatally wounded and had fled the scene at 10:30p.m. Alessandra Formica testified that while she was walking down the stairs that lead to Piazza Grimana (just near the cottage) she noticed a black-man with a dark puffy jacket, walking in a hurry with his head down in their direction. She said that the man bumped into her rudely and rushed off in a hurry. However, Formica could not say for sure whether this was Guede or not.

Nonetheless, Meredith's mobile phone records corraberate Formica's story, to some extent, helping provide the best possible scenario for establishing the time that the killer(s) and Meredith were interacting. Police inspector Letterio Latella testified that Meredith's cell phone made an attempted call to her answering machine at 9:58p.m., and the last call from Meredith's Erickson cellular phone was at 10:00p.m., to her bank in England. Inspector Latella also revealed that there was a data connection (GPRS) on Kercher's English registered (Erickson cellular) phone at 10:13p.m., again, to her English bank on the night of the murder, and again he claimed that it may have been unintentional, because it could have been a "messy touching of the phone keys." Inspector Latella also testified that later, at 12:10a.m., that same phone received a call that was intercepted at Via Sperandio, meaning that it was no longer at Via Della Pergola, but was in Lana's garden about a mile away from the cottage where it would be found the next morning by Giannetta Elisabetta.

From this we can safely hypothesize that that the attack was finished at sometime before 12:10a.m. But why would the killer have taken her mobile phones and dumped them in a different location? If Guede was the sole killer, what would be his motivation for doing this? It can be deduced that Knox and Sollecito had more of a reason to get rid of her phones—for as Judge Massei explained in his report, "The ringing of a mobile phone which had been left in the room would have created the risk, in fact, of drawing attention before time, and of greatly advancing the [time of] discovery of Meredith's body."

Amanda Knox's appeal is scheduled for the end of 2010. In the United States, the *conviction* carries the greatest weight and the *appeal* process is narrow in focus and scope. On the other hand, in Italy the *opposite* is true—where it is as they say, "no one is guilty until found guilty on appeal."

CPSIA information can be obtained at www.ICGtesting.com
Printed in the USA
BVOW021205231111

276805BV00001B/73/P